THREE PAMPHLETS COLLECTED

LINCOLN KIRSTEIN

Three Pamphlets Collected

BLAST AT BALLET • 1937

BALLET ALPHABET • 1939

WHAT BALLET IS ALL ABOUT • 1959

With a new Foreword • 1967

One of a series of republications by Dance Horizons, Inc.

1801 East 26th Street, Brooklyn, New York 11229

These are unabridged republications of the
original editions: *Blast at Ballet* was first published
in 1937 by the author; *Ballet Alphabet* was first
published in 1939 by Kamin Publishers, New York;
What Ballet Is About was first published in 1959
by Dance Perspectives, Inc., New York.

These collected pamphlets are for

VIRGIL THOMSON

on his seventieth birthday,

for telling me on my twentieth,

that ballet in America was not

a possibility but a necessity.

FOREWORD

The *Shorter Oxford Dictionary* tells us that "pamphlet" comes from a generalizing of *Pamphilet* or *Panflet*, from a twelfth century Latin comic poem, *Pamphilus, seu Amore*, so, at the very start, delectation was implied. We are further instructed that (as of 1642), the substantive "pamphleteer," means "a writer of pamphlets; often contemptuous,"—whether profession or product is not entirely clear. The three pamphlets here reprinted bridge thirty years to provide footnotes for some aspects of theatrical dancing in that period. Each was inspired by love of much ballet and contempt for most critics, feelings which, as years pass, increase. Also, as years pass, many problems here passionately proposed and sweepingly solved have become meaningless. New readers may well ask: why all the sweat?

Blast at Ballet (1937), named after *Blast!*, Wyndham Lewis' Vorticist Manifesto of 1914, appeared in an edition of one thousand, paid for by the writer, of which less than three hundred sold. Two or three hundred were given away to persons whom I hoped would be outraged. Barely noticed by the press, it turns up now and then in book catalogues at a flattering price. The two best things in it are in the Appendix: Gordon Craig's notes on Diaghilev, and Glenway Wescott's letter on the Gluck-Balanchine-Tchelitchev *Orfeo* at the Metropolitan Opera. There are other ghosts invoked or exorcised, who, active then, have faded. Explanatory notes, to give all their due, would by themselves make a book bigger than this. Pamphlets must trigger themselves from villainies, real or imagined. My villains were the then as yet un-Americanized Russians who formed, in my mind, a condign conspiracy to strangle the infant Hercules of American ballet in his cradle. Mr. Sol Hurok, in poor thanks for his heroic services, I cast as the wizard Kastchei. He must smile wanly should he recall an interview in which I presented him with this precious piece, prophesying the end of his sinister reign. In return, he later generously gave the New York City Ballet, the Chagall production of *Firebird* which was no longer wanted by the Russian company by which it was commissioned. The pamphlet was dedicated to the initials of Mrs. William K. Vanderbilt, the first of her generation to encourage an American ballet on the highest level of patronage. When one is sixty, eighty doesn't seem so *very* old. When you are twenty-five, it is simply: historic. In between memories of Nijinsky and Diaghilev, she forgot the name of a young man to whom she thought she might have once been engaged. I had been reading Dixon Wecter's book on American society as my homework. I recalled that name: Franklin Roosevelt's *father*. Mrs. Vanderbilt paid me the highest compliment an older person can pay a younger; she treated me with no mind to age or eminence. She was fascinated by the *idea* of ballet in America. We were both in league against "the Russians." Considering the talents and numbers of the Russians with whom I was then basing everything on, this now seems scarcely consistent, but even the oddest pamphlets have never been models of unalleviated justice.

Ballet Alphabet was printed by Mr. and Mrs. Martin Kamin, who for many years kept the best (and only) bookshop devoted to dancing in New York. I hope, but doubt, they recovered their costs. It has an article cribbed from Delsarte, on "Gesture," which has the virtue of compacting information otherwise hard to find, except as scattered through half a dozen sources difficult to obtain. It also includes technical gossip and information obtained from four graduates of the Russian Imperial (or State) Schools: Michel Fokine, Anatol Oboukhov, Pierre Vladimirov and George Balanchine. Gisela Caccialanza, herself a fine dancer, provided help on the Italian style in which she was schooled by her godfather, Enrico Cecchetti. I had briefly taken classes from Fokine and Vladimirov and had felt in my own body some of the basic muscular emotions by which dancers breathe. A footnote: Paul Cadmus' sketches were based on photographs of Michael Kidd, a talented young dancer in the Ballet Caravan.

"What Ballet Is About" was composed as the initial issue of *Dance Perspectives,* in gratitude to Al Pischl, for having the enterprise to start a new, serious magazine, along the lines of our own *Dance Index*. It is an addition to *Ballet Alphabet* and was graced by good photographs of the first *Agon,* by Martha Swope. These sadden me, since Diana Adams, Allegra Kent and Todd Bolender don't dance any more. *Agon* is still well done, but it has never been the same as when cast for the dancers for whom it was conceived. A gloomier thought: dance is the art of the momentary, immediate and evanescent. Its prose, read after the fact, is dusty. Here's an accumulation of three decades of dust. I hope traces of gusto can stop readers from sneezing. Marianne Moore, as usual, gives hope: "Gusto thrives on freedom in art, as in life . . . is the result of a discipline imposed by ourselves." The discipline of ballet produces freedom to dance which is a paradigm of all action, in its lyric essence. If anything rigorous remains here, it comes from associating with dancers, who, at the last, make all words dust.

L. K.

Washington's Birthday, 1967

BLAST AT BALLET

1937

BLAST AT BALLET

A CORRECTIVE FOR THE AMERICAN AUDIENCE

By Lincoln Kirstein

Acknowledgment

PART OF THE MATERIAL IN THIS PAMPHLET HAS APPEARED
IN A SIMILAR FORM FROM 1933 TO 1938 IN

Arts and Decoration

The American Dancer

Dance

The Dance Observer

The Hound & Horn

Modern Music

The Nation (New York)

The New English Weekly

The New Republic

New Theatre

The North American Review

Theatre Arts Monthly

The Saturday Review of Literature

Town and Country

Vogue

THIS PAMPHLET IS FOR

A. H. V.

TRUE FRIEND OF THE DANCE

WHEREVER IT'S FOUND,

AND IN PARTICULAR IN

THE UNITED STATES OF AMERICA

*Perhaps it will seem strange to austere Republicans that we occupy ourselves with the Arts while united Europe besieges the domain of Liberty. Artists do not fear the reproach of neglecting the interests of their country, they are free in essence; by their nature; the characteristic of genius is independence; and certainly in this memorable Revolution they have proved themselves to be the most zealous partisans of a Regime which restored to Man his dignity so long disdained by that class, which was the protectress of the ignorance that worshipped it.**

Description des Ouvrages de Peinture, etc., Exposes au Sallon du Louvre par les Artistes Composant La Commune Generale des Arts, le 10 août, 1793.

CONTENTS

PART THREE

PROGRAM AND MANIFESTO 94

APPENDIX

Advertisement

THIS pamphlet will not be favored with many reviews in the public press. In the first place, pamphleteering is not a familiar method in America. Anything bound in less than semi-permanent cardboards seems scarcely worth the trouble of scanning. And then, as you will see, the people who will be most hurt by my tactlessness are the very ones who would ordinarily be obliged to notice it in print. As Sir Benjamin Backbite admitted: "To say truth, ma'am, 'tis very vulgar to print: and as my little productions are mostly satires and lampoons on particular people, I find they circulate more by giving copies in confidence to the friends of the parties."

If, for example, this present pamphlet had been published in the England of Sheridan's day, and it should not have constituted a basis for libel action, which I hope my section on dance critics might be interpreted to do—there would doubtless have been a few paper-bound responses immediately issued in opposition to my point of view, with attendant letters to the *Times,* or at least to the equivalent of the *Dancing Times.*

In America, however, we have a different and perhaps more efficient technique for handling impolite, uncomfortable or brutal Blasts. We ignore them. A wall of silence costs little to build and is extremely effective. However, as author of an irritant, I am perhaps more fortunate than several of my colleagues who have lately issued similar works affecting the press, radio and films. Our vocative dance public may be comparatively small but it is very passionately interested in questions of theoretical practice, artistic policy, and even commercial dance management. It is to them, then, above all others, that this pamphlet is addressed, and to young American dancers whose futures are so vitally affected by the setup herein described.

Since I do not expect to receive much printed expression of opinion I should be delighted to receive letters from private persons or groups, who are to any degree moved by my ideas, either towards correction, amplification or coöperation.

LINCOLN KIRSTEIN

PART ONE

Our Back Drop

I. *INTRODUCTION*

> *We are dancing on a volcano,* SAID M. LE COMTE DE SALVANDY
> AT A FETE GIVEN BY THE DUKE OF ORLEANS TO THE KING OF
> NAPLES IN 1830.

1. *Ballet in a Bad Time*

Ballet, or the exact science of traditional theatrical dancing, survived the French Revolutions of 1789, 1832 and 1848. Nor did the World War kill it. It persisted during the Paris Commune of 1871. Its development has been uninterrupted in Russia in spite of 1905 and 1917. If any form of Western art is thought to remain in moderate health, then ballet is just as healthy. It may lag behind poetry or painting in its direct reflection of society, but not for long and not nearly as much as many might superficially think. It is still a form of art as practical and important to us as the two other great formal contributions of Western artistic ingenuity; aerial perspective in painting, and the symphonic form in music.

But ballet itself in America is in a bad way because Americans have been led to believe that *Russianballet* is one single word. *Russianballet* is not a single word. It is true up to now, there has been plenty of reason given us for thinking so. But it is my purpose to investigate that here. Russian ballet has meant world-ballet from 1910 up to about the year 1935. Yet, Russian ballet itself stopped being specifically Russian when Diaghilev, its unique promoter, quit Russia in 1909. From 1914, it was international ballet with an increasing French overtone. Its last direct contact with creative Russia was in 1929, the season of Prokoviev's *Prodigal Son,* and of Diaghilev's* death. If, but only if the still surviving Confederate veterans represent the American standing army today, then the White emigrés, their heirs and assigns represent Russian ballet today.

Traditional classic stage-dancing arose from a fusion of Italian and French sources, from theatrical usage and folk-custom. In 1738, ballet for Europe and the known Western world was *French* ballet and *only* French, but who can name a first-rate French dancer within living memory? In 1838, the monopoly was Viennese, or else Italo-Scandinavian. Today what Germanic or Italian ballerina has one seen? In 1938, we count off

---

*In this pamphlet I have used the letter *v* as a final letter, whereas the English use the double *f*. But the *v* is simpler and phonetically closer to the Russian sound.

11

ten Russian and only Russian. This, only to show Russianballet has not always been a single word.

Ballet is in a bad time in America today because the blackmail of the Russian organization, primed by publicity and patronage, still works. The Russian-ballet repertory, itself a vitiated and dying formula, is coasting down-grade on the prestige it has accrued over the last three decades. Its sunset manifestations in their clouded glory seem more brilliant and familiar to our audiences than the young, crass, naive, but healthy form which marks the beginning of an American classic dance. Our audiences are hired and instructed to aid the charming dotard and starve the yelping child. That is why ballet in America is in a bad time.

2. *Ballet in a Better Time: 1909-1929*

Under the unique dictatorship of Serge de Diaghilev, ballet enjoyed a better time. Released by accident or design on the one hand from direct connection with the crippling bureaucracy of the Imperial Theatres on Russian soil, Diaghilev on the other, employing the highly developed apparatus of dancers, musicians and designers attached to the subsidized theatres, could operate in Western Europe with comparative freedom. The security of the Czar's personal subvention had provided working and practicing conditions which produced dancers and choreographers with the training of Fokine, Nijinsky, Karsavina and Pavlova. Diaghilev himself was a serious and completely educated man. The economic substructure backing his first venture in Western Europe was the Franco-Russian political entente. Russian music and dancing aided the military alliance which is still operating. But that very substructure, resulting in the World War, would separate his ballet from its native Russian earth forever.

The inevitable snobbish reaction against Diaghilev just after his death, felt and voiced by his artistic heirs, has now faded for good. He can be judged as he would now judge himself. Ten years have elapsed and there has not appeared in our contemporary Russian companies either a single musician, painter or choreographer of value unknown to him. There can be no second Diaghilev. His taste was his own, but his breeding, background, instruments and resources were part of an epoch that is forever passed. Beware the little men who seek periodically to revive either his own work or those aims proper to his time, and to him alone. The Diaghilev-period is an historic chapter in the history of Western theatrical culture; recent talk among the White Russians of its revival is no less archaistic and unprofitable, than to revive the Romantic ballet of 1830 to 1850, or the age of Noverre from 1750 to 1780.

II. *THREE AGES OF MODERN BALLET*

    YOU HAVE THE PYRRHIC DANCE AS YET,
      WHERE IS THE PYRRHIC PHALANX GONE?
    OF TWO SUCH LESSONS, WHY FORGET
      THE NOBLER AND THE MANLIER ONE?
    YOU HAVE THE LETTERS CADMUS GAVE—
      THINK YE HE MEANT THEM FOR A SLAVE?

Don Juan, CANTO III

1. *The Golden Age: 1909-1914:* Gods and Heroes

The success of the Russian ballet in Western Europe is a phenomena so familiar by virtue of the memoirs of Mme. Nijinsky, Svetlov, Prince Lieven, Arnold Haskell, Gabriel Astruc, Jean Cocteau and Calvocaressi, that there is no need to push through it again. In 1909, only thirty years ago, Paris and London had heard very little Russian music. Post-impressionism in painting was still an unearned investment of the picture-dealers, and dancing as represented by the ballet at the Paris Opéra, had all the bourgeois security of an official finishing-school for naughty girls. Three-quarters of the first great success of the Russian ballet lay not in any of its inherent perfection of music, decoration, choreography or dancing, nor in any new social or moral ideas, but rather in the *contrast* to everything accepted by Western Europe as theatrical dancing at that time, and for the last forty years. As long back as 1892 Henry Adams had written "his heart sank to mere pulp before the dismal ballets at the Grand Opéra."

No one, of course, would recklessly attempt to underestimate the large personal contributions of Stravinsky, Bakst, Benois, Fokine or Nijinsky. But let us at least grant them their historic due by considering them in their real place in their own time. There is no need to wrench them out of their realistic position and make them do double duty for all time and every place.

Petrouchka for example; let us take *Petrouchka.* Stravinsky's delectable orchestral score remains intact for concert at least, and the story in essence at least, is still useful. Benois' successive remountings of his original scenery seem thin, patchy, and creased today. As for Fokine's choreography: in the original production, he had Bolm, Karsavina, Nijinsky in the chief rôles. The fragments of character-dancing, the vignettes of coachmen and the moujiks were then brilliantly executed by top-rank character artists from the School of Moscow. Even the smaller parts, some scarcely more than walk-ons, such as the gypsy, the organ-grinder, or the drunken Barin, were taken by first-rate performers like Theodor

13

Koslov, Bronislava Nijinska, and Ludmila Shollar. The holiday crowds in movement were organized, a sizeable crowd and not a stray handful of accidental supers picked up an hour before curtain time.

Now we have none of this former glory. To be sure, the best dancers available take the leading parts. But do they convince us as Blackamoor, as Ballerina, or as Doll? Do we see them as archetypes of tragedy we have been led by all the writers to look for? Are our hearts broken when Petrouchka's pitiful fluttering mittens crash through his paper house? We do not and they are not, at least if we're honest. We view with rapidly diminishing interest a vehicle once propelled by renowned artists. We see famous costumes nearly identical to those carried by Bolm, Karsavina, Nijinsky, covering dancers approximating the original gestures once electrified by Bolm, Karsavina and Nijinsky. But now, it is all a ghostly double-exposure, a spectral blackmail that the Golden Age of Russian ballet still exerts on our inert eyes.

The repertory of the Golden Age of Diaghilev still whipped like a staggering cart-horse over the ballet-trails of the world today, includes also besides *Petrouchka*, the dances from *Prince Igor, Les Sylphides, Carnaval, Papillons, L'Oiseau de Feu, L'Après-midi d'un Faune, Le Coq d'Or, Thamar*, and *Schéhérazade*. Of all of these, *Cléopâtre* alone, with its preposterous hobble-skirts and belly-mirrors of the vogue of 1909, was howled off a Newark stage in 1937. The rest smugly remain. The indiscriminate, pot-flung color of Bakst, the caramel orchestration of Rimsky-Korsakov, Glazounov or Tcherepnin, the old dancers' galvanic, drugging physicality has been something for our fathers and mothers to tell us about, like Dewey's triumph after Manila Bay, or their first automobile-ride. Wonderful for them, but not for us. For us, if we leave off the rose-tinted spectacles obligingly provided by the Great Conspiracy of commercial manager, dance and music-critic, and ballet patron, we will see only a dismal carnival in a theatrical storage-warehouse. The fatigued world-worn troupes stamp out the mechanical tunes to which our ears have long since refused to listen consciously. Yet these relics of the Golden Age of Diaghilev are the very backbone, the chief mainstay of Russian ballet today. When we see them again let us recognize them for what they are. We may harbor for them among other nostalgic souvenirs of our remote youth, an affectionate warmth. But to think that there is anything here to instruct, nourish or enlighten us for what we ourselves as adults will want to do or see, is like going to be taught or advised by a darling old nurse, or a favorite scoutmaster.

14

2. *The Silver Age: 1917-1929:* Experiment and "Modern Art"

This is the chapter of the Russian Ballet that isn't Russian, and it is the most interesting chapter. That is, we assume *Petrouchka, Le Coq d'Or, Thamar, L'Oiseau de Feu,* and *Prince Igor* are White Russian-Russian; *Schéhérazade* is Russo-Persian; *Carnaval* and *Papillons* are Russo-Biedermeier, and *Les Sylphides* is Russo-ballet. For Russian, read Russian tea-room, with the tea in individual tea-bags and not a samovar in sight. The difference between Diaghilev's *Ballet Russe* and Baliev's *Chauve Souris* was negligible at many points of contact. The tea-room Russian soon enough tired even the Russians themselves, and Diaghilev commenced an age of experiment which though by far the most valuable contribution of his career both in paint, music, theatre and poetry, is almost unrepresented in the present repertory of the Russian Ballet companies. Many of these works, to be sure, might not weather revival and, as we have recently seen, revivals are increasingly exhumations. But as long as revivals pay on principle, let them revive this period as well.

With the departure of Fokine and Nijinsky, passed Diaghilev's Golden Age, and the youthful Massine was permitted direct contact with the international collaborators of the School of Paris. "Permitted contact" is correct, because at that time there was no thought of a dictatorship by the choreographer, even by those as distinguished as Fokine or Massine. Diaghilev was the only dictator of dance, decoration or music. Massine and Nijinska worked with Erik Satie, Matisse, Stravinsky, Juan Gris, Picasso, Prokoviev and Derain. Revolutionary cubism hit the ballet with its ton of bricks and horrified the old-guard ballet-ballet lovers, which was Diaghilev's earnest intention. Social-satire, American jazz, the everyday continental vacation and boulevard life of the nineteen-twenties; dada, neo-classicism, the falsely naive, the falsely archaic, and decorative folklore no longer of Russia, but now of England, Italy, France or Spain were all exposed to the caprice of Diaghilev's ingenious combinations.

Why, with the exception of pieces deliberately old-fashioned at their very birth, such as *Le Chapeau Tricorne, La Boutique Fantasque, Cimarosiana,* or *The Good Humored Ladies,* is this experimental period unrepresented by the self-styled heirs of Diaghilev? Were the works of the Silver Age less amusing than those of the Golden Age? By no manner or means, and quite to the contrary. Nijinska's *Les Noçes* and *Les Biches,* Massine's *Parade, Mercure* or *Ode,* Balanchine's *Le Bal, Barabau,* or *Le Fils Prodigue* would be a great deal more fun to see today than the rabble-scrabble and bobtail we're stuffed with instead. Only these ballets do not *represent* the *Russian* ballet of the "original" period. *Les Noçes,* it is true, was admirably revived in London and New York two years ago, but its starkness and the fact that it demanded a largish chorus were seized by the direction as an excuse to end its appearance once and for all. *Les Noçes* and these others are not considered sufficiently antique. They might destroy the picture carefully constructed by idolatrous historian, wise ballet-manager, and lazy patron for the public's consumption. Remember the manager thinks the public is a stupid beast. *Russian ballet, Russian ballet, Russian Ballet*—repeat it ten times before each performance. What? A house-party, a steel-factory, a movie lot in *Russian* ballet? What would Petrouchka think, what Schéhérazade, what the Sylphs? The more sprightly inventions of Diaghilev's Silver Age, even lacking a large part of the original Imperial schooled dancers, Bakst's decor, and the political prestige, were the real contribution of Diaghilev to contemporary theatrical art. These represented the institution of ballet faced with the world we lived in. Maybe some of the ballets were half- solutions, part-failures, mere *succès d'estime* or scandal. They were, and still would be however, neither as preposterous, muddy or dull as the others which still stick like cinders in our eyes.

Don't think for a second all the Russian dancing artists themselves prefer the older repertory. Don't think their old-world hearts beat in dedicated sympathy to the tunes that pop-concert, radio, and school-band have worn bone-clean. Very often Zobeide's slave appears to be dying his death of ennui, a far deadlier sword than Shah Schariar's, and his ennui, dear manager, critic, and dear patron, is transmitted in its unadulterated wallop to us, blind as we are—the patient, hopeful watchers in the darkened house. Lord Chesterfield once remarked of two people dancing a minuet: "They looked as if they were hired to do it, and were doubtful of being paid."

3. *The Age of Iron: 1930-1938: a. Russian Ballet in America: 1916-1936*

Most of the original Diaghilev troupe came to the Americas in 1916. Otto Kahn, one of our entirely disinterested and understanding patrons of every sort of creative expression from opera to pure poetry, lost a very substantial sum of money on it since he undertook to fulfil the obligations of the Metropolitan Opera Association, with whom the contract was signed. Financially the tour was a disaster and prevented dancing being shown on a scale worthy of its scope in America for almost twenty years. The Italian intendancy entrenched at the Metropolitan Opera House were terrified lest Diaghilev with his experience in presenting Russian opera and ballet should not by chance alone supersede them, operatic hacks of whom the Scala was well rid. It was vitally necessary to them that his tour should fail, and on a commercial basis, fail it did. The routing and back-tracking, the placing of badly paying engagements and conflicting dates, safely secured the margin of their sabotage. Not only was the Diaghilev troupe pioneering in theatrically undeveloped territory, but aside from the big towns, it was pioneering in a vacuum where up to that time only a circus could have prospered. In our deep South, the negro slave in *Schéhérazade* was forced to put on all sorts of new and peculiar tights, colors and characterizations. The young dancer, Gavrilov, frequently appeared in *Le Spectre de la Rose*, although Nijinsky's name was usually on the program. Few in the audience were any the wiser. When people from the South and Southwest tell you, "Yes, of course we saw Nijinsky dance; he was incomparable," it is just as likely that they *thought* they saw him, even if they didn't. For example, though long announced, he did not actually appear in Boston, due to passport difficulties. However, the effect was always the same. Even then the press-agent knew his business.

And although the great tour was a failure financially, it rocked a widespread minority of interested people all over America to their imaginative foundations. There is a curious little poem to be found among the juvenilia of Hart Crane, with a mispronunciation of *Daphnis et Chloë*, to fit a rhyme of *Cloh*, testifying to his amazement, his rapture at the Russian ballet. Likewise, other painters, poets, musicians, and stage artists all benefited from the Russians' first American visit. Robert Edmond Jones, for example, received his first great impetus towards his remarkable career, by his designs for Nijinsky's *Tyl Eulenspiegel*, and for the unproduced *Mephisto Valse*.

But far more than the Russian visit, Americans have benefited by the Russians' stay. Michel Fokine, Jove of the Golden Age, remained in New York, and has taught with his unique pedagogical mastery many of the best of the present generation of American-born dancers for the last twenty years. The choreographic works that he has created since 1914, seem minuscule in comparison with his influence as a source of choreographic information, style and theatrical presence. It is exactly as if our contemporary poets had had for the last two decades personal contact with Browning or Tennyson, or our musicians personally could have talked to Tchaikovsky or Debussy, our painters to Monet or Renoir. Few have been aware of it, because many of the more conscious ones have been thrown off Fokine's teaching by the shabbiness of the productions he has himself arranged here, by their down-at-the-heel repetition with no dancers but weak pupils of his own, performances which even in comparison to his works in the Russian troupes have been shameful. I remember, only four years ago, seeing his rearrangement of a ballet to

17

the Tannhaüser *Bacchanal,* danced on a raised square platform erected in the middle of a remote Brooklyn armory, with the amplifying system which provided the recorded music placed under the shadow of a large field-gun. It was miserably stamped out by his students, and yet it had a certain interest, for it was full of the bas-relief gesture which he insists Nijinsky took from him for *L'Après-midi d'un Faune.*

Other dancers of the Golden Period trained in the Russian Imperial academies before the war, who later settled in America, were: The Bekeffis, Bolm, Bourman, Gavrilov, Koslov, Kobelev, Kotchetovsky;—later, Novikov, Mordkin, Oukrainsky, Pavley, Shollar, Simeonov, Tarasov, Vilzak and Vladimirov. These have taught and produced ballets in the Russian tradition from Washington to Los Angeles, from Houston to Chicago, and from Hollywood to New York. Since their arrival, American dancers of our generation have naturally accepted Russian teaching as normal. Before, it had been primarily the Italian pedagogical tradition of Albertieri, Bonfanti and the school of Milan, favoring a small, detailed dancing-style and almost completely discouraging the male dancer. The actual training our dancers have received from the Russians, with the possible exception of Fokine, Bolm, Balanchine and Vilzak, who had each in his different way danced or created ballets quite apart from Diaghilev, was what the older artists themselves had been taught by the Imperial Russian School masters during their own adolescence from 1900 to 1910. These teachers continued to profess the technical groundwork which made possible the great late-nineteenth century repertory of Petipa, Ivanov, and Gorsky. It was excellent training as a theatrical basis, even if it may seem to us needlessly rigid today. Some influence from Fokine's early period may have been apparent in their own lessons, but general Russian instruction of American pupils has hardly even been touched by the choreographic experimentalism of the Diaghilev Silver Age, from 1917 to 1929. Most of these teachers had left Diaghilev by 1916, for America. Fokine himself, has considered every subsequent innovator in choreography as a rank upstart. Massine's symphonic work was mere *Wigman sur les pointes;* Balanchine's creative effort, which Fokine had influenced in the old Petersburg School, was *La mort de l'Art et la décadence de la danse.* Fokine pays his respects to the talents of Serge Lifar in an amusing and malicious article published in the London *Dancing Times* for July 1938. Separation from the source of development of the advance-guard movement in the dance tended to crystallize and age the elder Russian teachers' own ideas before their time. Imaginatively, they became fixed in their own first great golden period. They were heroes of the Golden Age, not only to their

18

pupils, but to themselves as well. They naturally instructed their little American pupils to emulate them, the only real dancers in the only real florescence of dancing they had ever known. This was only logical, but Russian dominance in the American teaching profession has further intensified those notions of the American audience which are susceptible to the blackmail by the traveling Russo-International ballet troupes. It is obvious that older Russian teachers should prefer *Petrouchka, Prince Igor, Les Sylphides,* to more recent choreography. They recall the good old days before their long separation from their lost homeland. But there are half a dozen Russian teachers of the younger generation in America who encourage and applaud the efforts of their young American proteges, with a devoted and unselfish interest which is characteristic of the best traditions of the Imperial Schools. After the debut of Fokine's first ballet, he received a card of generous praise from Marius Petipa, who after three-score years, and still a Frenchman, had become the fountainhead of the Russian classic dance.

On the whole, however, this historically inevitable Russian groundwork has been more than advantageous for America. The Russians have been proud of their American pupils, and if they have made them memorize Cossack or Persian dances from the repertory of their own youth, then they have also mounted for them their idea of Navajo and Mexican numbers as well. Petipa early in his Russian career invented what was then a surprising novelty for the Marinsky Theatre—a Russian ballet, that is, a work with a native folk subject. By school recitals, or semi-professional performances with local student ballet-companies, our Russian teachers have stimulated sectional interest and local pride in American dancing. They have, by their association with the renowned Diaghilev, given the dancing profession a dignity and a prestige which it never enjoyed before. Without their aid, direct or indirect, the recent Russian ballet tours would have been as much a failure as the first one.

In spite of numerous proposals, Diaghilev never would return to America, and this country at large has never subsequently seen the influential experiments he activated by collaborations with the School of Paris. However, the music has mostly been heard in our concerts, the painting has gone into our Museums, even the great part of actual sketches for costume and decor of his last period, from the collection of Serge Lifar, now reside in the Avery Memorial at Hartford, Connecticut. And of course, there were many American tourists in London and Paris from 1922 to 1932.

After the death of Diaghilev in 1929, his choreographers who seldom, it is true, had ever worked for him all at the same moment, disbanded.

19

Massine came to America from Italy, worked unsatisfactorily at the old Roxy Theatre, but on the side, mounted the first American stage performance of *Le Sacre du Printemps* in his own version, with Leopold Stokowski and Martha Graham. Nijinska went to South America, Balanchine to the Theatre Royal in Copenhagen, Lifar to the Paris Opéra. Boris Romanov, who had been working in Monte Carlo, Italy and South America, was later to replace Balanchine at the Metropolitan Opera in New York.

The Monte Carlo Ballet, founded in 1932, was a reassemblage of forces in the name of Serge de Diaghilev. The direction consisted of René Blum, long interested in the direction of the theatre of Monte Carlo, and of Colonel de Basil, an alleged ex-Cossack concert-manager. They made Balanchine ballet-master, entrusted him with the formation of a troupe. He requested and received Massine's coöperation. The ballets *Cotillon* and *Concurrence,* by Balanchine, and *Jeux d'Enfants* by Massine, were new. Later came the large symphonic works of Massine. Yet as a bridge with the past, were also included *Les Sylphides, Prince Igor, Petrouchka,* and *Les Matelots,* as well as *Le Beau Danube,* which had not been created for Diaghilev originally, but for *Les Soirées de Paris* of Count Etienne de Beaumont.

From now on we are all on pretty familiar ground. The Monte Carlo Ballet was substantially the late Diaghilev ballet, except for the apparition of the much heralded new baby-stars: Toumanova, Riaboushinska, and Baronova, whom Balanchine discovered in the dancing-schools kept in Paris by the four last great Imperial Ballerinas. It was a working ballet mechanism in every particular, complete with its own slight novelty and some success. It delighted the Diaghilev audiences who feared that with him, his ballet was dead.˙It only lacked the one vital element to make of it a genuinely creative enterprise—Diaghilev himself.

To remedy this lack, after realizing the entirely retardative and dominantly commercial aims of de Basil, which took most people five years to admit, George Balanchine, Diaghilev's last choreographer-in-chief, with Boris Kochno, Diaghilev's close aide for the last period of his life, and Vladimir Dimitriev, for the last five years director of the School of American Ballet in New York City, founded *Les Ballets 1933.*

It was not any easy task, for after a single season the Monte Carlo Company had appropriated unto itself the prestige of the "true" mantle of Diaghilev. However, when the first nights of both companies arrived in June of 1933, the actual hereditary distinction of Diaghilev was found to be resident not in the old Châtelet, the scene of the triumph of *Les Sylphides, Igor* and *Petrouchka,* but in the newer Champs Elysées, the stage of the scandal of *Le Sacre du Printemps.* The creators of the 1933 Ballets, were mostly an amplification of the Silver Age collaborators: Derain, with his marvelous Etruscan decorations and clothes for *Fastes* and *Les Songes,* and the musicians Sauget and Milhaud. Pavel Tchelitechev set his white, hysterical and crystalline stage for *Errante,* with Charles Koechlin's splendid orchestration of Schubert's *Wanderer* fantasy. Among the artists who had not worked for Diaghilev were Christian Bérard (subsequently designer of Massine's "symphonic ballets"); the dancers Tamara Toumanova and Tilly Losch of the Vienna Opera; the German poet and creator of contemporary epic-drama, Berthold Brecht, and his composer-colleague, Kurt Weill; the surrealist architect, Emilio Terry, and the brilliant young German stage desginer, Caspar Neher. Their dozen or so evenings of ballet in London and Paris in the summer of 1933, were in reality, the swan-song of the Diaghilev period. Here was real artistic discovery, real theatrical invention, true collaboration on Diaghilev's own ground, even without him. It could not have been greatly different even had he been alive to supervise the scene, for every new talent of the day with the possible exception of Salvador Dali, and the surrealists (who had refused on idealogical grounds to be included), was somehow involved. Significant and novel ideas in music, dance, poetry and social-comment were presented. Nothing as powerful, influential or original as this has happened in the world of theatrical-dancing since that time.

If the responsibility for the success of *Les Ballets 1933* was due to any one person, it was to their choreographer, George Balanchine. He is not a person easily described. I had first remembered seeing him in 1926, during Diaghilev's London season, not in the "modern" ballets which he was then helping to create, but in mimed rôles such as the enchanter Katschei in *L'Oiseau de Feu,* and the Corregidor of *Le Tricorne.* He invented something extremely personal and distinct for parts which can so easily be ciphers if only filled by a dancer for the sake of the printed program, while having no connection with the rest of the action.

Balachine had been with Alexandra Danilova and Tamara Geva, Diaghilev's last connection with the Russian academic tradition, now continued in the State Schools of Leningrad, which after the 1917 Revolution still employed the masters of Imperial days. Balanchine had danced at the Marinsky Theatre for seven years after the Revolution, ever since he graduated from its ballet-school, and had only left Russia on a summer-vacation tour to dance with a small troupe organized by Vladimir Dimitriev, a singer of the State Opera. Failing to obtain a passport to perform in Japan and China, they found they would be permitted to work in Germany and France. Diaghilev signed them for his own company in London, and they did not return to Russia. It was the midst of an age of experiment in the West, and it seemed too exciting a chance to pass up. Balanchine at once become a choreographer of the Russian Ballet in Western Europe, and later when Massine left, its last balletmaster.

In spite of Balanchine's phenomenal American success in the popular genre of musical-comedy, he has tended to remain in the minds of the serious dance public as at best a choreographer's choreographer, and at worst as a perverse and mysterious talent. That is, in his serious work he has been found not to be interested in producing ballets which have any interest other than that inherent in music, or in the dancing as it stems from this music. He has always avoided crass pageantry, showy stage pictures of living models, pictorial build-ups, and parades in which there is no *dancing* as such. For that reason he has never had the obvious popular fame of the Russian ballet-ballet choreographer. He has, nevertheless, an extraordinary instinctive gift for finding the quality of coherent gesture to fit the exact shade of quality in the chosen music. His movement is a continual homage to music; the better the music the more effective is his choreography. I have come to feel that music unduly tyrannizes him, but then I am not a trained musician nor a trained dancer, as he is, and hence, have less right to speak of it. Balanchine's greatest pleasure is derived from his collaborations with the scores of Gluck, Mozart, Chopin, Liszt, Tchaikovsky, Stravinsky, Prokoviev, or Hindemith. Balanchine has an inborn choreographic sense so acute as to amount almost to that of a painter's extra gift, giving him an eye so delicate that he can see color spectre past the range of his fellows, or a musician hearing more delicate and quite different sounds that the rest of us, even with some musical training. Balanchine's employment of the material with which he chooses to work is not only exceptional musically, but from the plastic results he obtains. His choreography is not ever literally narrative; it seldom tells a consecutive story. It weaves, however, a dominating but eventually a climactic and profound atmosphere which is frequently romantic, but just as often so odd in its romance as to seem a genre of romanticism the like of which has seldom been seen before. It is the poetic romanticism not of a Rousseau or Chateaubriand, but of the cruel tales of E. T. A. Hoffman, Grimm or Andersen; the sombre verses of Lenau, Heine and Hölderlin, the cynical self-contempt of Byron and Poushkin. It is a romantic attitude divested of sentimentality. It is an atmosphere at once nervous, individual, spoiled, tender and tragic. Balanchine utilizes no ordinary academic pantomime. Instead he amplifies and broadens ordinary conversational gestures from our familiar lives to connect and correlate the specifically danced portions of his design. If he is deeply moved by his music, Balanchine visualizes amazing cross-currents and short-circuits of representational emotion. These representational fragments are not literal, and hence, have to be watched more closely than the ordinary corroborative mimicry which is easily familiar to superficial audiences. The dancers clutch no fists nor beat any brows, nor point at, nor manually identify each other by vigorous threats or parries. Nor are his gestures "symbolic"; they do not *symbolize* anything; they are in themselves deeply and completely lyrical. They are like the statement of joy or grief in German *Lieder*. The printed words may quietly say that the postman is coming with a message from my love. But Schubert's horn-call annihilates the verses and at the same time, makes them sing and burn in an emotional counterpoint. Balanchine's choreography for Gluck's *Orpheus*, with its grave, sonorous sensuality; for his nervous, tender and diabolical games in *Cotillon;* and for the controlled hysterical transparent nightmare of *Errante*, are to me as wonderful in their way, and in a parallel way to the floating melodic line of Schubert or Mozart. The gestures have a quality of independent rightness exhausting the motor impulses in the music and in the lyrical substructure of concepts on which the music is founded. I have never seen anyone who can approach his mastery of the poetry of dance pattern in a symphonic form. I do not mean by his utilizing the symphonies of Brahms or Tchaikovsky, but in his orchestrating dancers to move in his given space, as sounds exist in their given time in a symphony.

When Balanchine uses solo figures moving against the choral background of his corps de ballet, with this background not visually muted, but with gestures controlled by their further distance from, and hence, less importance to our eyes, as in his *Serenade*, I always think of the uses of the piano against a string-background in the Beethoven or Chopin piano concerti. Balanchine is too fine a musician to succumb to the literal transcription of an entrance for a solo dancer to correspond to the entrance of a solo instrument. He would never have been so naive as to reiterate the individual air-turns of the opening of the fourth movement of Massine's *Choreartium*, where a brave attempt is made to connect the dance-steps with the initial ascendant chords of Brahms, only up to the place where the symphonic structure becomes too complex for a choreographer to follow literally—at which point he simply abandons the note-for-note pattern and just turns the ballet into what Arnold Haskell calls "being effective." Balanchine would never be guilty of the niggling closeness to Mozart's intervals, which makes Fokine's *L'Epreuve d'Amour* look like a literal translation from the Franco-Chinese. Balanchine's musicianship is essentially, not literally poetic. He uses his music with the utmost tact as well as with the utmost freedom. The divisions in his corps de ballet do not have to correspond to exact divisions to strings, brass and wood-wind. His patterns are not musical "visualizations" but movement created in and from tonal cadence and harmony. The dynamics of his broad movement are not correspondents but equivalents to the dynamics of his orchestra. In any given Massine danced symphony, you will find four entirely dissimilar stage-pictures, each one having been conceived, as far as the underlying quality of gesture goes, apart. In a Balanchine symphonic work, he will take a certain grain or quality of movement, rather like a chord based on the original theme of an orchestral piece, and exploit this grain to its utmost. The grain, for example, in his *Mozartiana*, had a curious feeling of outthrust, expectant, bold and capricious high-stepping wilfulness. This grain, chord or quality was never lost, however much it may have been developed on the original statement. He chooses his scale and makes his pattern change on a consistent texture. I know of no one else who has the skill both to hew to the music, and to create a musical counterpart to such a degree. Watch the running, fresh, transparent tone of *Serenade*, or the abrupt, brusque, pettish deliberately delayed motor intervals in *Concurrence*. It is hard to realize the extent of the theatrical information and specific dance experience which has been accumulated, rejected and assimilated to produce the purity and sophistication of Balanchine's best works.

My admiration for his inventive genius or taste has never for a second faltered, whether or not I have agreed with his interest in a special subject-matter or rather in his lack of interest in any subject matter whatever. I think he has more to teach a young choreographer about formal gesture in the developed classic tradition than anyone now working in this field. He continues to amplify the range of possibility in the classic dance to such an unfailing degree that he seems a mine of choreographic information. The more you take from his ideas of movement as model, the more there is to be taken. He is here to be used by Americans of less experience, and from the moment I saw *Les Ballets 1933*, I knew he should be used by Americans in America.

Les Ballets 1933 was an international European and not a specifically Russian effort. In one sense it was an end of an epoch; in many others only a beginning. Of its collaborators, the Germans are, of course, all exiled. Bert Brecht continues to influence the American stage. His version of Maxim Gorky's *Mother* was produced here in 1935. Marc Blitzstein's labor opera, *The Cradle Will Rock*, bears its dedication to Brecht. Kurt Weill composed music for *Johnny Johnson*, for the Group Theatre, for Reinhardt's *Eternal Road*, and is currently in Hollywood where he has been actually the first composer of note permitted to orchestrate his own films. Caspar Neher works for John Christie at Glyndebourne, for whom this year he designed the revival of Verdi's *Macbeth*. Sauget's opera, *La Chartreuse de Parme*, based on Stendhal's novel, is in preparation at the Paris Opéra. Milhaud is making ready his huge *Christopher Columbus*, for the 1939 World's Fair in New York, in collaboration with the French Government. Pavel Tchelitchev's enormous dialectical painting, *Phenomena*, has just created its scandal in London, preparatory to an American exposition, and he has designed the new Hindemith-Massine *Nobilissima Visione* (St. Francis), a collaboration Diaghilev had indicated, but which he did not live to present. Bérard, last year designed *La Symphonie Fantastique*, and this year, Beethoven's "Seventh" for Massine, besides sets for the Comédie Française. Derain invented the chinoiserie pastiche for the Blum-Fokine-Mozart's *L'Epreuve d'Amour*, besides frequently collaborating with Serge Lifar at the Paris Opéra. Charles Koechlin just completed an able sound-track for Henri-Cartier's Spanish documentary war film, *Return to Life*. Thus a brief indication of results stemming from *Les Ballets 1933*, an effort small in scale but rich in possibilities, and in the normal tradition of Diaghilev's anti-academic experiment.

Compare it to the subsequent record of the collaborators of the so-called Russian Ballet. The decor by André Masson, for *Les Présages*, was for a while abandoned, only after its full hideousness had been allowed to baffle the world for two seasons, but now the Australians will get a chance to look at it. Three obscure White-Russian Parisians were responsible for the tepid back-cloths and clothes for *Choreartium*, which even Arnold Haskell, de Basil's most passionate apologist, could not stomach. Jean Victor-Hugo did his usual clever pastiche of his own old sets for Cocteau's *Romeo et Juliette* again for the wealthy musical amateur, d'Erlanger's opuscule, *Les Cents Baisers;* Dukelsky's (Vernon Duke's) fatuous score for *Jardin Publique* received two complete extremely expensive decoratings and costumings in two seasons, was a failure in both, and junked in a third.

The musical collaboration of the de Basil Ballet, however, was more distinguished than the inheritance of *Les Ballets 1933*. It included Brahms, Tchaikovsky (four times), Berlioz, Beethoven, with revisings of Händel, Scarlatti, and Rimsky-Korsakov. The unqualified distinction of these composers has not been questioned for some time. A gesture in the direction of American folk-lore was conceded in the concoction of *Union Pacific*. The published libretto signed by Archibald MacLeish, had little connection with what we saw on the stage; but the costumes and scenery were both by American Broadway designers. Music was by the talented Russian, Nicolas Nabokov; choreography as usual, by Massine. Arnold Haskell placidly hailed it in London as "living tableaux from Currier and Ives prints," but that was a forgivable lapse; he had probably never seen any. It was as authentically American as English jazz, the average French notion of New York, or Puccini's *La Fanciula del Far West*.

The one new choreographer presented by de Basil entirely *faute de mieux*, has been David Lichine. His first five ballets: *Nocturne* (1933); *Les Imaginaires* (1934); *Pavillion* (1936); *Le Lion Amoureux* (1937); and *Les Dieux Mendiants* (1937) were failures indistinguishable from one another, and scarcely remained in the repertory long enough to be seen. The capriciousness of Balanchine's latter perversities for Diaghilev was presented seven years afterward, undigested and without comment. The Tchaikovsky *Francesca da Rimini* (1937) was an unwieldy and retardative spectacle based on visual memories of the Italian Renaissance as seen by a Hollywood decorator. It could easily have been presented without surprise by numerous pupils of Fokine, who had, indeed, himself staged it in Russia in 1915. Lichine is a flashy dancer with a very weak technical basis. As a performer he is a good showman and an excellent grotesque mime. However, his selection as a dance-designer is only an indication of the thin end of the Russian ballet's choreographic strain. He has just mounted *Protée* to Debussy's *Danse Sacrée et Profane* for harp and orchestra. The scenery is by de Chirico, and the whole piece is consciously or unconsciously formulated as a revival of the neo-classicism of the 1920's. Here is the Diaghilev decorative formula reduced to its ultimate absurdity: a revival of a revival of a revival, Russian-Greece, 1938, superimposed on Paris-Greece of 1922, which itself was a double-exposure of Roman-Greece, Louis Philippe's Renaissance and Picasso's post-war classicism.

Except for the dubious quality of the innovation of Massine's symphonic ballets and the fine dancing of certain principals, notably Massine himself, Toumanova, Danilova, and Shabelevsky, the artistic heritage of the official Russian Ballet has been almost completely bankrupt.

I cannot pretend that watching the Paris and London season of *Les Ballets 1933* was an unheralded revelation to me, nor that I immediately took them for *my* private and personal Golden Age of Ballet. I had been seeing every Diaghilev season since 1925, with Pavlova, the Swedish

Ballet, Bolm's and Mordkin's troupes in between times. As a matter of fact, I have never as yet seen anything on the stage comparable to what I imagine it could be under the proper circumstances. All my time and energy is devoted to realizing what I imagine. Rather than discovering everything new and wonderful in *Les Ballets 1933*, I did, however, find much of a healthy creative direction, which after the long interregnum since Diaghilev's death seemed almost more satisfactory than novelty.

I will not permit the rest of this résumé to become irritatingly personal because I am not myself irritated, either by what has happened to me or because the general economic, artistic or political situation is what it is. Even if I accidentally became involved with the ballet business in a very personal capacity, I refuse to let this fact disqualify me from writing about it. The question of my personal prejudice will naturally arise from my readers, and I would hesitate to plead any more unselfishness or objectivity than anyone else. However, our record stands in spite of us and will be regulated and attested by other remoter historians. I do claim that my actual connection with this narrative fits me, rather than strips me of a chance to be frank about it.

Since I was very young, I had always wished to be connected in some way with the ballet. My parents did not allow me to see the original Diaghilev Company when it came to Boston in 1916, not because they thought it was something the young should not watch, but probably because a nine-year old's wishes weren't taken very seriously. For this denial I harbored a deep-seated resentment against them for years, formulating revenges and astounding retributions. I thought of running away to become a dancer, and watching my astonished family, who as a matter of fact would not have minded, across the footlights on the night of my successful debut. Only lately have I been glad, for my many present reasons, that I never myself saw the real Golden Age, but only its faded echo. It somehow separates me as a worker in this art, instinctively and essentially from its deadliest period. As Max Beerbohm wrote in 1906 of the dancing of Adeline Genée, "For all men the time of their fathers is the most delicious time of all; just near enough to be intelligible, just far enough to seem impossible. I am glad I never saw Grisi, never saw Taglioni."

My education was accelerated and intensified, however, by an intense exposure to the Silver Age of Diaghilev, and to the public and private lives of Paris, London, and the Riviera in the 1920's, which was the essential subject matter of the works mounted under his direction. Even then, I never wanted to live "abroad," and I began early to translate into American terms the experimental artistic formulae I saw worked out every summer; creative formulae for the most part already affected by American ideas in music, clothes, books or architecture. So when I saw *Les Ballets 1933*, I felt here was a point of contact and a place to start. I was lucky in arranging for its prime-movers, Balanchine and Dimitriev, to come to America, and I have been continually fortunate in working with them.

Over the last five years since we founded the School of American Ballet together, I have learned many things; every mistake, every error in judgment, every false-step, seemingly at the time a disaster, has in compensatory retrospect proved inevitable and for our own best education. With the aid of Edward Warburg, who has involved himself more whole-heartedly in the support of ballet in America than anyone since the late Otto Kahn, we made the start of it financially possible. Strangely enough, almost the very last letter Mr. Kahn wrote was one to us expressing pleasure, interest in, and hope for our new venture.

There have been other ballet-schools founded in America before us and probably many will be founded after, but I think few have started with such complete plans, or with such a root-grounded base of organization or instruction. The bulk of the teachers are still Russian, with one distinguished American member of Pavlova's company. The Russian State School pedagogy is still incomparable. Only now, after five years, our own pupils are beginning to be in a position to teach themselves and other younger generations. At the present in our winter and summer courses we have nearly two hundred students from all over the country.

The first performances of the American Ballet Company in New York City and on tour in 1935, pleased many people and disappointed others. I think it was John Martin who called it *Les Ballets 1935*, and with some reason. Balanchine, since he had brought over with him the costumes and scenery, remounted *Mozartiana*, *Errante* and *Les Songes* from his 1933 repertory. However, *Les Songes* had a witty new score by the American composer, George Antheil. The most popular ballet produced was *Alma Mater*, a satire on our recent college days, which Eddie Warburg arranged with Balanchine to Kay Swift's comic music and John Held, Jr's perfect costumes. I personally liked *Transcendence* best. This ballet had a strange history: to music by Liszt, with remarkable painting by Franklin Watkins of Philadelphia, it independently anticipated both Frederick Ashton's *Apparitions*, Nijinska's *Well-Beloved*, and Massine's *Symphonie Fantastique*, all ballets on the same theme, all produced within a year and a half of each other, by choreographers working independent of one another. In *Transcendence*, the Fokine-trained St. Louis-born dancer, William Dollar, made an unforgettable impression. As a ballet based on the life of the virtuoso Nicolo Paganini, with overtones from "The Golden Bough," it was a perfect example of Balanchine's framing an individual artist of exceptional and very personalized gifts. *Serenade* was one of Balanchine's most beautiful lyric works, in the uniquely human manner that only he can realize.

b. *The American Ballet at the Metropolitan Opera House: 1936-1938*

The remoteness of the auditorium of the Opéra is nearly negligible for those people who possess their own carriages; but one cannot deny that the less opulent classes of honest citizens which the spectacle attracts, are constrained from coming more from the difficulty of getting in, than from the trouble of getting home, due to a lack of public means. The net loss cannot be valued, for this reason, at less than the sum of sixty thousand livres. The deficit, since 1783 and up until 1785 is then, the result of an infinitude of false operations to which the Direction has not had the power of opposing.

Memoire Justicatif des sujets de l'Academie Royale de Musique en reponse à la Lettre anonyme qui leur à été adressée le 4 septembre, 1789.

It is as hard work as any other to create from scratch a ballet school and a ballet company. It is unwise, as in any other work to go too fast, because you'll have to pay high for your high speed later on, but it is almost impossible to resist the temptation to permit oneself to be pushed "ahead" if people are willing to do it even if, on a considered basis you aren't ready for it, and it really isn't "ahead." When Edward Johnson assumed the intendancy of the Metropolitan Opera Association, ending the Italian succession, he asked the American Ballet to come in, create the opera ballets and present their own repertory. The invitation was so unsuspected, the opportunity seemingly so wonderful, there was scarcely a thought of refusal.

Balanchine withdrew the American Ballet from the Metropolitan just three years later. A tabloid columnist said it was just another case of "You can't fire me; I quit." Possibly, only it was not quite so simple as that. The whole arrangement with the Metropolitan was hopeless from the very start. Although Balanchine had long created opera-ballet successfully for London, Copenhagen, Monte Carlo and Paris, the particular situation in New York was something no one could foresee.

Perhaps Opera Houses are the same all over the world, have ever been the same, and will ever be so. Perhaps we were wrong to expect anything else. Indeed Thackeray had his Mr. Cox, the shop-keeper, visit the London opera of 1838.

After the aperture, as they call it, comes the opera, which, as I am given to understand is the Italian for singing. Why they should sing in Italian I can't conceive; or why they should do nothing *but* sing. . . . . Fancy old men dressed in old nightgowns, with knock-knees, and dirty flesh-colored cotton stockings, and dabs of brick-dust on their wrinkled old chops, and tow-wigs (such wigs!) for the bald ones, and great tin spears in their hands mayhap, or else shepherd's crooks, and fusty garlands of flowers made of red and green baize. . . . Such dirt, darkness, crowd, confusion and gabble of all conceivable languages was never known.

As for myself, I was so enchanted to work in the dusty labyrinth of that palatial mortuary under the cracked gilt plaster, powdery scenery, and bundles of rotting costumes, that my *zeal* exceeded a crusader's. I had not yet learned the first rule of diplomacy: *Surtout point de zèle.* We all naively believed what they said when they asked: "Give us something fresh in the ballet, something new." Everything proceeded on our part with a fatal and precipitate enthusiasm.

For example, we decided to put a little Egypt into *Aida,* an opera the locale of which is ostensibly Egyptian. It is indeed a fact that this opera had been written for a Khedive, was first heard in Cairo, but since then, Verdi's original ideas have been somewhat improved. As we all know from having frequently watched it at the Metropolitan, *Aida* is a concert of duets and choruses sung in fancy-dress, with two real horses in rubber-boots, twelve real negroes somewhat paler than the made-up Nubians of the ballet, a brass-band in horn-rimmed spectacles marching on the stage, decked out by amazingly rickety canvas representing the wrecked interior of the Scala Theatre before a recent renovation. We did not wholly permit ourselves this realistic picture in the beginning, but we quickly learned. Balanchine's acrobatic divertissement for the "Victory" dance, his *danses du ventre* for the priestesses based on religious sculptures at Sakkarah, at Beni-Hassan, and from La Fage's archeological engravings, were a scandalous failure. Balanchine rearranged these same dances three times after his initial try, and finally signed them *"after* Petipa," *after* which official silence gratefully closed over them. But we might have known after our first *Aida* that we were through.

For the *Tannhaüser* Bacchanal, Balanchine read Richard Wagner's correspondence, his printed stage-directions, and Isadora Duncan's adventures in her own novelties at the Bayreuth Festival. No one else on 39th St. had this information, if so the Metropolitan stage had never been sulled by the results of this patently pornographic research. *Tannhaüser*, had we the brains to think it out, should have been arranged in pre-Duncan dancing-school drapes, on the symmetrical pattern of the academic French opera. Balanchine's Bacchanale was so convincingly orgiastic that although they used to turn out almost all the stage lights, still the paying-guests in the boxes who infrequently arrived early enough to see it, objected, and from their point of view, rightly so. They were cosily attached to the moth-eaten vision of Leda's stuffed swan and Europa's plaster-of-Paris bull. The dancers were somehow and unaccountably alive. The same confusion arose over the dances in *Lakmé, Samson*, etc., etc. Yet some of the opera-ballets, oddly enough, were a success with parts of the public, some of the newspapers, but hardly with any of the box-holders, and after all, who runs the Metropolitan? Balanchine's *Carmen* divertissement, for example, always saved the opera after the Met's favorite Carmen lost her voice. Even the management admitted that. The "Kermesse" scene in *Faust*, for absolutely no reason, was highly praised by the newspapers. I think Balanchine must have composed it in a deep sleep.

It was soon discovered that due to the cost of extra rehearsals, it was wholly unfeasible to present our own ballet company, one of the main reasons we had been invited to enter the Metropolitan in the first place. During this epoch, however, the Metropolitan found enough money to rehearse and present two entirely new operatic works by American composers. The first, *Caponsacchi*, by Werner Hagemann, was longer and more embarrassing than *The Man Without a Country* by Walter Damrosch.

Yet Balanchine arranged *The Bat* to Strauss' *Fledermaus* music, which the orchestra already knew, and could, hence, play without extra rehearsal. *The Bat* must have been performed nearly as many times as Massine's *Le Beau Danube* and always pleased the public. Keith Martin's pretty costumes helped, but it was never one of my favorites. William Dollar mounted the Chopin F-Minor Piano Concerto as a ballet. It was a remarkable piece of invention with respect to the mood and form of the music, all the more so, since it utilized forty dancers, and was this fine artist's debut as choreographer. This piece was also chosen since the orchestra had it in repertory. It was presented only on Sunday evening "gala" concerts, and was never noticed by the critics of the daily press. John Martin was invited to a piano-rehearsal (there was no "dress" rehearsal permitted), since he had other duties at the time of the actual performance, but caretakers at the door forbade his entrance, since they could not believe a critic of the *Times* could legitimately want to see *dancing* at the Met. I don't blame Mr. Martin for never coming back. This, however, was only an indication of the official attitude at the Metropolitan towards the position of its American Ballet Company. Then, I guess it was, that Balanchine indulged himself in a fanciful interview with a morning newspaper reporter. He said music critics knew nothing about dancing, and not much more about music, as they were continually proving in their columns. That fixed him, and with him, the American Ballet as a possible collaborator with the Metropolitan Opera Association.

The *coup de grace* was, however, reserved for our production of Gluck's *Orpheus*, in the spring season of 1936. It is too long and too special a story to tell here; I am reserving it for a detailed study elsewhere, when I can print pictures. We were, naturally, all eager to put into immediate action all our theatrical ideas we had developed from Diaghilev's day to our own tenure at the Metropolitan, concerning the proper contemporary presentation of lyric drama. These ideas were in essence revolutionary, and hence, unsuitable for the Metropolitan. The Metropolitan is scarcely the place for experiment, even in an "experimental" spring season. We knew that even at the time, but there was little enough to lose and everything to gain by going ahead. By a curious relaxation of the general managerial inertia, or on account of it, or because everyone was so preoccupied with postponing their much publicized reforms promised ever since Johnson took over, or because Mr. Warburg agreed to divide the expenses for new scenery and costumes, we were permitted to stage our *Orpheus* with chorus, soloists, orchestra, and stage crew of the Metropolitan Opera House. It was by way of being a reckless manifesto designed, rehearsed, and produced within three weeks' time; but as Whistler replied when the Lord Justice asked just how long it took him to paint a certain landscape, "My whole life-time."

After considerable study and discussion of the legend of Orpheus and Eurydice, we decided to present what was most living for our epoch in the Orphic myth. We saw it as the eternal domestic tragedy of an artist and his wife, with Love himself a male angelic embodiment, with real feather wings and real muscles for flying, not a girl androgyne, which was the tradition of the Paris Opéra. Balanchine also had suggested that the singer who sang the rôle of Orpheus while Lew Christensen danced, should not have a woman's voice, in the Franco-Italian tradition of the *castrati*, but instead a tenor. This replacement had long been achieved in the Russian Theatres. Instead, the Metropolitan permitted the dancer to be a male (which even Paris still refuses), but insisted his voice should remain female.

We saw Hell as a concentration-camp with flying military slave-drivers lashing forced labor; the Elysian Fields as an ether dream, a dessicated bone-dry limbo of suspended animation, and Paradise as the eternity we know from a Planetarium arrayed on the astronomical patterns of contemporary celestial science. The movement was danced and mimed in some of Balanchine's most accomplished erotic patterns, touching and electric encounters, and noble plastic groups. Attic vase drawings, themselves, and not polite dancing-school scarf dances, in his love-knots and amorous garlands had really come to life. Pavel Tchelitchev's scenery and costumes, which in tonality and atmosphere recalled Massacio, Piero della Francesca, and our everyday work-clothes, clad pseudo-Eleusinian mysteries equal in dignity and grandeur to Gluck's superb score.

The actual production was a complete failure; a failure echoing with dog-howls of triumph from an opposition that was already vocative; partly outraged box-holders, partly the displaced professional Italian claque. It was a complete official failure because it was neither a castrated Puvis de Chavannes mural, nor yet an archeological 18th century reconstruction; it treated the emotion of love in an adult manner, and the theatre as an adult occupation, both serious mistakes in such a house. It was only presented twice. It offered the music critics the best chance so far to ask those rhetorical questions which rank them as *Messieurs les Ennemis*, the hardy perennial complacent censors of new life. They demanded with Olympian satisfaction: "Who are these unknown presuming persons, who have been vouchsafed the sacred scene of this great house, etc.?" Indeed, the audience, in several places had tittered because the human flesh of the dancers was designed to be seen in loving contact. *Orpheus* is about love, and sex does enter it. We made a triumphal arch for love to enter, but the shy-eyed and weak-minded were very upset. The critics loathed it because it made them think. Rather, it didn't quite make them, because most of them were incapable of the function. However, the act of thought was indicated, and they punished us for their incapacity to face it.

Orpheus, then, was a complete failure except for the forty dancers who performed it as a conscious dream; the few artisans and stage-hands who created the wonderful ritual objects, the crystal lyre of Orpheus, the white ghastly whips of the military Furies, and the white-silver branches of the Shadows which the dancers handled. A few American painters, poets, architects, writers, musicians, actors, and stage-directors on seeing it at both performances have never forgotten it. Take it or leave it, here in 1936 was an attempt towards living theater. The critical disdain was effective. When the Met announced *Orpheus* for a new production for the season of 1938-39, the press release stated it had not been in the repertory (of the regular season) for fifteen years. The American Ballet was rewarded for the production of *Orpheus* by never being allowed to create even a suspicion of such an arrant indiscretion again. But the genteel mockery of the Metropolitan management politely continued. Still agreeable and tantalizing requests were forthcoming from the General Manager's office for "something fresh, something new." Sometimes back-stage we could not avoid encountering Mr. Edward Ziegler, the ironic and able controller of the mechanics of the Metropolitan management. We feared his smile more than his wrath. It is indeed Ziegler, more than any other man, who makes the Met work. Hence, he is a miracle man. His candour about the ballets' chances was delightful; here at least, was a genuine realist. He knew to the ground the difficulties of the conditions under which the opera was conducted, and had developed a manner of cold-steel, the only manner which could be effective in such a house. But sometimes he would discuss the dancing. I still occasionally recall with fright the look that would freeze his face when he permitted an icy criticism to crack his lips. Heinrich Heine thus described M. Duponchel, director of the Paris Opéra in 1835; "To judge from his outward appearance one would take him for the overseer of the Père Lachaise cemetery rather than for the director of the Grand Opéra."

There is to be found in the September 1938 *American Dancer* an interview with Mr. Edward Johnson on "What is Wrong with Opera Ballet?" The remarks credited to the General Manager of the Metropolitan Opera Association are recognizable for their scrupulous good taste. His recent unpleasant experience with the American Ballet is never alluded to once by name. This is, for those who know, a mute rebuke for the outrageously frank tirade of which Balanchine delivered himself when he shook the dust (no metaphor) of the Met from his heels. Mr. Johnson says that the trouble with opera-ballet is that it usually tries to compete with big-time Russian ballet when it should be only an incidental and indistinguishable cog in the complex mechanism of traditional opera production.

Even in the face of such handicaps, choreographers complain that they are not given the opportunity of rehearsing their ballets. It can clearly be seen that this is impossible. It is for this reason, therefore, that intact ballet groups are engaged. Ballets must be previously rehearsed to such an extent that they can fare alike with musicians, choristers, and singers while in the Opera House.

The American Ballet learned to its sorrow that the Metropolitan found it indeed impossible to afford the ballets' necessary rehearsals but there is one single point in our favor, of which we could never convince the Metropolitan general management. This was concerning the age of the dancers. They had specified that the dancers must be "fresh, charming and youthful," and hired our ballet on that basis. Hence, in most cases, these dancers were quite new to 39th Street, their average age being not over twenty-one. Unlike the musicians, choristers, singers and supers, they had not been repeating identical stage-business for the last twenty-five years, until they could move automatically like trained somnambulists in a noisy nightmare. Our young dancers were continually thrown on the most famous operatic stage in America, so badly rehearsed from a musical standpoint, that on one occasion during a performance of the Polka from Smetana's *Bartered Bride*, the ballet found, to its grief, that the orchestral score had had cuts made in it from a previous production, which were not restored for the present one. The rehearsing had been done in the studio to save money. When the dancers were approaching their climax on the stage, the orchestra stopped suddenly. The conductor had forgotten about the cuts, and the dancers were left in mid-air. The critics wrote that the dancers couldn't keep step. The publicity department of the Metropolitan agreed, and naturally enough, gave no extenuating explanation.

Why did the Metropolitan imagine they wanted "freshness, youth, novelty" from our ballet, in the first place? Quite simply, because they thought that it would be cheaper and easier to hire a troupe with a repertory already rehearsed and proven, because the ballets in this repertory could be utilized as part of the general operatic program without extra cost (except for rehearsals, which were "impossible"). But the physical conditions (the lack of rehearsals, clean costumes or proper shoes), attendant upon the production of ballet-divertissement in the regular operas themselves, were so unjust that the box-holders became prejudiced against the American Ballet as an entity almost from the start. Hence, they gave it little or no encouragement to demonstrate what it could do, independent of the singers, and with a decent presentation. The Metropolitan was continually embarrassed by Balanchine's integrity as an artist when he attempted to defend the rights of his troupe. It was, after all, the dancers who were ultimately to suffer, not himself, as he had plenty of work for the future on the outside. The mechanism of the Metropolitan is so antiquated even with all the extra-musical odds in its favor, that I understood only too well how much the ballet question pricks them. But they give it less thought than new uniforms for their ushers.

However, I refuse to be silent in the face of the genteel if hurt accusations, the well-bred blame which the Metropolitan now levels at Balanchine and his ballet, for treatment over the last three years. The Metropolitan Opera Association, as a specimen of inert survival, is a diverting relic. It inhabits a physical plant in which all the effort of an extremely efficient, technical staff is forced to manufacture an eighty per cent efficiency out of a mechanism not capable of fifty. They could have sold the building and land five years ago to house them well in a new place, but they waited for a "better" price. The market dropped, and they are still waiting. If the single voice of Kirsten Flagstad were removed from their box-office attractions, I, for one, would not tremble much to think of what would happen to their receipts. They have created a popular German repertory entirely on the basis of one great voice and two composers, Wagner and Richard Strauss. Their seven-dollar top, their comparatively short season, their heavy subsidy, their lack of any French, Russian, or Anglo-Saxon repertory or singing actors, their contempt for American singers and composers of our generation, and for any music since 1914, is only compensated for by a persistence of the accrued prestige of by-gone glory, and the persistent interest of the box-holders in the value of the real-estate if and when the house can be sold.

But I still think that given half a chance, ballet even by Americans, would please an opera-house audience if the atmosphere were a trace less snobbish, and if it were given only half the physical consideration, for example, that Radio City Music Hall's ballet automatically receives. The Music Hall is almost as difficult a mechanism to operate as the Metropolitan, with a new stage show every week, with two large dance troupes beside chorus, orchestra and soloists. Yet Miss Florence Rogge, the ballet-mistress, is treated like a human being, and she produces work in return which is of a superlative average quality, and whose popularity increases year by year. Under proper conditions ballet would be as useful to the Metropolitan as Serge Lifar's weekly Monday evenings of ballet have been to M. Rouché of the Paris Opéra since 1930.

At the same time and before this, there was parallel activity in the ballet in other parts of America. In Philadelphia, Catherine Littlefield had been long working with the Philadelphia Opera Company. She had been subjected to similar European sights and sounds as all the rest of us. Among other works, she redesigned Stravinsky's *Apollon Musagète*, and recreated Poulenc's *Aubade*, both of which had been presented in Paris by Balanchine before. She staged the first complete choreographic performance in America of Tchaikovsky's *La Belle au Bois Dormant*, the last act of which in one way or another has long provided the Russian

Ballet with *La Mariage d'Aurore*. Miss Littlefield also presented Ravel's *Bolero*, and his *Daphnis et Chloë*, not seen in America since Fokine's version in 1916. Her performances had the excellent musical background of the Philadelphia Symphony Orchestra, with Leopold Stokowski's or Alexander Smallens' direction, and were enthusiastically received.

In Chicago, Ruth Page occupied a similar position. She had worked in Monte Carlo with the Diaghilev Company. She had danced in Bolm's production of *Le Coq d'Or* when he presented it in the Metropolitan Opera House without acknowledgments to Fokine who surely should have been, but was never asked to be *maître de ballet* there, on account of the Italian supremacy. Page created the rôle of the Dancer in the League of Composers' American debut of Stravinsky's *L'Histoire d'un Soldat*. She has toured extensively in America, the Orient and Europe with Harald Kreutzberg, alone, and with her own company.

Mikhail Mordkin, one of Pavlova's most famous partners and an experienced artist of the Golden Age, mounted for his own company of professionals and pupils, perhaps the oldest ballet of which we have any clear record, Dauberval's *La Fille Mal Gardée*, and also revived *Giselle*, both in his own rather than in their original version. He also produced other dance works to the music of Glazounov, Tcherepnin, and the stock Golden Age Russian musicians, to subjects from Russian fairy stories, Poushkin, etc.

In the far West, in Portland, Seattle and San Francisco, William Christensen, an American dancer of Danish tradition and Italian training, working with the orchestral conductor, Willem van Hoogstraten, produced dance versions of Enesco's *Rumanian Rhapsody*, and Tchaikovsky's *Romeo and Juliet*. Adolf Bolm of the Diaghilev Company, mounted for a John Barrymore film, *The Mad Genius* (vaguely supposed to have been based on the life of Diaghilev and Nijinsky) Mossolov's *Steel Foundry*, as a "modernistique" ballet, and later staged it completely for the Hollywood Bowl. As early as 1922, with the Chicago composer, John Alden Carpenter, he had presented Herriman's famous comic-strip character, *Krazy Kat*, as a ballet, and in 1928 had given the world première (before Diaghilev's) of Stravinsky's *Apollon Musagète*. Bolm has frequently worked with American music by Carpenter, Griffes, W. G. Still, Eicheim, besides Bach, Ravel, Rimsky, etc.

Fokine, on the other hand, in his long career has never created a single work on a contemporary subject, and has scarcely ever invented on an historical or traditional American background, although he has been located in New York for nearly twenty-two years. In September 1921, however, Fokine designed a new ballet for *Get Together*, a revue at the

New York Hippodrome. It was "The Thunder Bird," in one act, adapted by Vera Fokina from an old Aztec legend. The music was an arrangement of selections from the works of Balakirev, Borodin, Glinka, Rimsky-Korsakov and Tchaikovsky.

Over a number of years, the League of Composers in collaboration with Leopold Stokowski and well-known American or Russian-American dancers and designers, presented works in the gamut of Diaghilev's repertory. Stravinsky's *L'Histoire d'un Soldat, Le Sacre du Printemps,* his *Les Noçes,* and *Oedipus Rex* were all given their first New York (and frequently Philadelphia) performances. So was Prokoviev's *Le Pas d'Acier,* de Falla's *El Retablo del Maese Pedro,* and Schönberg's *Die Glückliche Hand.* The productions were admirably presented from a musical standpoint, but the dancing and mise-en-scène were seldom successful, as there were neither first-rate collaborators nor a permanent dance organization to execute them. They frequently were second-hand reworkings of Diaghilev's ideas, but without his apparatus or, above all, his taste. Hence, these American productions gave many people who had not seen the Russian Silver Age, a false or confused conception of the work actually being done at this time, or shortly before, by the School of Paris.

This, then, was the activity of Russian Ballet on American soil, either by Russian dancers or by Russian choreographers with American dancers, or by American dancers with choreographers under the influence of Russian notions. At this epoch Russian ideas in ballet were as dominant as German standards in music at the end of the last century, and Italian of the century before. It was a normal historical development, a necessary appropriation to our techniques and imaginations of certain standards and tendencies important for our future. I think in no case was there any competition intended with the "legitimate" Russian ballets. These efforts of our American Age of Iron were considered as individual initial solutions of our immediate personal problems. They were accepted by the local intelligentsia with the patronizing air of parents at a dancing-school's graduation recital, which perhaps they rather were. Only, they seldom considered the performers as their own kids, but rather as those of the poor people next door. Yet many audiences and local folk who had never been able to see ballet before, liked them. They wanted more of them. And these audiences formed the basic nucleus of the mass public for the popular future of ballet in America.

c. *American Ballet in America: 1936-19---*

The American Ballet Company returned gloomily to the Metropolitan

IVOIRE
DE
BALMAIN

le parfum qui est une femme

Opera House in the fall of 1936, primed with rumors of all sorts; threats, admonitions and tacit warnings. Something palpably had to be done if they were to be allowed to stay even another year. The Metropolitan management, distressed over receiving hardly less than equivocal notices in the newspapers, and by no means satisfactory services in the opera ballets in return for their entirely uninterested collaboration, made it quite clear that Balanchine and his troupe were there on sufferance only. Something plainly had to be done. The result was the American Ballet's Stravinsky Festival in the spring of 1937.

Balanchine had always had an admiration for Stravinsky bordering on filial idolatry. One of the first things he had set for Diaghilev had been a restaging of *Le Rossignol* (1926) in Monte Carlo, with the English baby ballerina Alicia Markova (Alice Marks) as the Nightingale. In 1928, with Stravinsky's close collaboration, he had mounted *Apollon Musagète* for Serge Lifar. In Russia, as far back as 1922, he had worked on *Pulcinella.* Stravinsky's generous homage to Balanchine as dancer, musician and choreographer, may be found in the composer's memoirs. Balanchine now decided that it should please the Metropolitan Opera management, establish the American Ballet once and for all as a major institution in the American theatre, and in order to give himself a great personal happiness, he would mount two Stravinsky ballets unfamiliar or unknown to America, and one new work to be written for the occasion. The Metropolitan stage would be used, the Philharmonic orchestra would play, and the composer himself would conduct.

From the very first I was, in company with our older colleague, Vladimir Dimitriev, opposed to this ambitious scheme. I felt that as great a dance-musician as Stravinsky is, he had already had his due from his own Russians, that he would never lack a chance to produce his own work, and that the ballets, chosen to be mounted were every one in a different way retardative. Balanchine wished to produce *Apollon,* for which both he and the composer had a considerable personal affection. He wanted to present *Pulcinella,* but Massine had then announced it for his own immediate production, and since he had originally designed it in 1920 with Diaghilev, Balanchine now stepped aside, though Massine has not yet (1938) reset it. *Petrouchka* and *Firebird* were too familiar to be considered. He felt *Le Sacre du Printemps* was not possible as ballet-music today. Nijinska had just done a fine production of *Les Noçes* in *New York,* and *Le Rossignol* was known as an opera at the Metropolitan. *Renard* and *L'Histoire d'un Soldat* were too small for a large house. So inevitably *Le Baiser de la Fée* was chosen, Stravinsky's homage to his master Tchaikovsky, and Balanchine's to the choreographers Petipa and

Ivanov. The new ballet was *Jeux des Cartes,* or "The Card Party," upon which the composer was engaged when Mr. Warburg approached him. I disliked the idea of this dictatorship by a musician, even if the musician happened to be Igor Stravinsky. For Balanchine, on the other hand, music as always was his prime-mover. He considered the dancing nearly incidental. Balanchine said he would almost prefer to be the conductor of an orchestra for dancing, as much or more than being a choreographer. Anything Stravinsky chose to do was O.K. with him. It was more than O. K.; it was a direct commandment whose fulfilment was joy.

The Festival was admirably rehearsed, ably presented, brilliantly received, and almost paid back its considerable cost in two nights. Lew Christensen in the rôle of *Apollon* achieved a human nobility and technical mastery which he had promised in *Orpheus.* His distinguished interpretation of this difficult part was more golden baroque, more the Apollo Belvedere than Serge Lifar's dark, electric, archaic animalism of nine years before. But at last here was an American dancer with his own individual classical attitude, using his six feet of height with a suave and monumental elegance which was wholly athletic, frank, musical and joyful, and wholly unlike the smaller-scaled grace of the Russian prototype. Martha Graham thought it held the most beautiful contemporary ballet gesture she had seen, and said so. So did a few others. "The Card Party" was ingeniously worked to the regulations of Stravinsky's very rigidly indicated libretto. In spite of witty music, fascinatingly orchestrated, dainty perversions of Rossini, Delibes and Stravinsky himself, I found the literal unfolding of a poker-game according to Hoyle, undramatic and even flat. The audience, however, thought they adored it. A poker-game; marvelous; poker is such a definitely American game; *The Poker Party* must be an *American* ballet. Balanchine's choreography was tricky as the game itself. It was difficult to dance, and it was very well danced. At least three Broadway revue producers wanted to whittle it down for their own shows. *Le Baiser de la Fée,* with Alice Halicka's tender decorative investiture, was a touching evocation of the early period of the Romantic ballet of the 1830's, the lost epoch of Philippe Taglioni's *La Laiterie Suisse* or *La Fille du Danube.* Balanchine recalled the Marinsky Theatre of his youth, only his choreography was not a reproduction of, but a sophisticated comment on the school of Petipa and Ivanov, turned towards an epoch in the dance fifty years before their time. A Russian friend, sitting in what would correspond to the Imperial loge at the Metropolitan, said: "I can't help it, and it may be terribly depressing, but it reminds me of Petersburg, 1914, before the Revolution." But no, it was only New York, 1937, a long time before another revolution.

John Martin, the suggestive dance-critic of the New York *Times*, even said he liked *Le Baiser de la Fée*, that it was the best thing Balanchine had done since he had been in America. Of this, much more later. The evening of the première was a great success. The congratulations were colossal, Stravinsky beamed, and the result was completely zero, although it did prove this American Ballet Company was a splendid technical organism. For me, however, it was a triumph in a vacuum. It had been hoped that in the next season at the Metropolitan the three Stravinsky ballets would be presented as part of the regular operatic repertory. Such, however, was scarcely the case. When Mr. Warburg, having paid for everything else, refused also to pay for the Metropolitan's additional rehearsal time necessary for presenting the ballets, the plan understandably fell through. *Apollon*, since it had only a string orchestra and hence required (so the Metropolitan considered) next to no rehearsal, was actually given twice in the regular operatic season of 1937-38. The least interesting of the ballets from a popular viewpoint (although my favorite), was dealt its death blow by the excruciating orchestral performance which the Metropolitan permitted it to receive.

The only tangible result of the Stravinsky Festival seemed to be that the American Ballet did return to the Metropolitan in the Fall of 1937 for its third and final year. In the summer, Balanchine took the company to Hollywood and successfully mounted two ballets for *The Goldwyn Follies*. I did not go. I was neither disillusioned, disappointed, alienated nor sad, with either Balanchine or the American ballet. I knew that my service to this American Ballet was over because there was absolutely no chance for the young dancers in whom I was more and more interested, getting any opportunity to perform in the kind of dances which I wished them to create. Balanchine had Hollywood and his enormous popular success on Broadway. Rouché of the Paris Opéra was always after him to return, and he had agreed to collaborate with Massine's new venture while protecting the integrity of his own American company. His future was more than assured. He had done much to instruct and influence our American dancers who worked with him.

So I organized a small troupe of dancers from our own school, which had been incidentally very successful, and from among those of the American Ballet proper who were dominantly interested in classic ballet choreography applied to native themes. We found in Frances Hawkins an energetic and humorous independent manager, who heretofore had only worked with the "modern" concert-dancers, Martha Graham and Harald Kreutzberg. In six weeks we made a little repertory and gave our first performances in July 1936, at the very centre of the bitterly anti-ballet,

41

"modern-dance" school in Bennington, Vermont. That debut was a nightmare, although the Bennington audience was a great deal more patient, tolerant and interested than many other people for whom we would dance when we became much better known.

"The Ballet Caravan" has been in microcosm a permanent laboratory for classic dancing, by, with and for Americans. So far we have given over a hundred performances from Skowhegan, Maine, to Havana, Cuba, and are embarking on our first transcontinental tour in 1938-39. It is a company neither as old nor as large in repertory or personnel as the Littlefield Ballet or Ruth Page's troupe, companies dedicated to the same principles and working along the same general directions. The story of the Philadelphia Ballet or of the Chicago Ballet is probably in every way as instructive and entertaining as my story, only the creation of the Ballet Caravan is an important part of *my* story, so I'm telling it here.

I intended to create a small company of good dancers which could one day be amplified into a big company with a similar repertory. The music was to be good enough to serve both, and it did. The dancing was to be a foundation for further developments, and it is. Realizing the danger Diaghilev risked at never having more than two choreographers at his disposal at one time, and only five in his entire career, I started off by mounting four works by four different dancers. The first season of the Ballet Caravan with a tour in New England was of not much interest except to the dancers and myself. It was more of a hard vacation than work, a feeling-out for our future. But William Dollar's dances for Ravel's *Valses Nobles et Sentimentales,* and Lew Christensen's to Mozart's *"Haffner" Serenade* are still in our repertory. Elliott Carter's *Pocahontas* offered too many technical problems of stylistic handling to be immediately successful; the music was so good that now, two years later, we are reviving it with all the means we have at our disposal.

For the second season we mounted our first American works successfully, and appeared with the Philadelphia Symphony orchestra. Our musicians, while they are all native-born Americans, had everyone of them been exposed to the School of Paris, directly or indirectly, through Nadia Boulanger, the heirs of Erik Satie, *Les Six,* and the principles of *musiquette;* or else they had refused to be affected by the Franco-Russians and were hence influenced in reverse. Each of them used American folk-material. Robert McBride had long played and arranged for a jazz band; Paul Bowles knew Kentucky and Mexican folk-songs from first-hand; Virgil Thomson, the composer of *Four Saints in Three Acts,* had just finished music for the United States Government film, *The Plough That Broke the Plains,* and would soon start on *The River;*

Elliott Carter, Jr. had studied with Loeffler, Piston and Gustav Holst, and had conducted a workers' chorus all over France. All of them were in the lively traditions of *les Jeunes*. They knew and loved Russian ballet as much as I did, shared my opinion of its uses and abuses, wanted to collaborate on American subjects.

The American subject-matter gave me a lot of thought. I had only a small company, so that anything involving pictorial pageantry was out of the question. Trial and error had showed me the danger of competing with the Russians on any ground at all upon which they might choose to perform. Finally, there must be no Spanish, Russian or Italian manual pantomime or character-dancing. We needed something that would seem familiar to our hoped-for audiences, something with which they could feel at home, and yet something in which our specifically American-styled dancers could be shown to their best advantage. The familiarity of our subject-matter must never duplicate the familiarity of the Russian formula. The American classic style should never be dulled by a veneer of Russian glamor.

Just as there is always a literary diction like Tennyson's as opposed to lyric speech created from the vernacular of our every epoch, by poets like W. B. Yeats or A. E. Houseman, so is there an opera-house post-Imperial ballet-ballet style in dancing, as differentiated from that simple stage elegance which always distinguishes a true classic dancing-artist, whether he or she be Russian, Polish, Danish, French or American. Due to the effective blackmail of the Russian Ballet, the only *style* which is now recognized as legitimate, is a stylization stemming from the specifically *Russian* ballerina. Some idea of Soviet Russian style as opposed to the Imperial Russian style could be gained from watching the remarkable performance of Wachtang Chabukiani of the Bolshoi Ballet at Carnegie Hall three years ago. He was an exultant acrobat of extraordinary physical power and nervous strength. His effects were broad rather than refined, but his vitality was intoxicating, like the pictures of demonstrating athletes one seems in newsreels of Moscow May Day parades. The post-Imperial style-type springs from Fokine fragments for Pavlova, as exemplified in her popular "Death of the Swan." Pavlova herself was probably not responsible. Only her diluters appropriated a certain half-shut-eyed, strangling, ecstatic agony of beauty felt-to-be-unbearable, peculiar to this one short number, and developed it as a consistent manner of stage-behavior. I have seen Tamara Toumanova in the Grand Variation from *La Mariage d'Aurore*, for example, when if you let the activity of her eyelids or nostrils serve as any symptom, you might have thought that she was fighting off a syncope or some other more intimately painful shock. The Russian ballerina has gotten to be considered some faintly fairy creature, some celestial Grand Duchess vouchsafing an aerial apparition to her enslaved terrestrial fans. She is bent on being remote, bloodless, apart, glittering with crown-diamonds, socially aristocratic, with a sex-appeal as artificially frigid as it is definitely provocative. This style is a reflection of the society of pre-war Russia. Its present use echoes the maintenance of the lost Imperial myth by Parisian White Russians. It is a style that needs overhauling, since it is no longer an index of human dignity, but rather a decorative hangover and a sentimental imitation. It's all very *vieux Russie;* tiny champagne suppers for two, crushed vapors of snowy tarlatans, and bubbly sentimental toasts quaffed from pink ballet-slippers. This is the vulgar cliché that has been far too long hammered into the eyes of most of our audiences. It makes dolls of the dancers, only perhaps a wooden puppet would be less irritating. One recalls the remarkable notes of the German romantic poet, Heinrich von Kleist (1777-1811) when he visited in company with a brilliant young dancer a provincial marionette theatre.

And what advantage would this puppet have over a living dancer?

What advantage? Above all, dear friend, a negative one, to wit, it would never behave affectedly. For you know, affectation is shown when the soul (*vis motrix*) is at a point other than that of the centre of gravity of the movement.

Now, the dancers I have to work with in my own small troupe can put on some very droll imitations of Russian ballerinas of the antique genre if they have themselves performed well that night and someone is giving a party afterwards. But it is not *their* style. Dancing style is merely a heightening, a theatricalization of the personal gifts of the artist, a conscious projection of their delight and security in their work, a direct and transparent reflection of their essential value as human beings, which takes its color from their training and from their environment. The style of the Russian dancers whom we are now privileged to see, echoes the faded aristocracy of the Imperial schools or its Parisian reflection. The style is not a simple affectation. It is an accurate reflection, and for thirty years has framed the most intense and vital lyric theatre we have had. The American style will not imitate the Russian, but instead be its equivalent for our time and place. Our legitimate reflection of a Democracy is of necessity not distant, but immediately intimate. There is *pride* in both styles, the awareness of the human body in all of its super-human released essential energy. I leave with my readers their choice of future style in the dance. The choice ultimately depends among other things on which political or economic system has the best bet in America. American style springs or should spring from our own training and environment, which was not in an Imperial School or a Parisian imitation of it. Ours is a style bred also from basket-ball courts, track and swimming meets and junior-proms. Our style springs from the personal atmosphere of recognizable American types as exemplified by the behavior of movie-stars like Ginger Rogers, Carole Lombard, or the late Jean Harlow. It is frank, open, fresh and friendly. It can be funny without seeming arch, and serious without seeming pained. These actors or dancers like them, wish to establish a direct connection, approaching personal intimacy or its theatrical equivalent with their audiences, like Helen Morgan perched on her piano, or Paul Draper appearing not as a dancing-entertainer, but as an artist-guest and host from his own dance-floor.

The Russians keep their audience at arm's length. We almost invite ours to dance with us. Anyone of us would like to know Fred Astaire, since we have known other nice, clever, happy but unassuming boys like him. The same is true of Paul Haakon's clean, manly brilliance, his brilliant apparition like a pocket-Hercules; Buddy Ebsen, a contemporary Daniel Boone or Davy Crockett, seems to have just hoofed out of the sticks; and Ray Bolger is the eccentric dancer's paragon for the "Tin Man of Oz." These dancers have the American style, and so has the cynical footwork of Donald Duck and Popeye, the Sailor. It is this kind of feeling we will have to find and accentuate in order to provide American dancers with their best background, and American dance audiences with their best entertainment.

> You can't expect a cowboy to agitate his shanks
> In etiquettish manner in aristocratic ranks,
> When he's always been accustomed to shake the heel and toe
> At the rattling rancher dances where much etiquette don't go.*

Partly because The Ballet Caravan was touring the Maine and New England Coast, partly because I had a great fondness for Melville's marine narratives, we pursued our American subjects with *Yankee Clipper*, which chronicled a farmboy's adventures in the ports of the world and on a merchant-ship of the "fifties." Eugene Loring did a charming job of parodying the native dances of Argentine, Japan, Bali and Africa. He put his Tahitian girls on toe-point. The folk numbers were episodic, like a newsreel-travelogue. The Adagio for the farmboy and his Quaker girl recalled Balanchine, as was only natural. Lew Christensen's *Filling Station* had the benefit of Virgil Thomson's music and inclusive stage information and Paul Cadmus' comic-strip clothes. This was a ballet

---

*J. B. Adams. (Songs of the Cattle Trail and Cow Camp, by John A. Lomax.)

with a contemporary background. It started out quite differently on an idea I had the year before. This was to have been called *Bombs in the Ice-Box*, or *Everyone is Equally Guilty*. It would probably have been a very flat American danced imitation of Auden and Isherwood's *Dog Beneath the Skin* or *Where is Francis?* It would have required a gigantic frigidaire full of rubber-tubing and tear-bombs, a swing-session of gas-masks, and a hero-surgeon who with a miner, a fireman, an aviator and a diver (the four elements) destroyed the war-mongers. All these bad ideas, however, resulted in some good ones. *Filling Station* has only a few characters, but each, either alone or in combination, has its reason for being, each represented an actual facet of American civilization. Each was a recognizable social type, and each had its choreographic climax treated in a manner to heighten each individual dancer. Lew Christensen's choreography had a virtuosity and showmanship to which his long years of training in big-time vaudeville had accustomed him. The two truck-drivers' tumbling act was a sure-fire hit. The group dances in which he freely used the Big Apple were simplified past any actual resemblance to a dance fad which might date it in six months, as our repertory almost must last us for many seasons.

Now we are working on Aaron Copland's *Billy the Kid*, Elliott Carter, Jr.'s *Pocahontas*, and a contemporary treatment of the Minotaur legend, more modern Nazi than ancient Greek, with music by Charles Naginski, who sometime after starting our ballet, won the *Prix de Rome*. Our plans include works based on the subject-matter, if not on the actual plots used by Melville, Hawthorne, Mark Twain, Whitman, Henry James, Stephen Crane, Hart Crane, Thomas Beer, or James Farrell; folk or popular material that is comprehensible to all of us whether we've read these particular writers, or have ourselves had experiences on this continent which they have already recognized. Our treatment, we hope, is moral rather than rhetorical, although there is plenty of work to be done along this line. By moral, I do not mean ethical. By moral, I mean having some connection with the manners and behavior of men and women with whom we are familiar, as directly or indirectly displayed in theatrical settings which have a real, not a rhetorical or decorative relevance to ourselves.

Consider *Billy the Kid*, for example. Instead of take a picturesque cowboy legend and making it the tragedy of an individualistic, romantic desperado, *à la* early "Western" serial movies which, following the Russian formula, would have been the obvious thing to do, we saw the Kid's life as only a fragmentary, if symbolic, incident in the expansion of our vast frontier. Billy's career was doomed, not by implacable fate, but by the collective necessity of establishing law and order so that people could live in a new place in peace. Billy was used as the symbol of an order of reckless individuals which, however charming or picturesque, was doomed by the historical process of the developing Frontier. Billy was not a tragic poet but a little bad-man, like others we know and even like, and are forced to shoot to keep them from shooting us first. Realism in the ballet may be an anachronism. I, for one, haven't the slightest intention of adapting the means of the realistic theatre to the lyric stage. Only a realistic historical attitude can be used for far more powerful lyrical ends, because they will be truer ends for our time and place, than a persistent prejudice for a romantic, story-book, unrealistic and essentially decorative ideal as exemplified by the "poet" of *Les Sylphides*.

Coincidental with our activity, Catherine Littlefield had been working on a series of ballets with American subjects which she later presented in Europe with considerable acclaim. Although Isadora Duncan and Ruth St. Denis had toured abroad two decades before her, Miss Littlefield took the first contemporary classic ballet company from America to Paris, Brussels and London. She had arranged the dances for Carlos Chavez' *H.P.* (Horse Power), with decor by Diego Rivera. Her *Terminal*, set in a railway station, *Let the Righteous be Glad*, a negro ballet, and her *Barn Dance*, gaily conceived as an integrated suite of American square-dances, have been particularly appreciated.

At the same time, or slightly before, Ruth Page in Chicago had presented *Hear Ye, Hear Ye*, a court-room ballet with tabloid-burlesque and night-club interludes, to the music Aaron Copland had written especially for her. She also presented George Gershwin's *American in Paris*, with the virtuoso tap-dancer, Paul Draper, who had been benefitting by strict classical ballet training. Recently, Ruth Page's *Frankie and Johnnie*, score by Jerome Moross, has been the big hit of the past Chicago season. Catherine Littlefield is preparing her *Ladies' Better Dresses*, with the composer Herbert Kingsley, as well as a satire on *Café Society* (Ferdy Grofé) for immediate production.

In San Francisco, Portland, Seattle, Los Angeles, Pittsburgh Washington, Boston, Baltimore, Newark and Detroit there are the first healthy signs of local American ballet companies. In Rochester, New York, Thelma Biracree has mounted several ballets by younger American musicians at the Eastman Conservatory of Music, on subjects ranging from Anthony Comstock's vice-crusade, Ladies' Day at a Ball Park and Haiti voodoo, to dictatorship and Mexico. Before about 1870, there was scarcely a permanent endowed civic symphony orchestra in America, and yet we all are familiar with the presence of an endowed orchestral institution in almost every one of our fair-sized cities. Now, it is not too much to

47

hope with some encouragement and the employment of taste and efficiency on the part of the companies themselves, that we may be able to have one day as many ballet organizations as there are orchestras. All sorts of reciprocities and collaborations are open to alliance between ballet-company and orchestra. The literature of dance-music and its subsidiary tone-poem is extremely attractive to popular audiences. American ballet in America is rapidly approaching the proportions of a national movement. And all this in spite of my inconvenient villain, the "Great Conspiracy."

Our future in dancing, however, is by no means assured. We can no more believe that Americans can create ballets to cancel the Russian repertory's popularity in the next five years, than we can hope for peace in Europe for a same length of time. But the question of time happens to be the most important. Now, not five years from now, is the time to encourage our American companies, since lack of interest, or consistent setbacks can kill their initial efforts without too great pressure. This is what the managers of the Russian troupes count on; not consciously, perhaps, because consciously, they would never admit any competition whatever. We are naturally grateful for the tours of their international companies, who from the snow-balling of their accrued prestige have dug our groundwork for us. I, for one, want to see Massine create for many years to come, because his choreography has always elements for our instruction, his great dancing always fills us with delight, and his appreciation of theatrical values is a model for the young American dancer. The question is now, at this moment, and within the next five years, whether or not there's enough backing, private interest or public energy for both. Or will the "Great Conspiracy" manage to draw the teeth of an American Movement by consolidation and compromise. Can the appropriation and Russification by flattery and pigeon-holing of our best young American dancers proceed? Can the Russian companies Americanize themselves in every way but the essentials? Will the "Great Conspiracy" succeed?

PART TWO

The Great Conspiracy

I. *THE MANAGER'S STAKE*

The promotion of ballet in America may be a nervous excitement full of frustration and love for some of us, but for others it's big business pure and simple. As a matter of fact, it's pure business for both, because no one any longer has independently enough cash to take dead losses year after year on the scale Diaghilev, Ida Rubenstein, or Rolf de Maré of the Swedish Ballet did. Russian ballet in America has paid extremely well, considering the fantastic complexity of the organization needed; boat-fares back and forth, train-fares across the continent, the reams of publicity bought on the line, and the over-balancing size of personnel and machinery. The Russian Ballet has been treated in our Provinces like a road-show, a circus, an old-time "Ben-Hur" production, because that's been the only way up to the present that a mass-audience can be hooked. The general impression one gets from talking to dance-managers is that ballet costs a fortune, brings in a fortune and loses a fortune. This partly arose from the mythical rumor that although Diaghilev in his first Paris season made two million gold francs, he lost three and went on doing so for twenty years. In America, the dance-managers behave as if they were patient but feeble-minded altruists; unfortunately for them, the ballet's got into their blood; they seem doomed to haul it back across the wide ocean year after year, to satisfy their own exigent artistic hunger. They somehow have to drag it all over America for seven or eight months, playing one or two-night stands because America just simply *needs* it. However, the managers are not, to say the least, feeble-minded. Their actual financial stake in presenting such a complex attraction as ballet is ridiculously small, because they are not in reality either general-managers or even impresarii. They are booking-agents, pure and simple. They are more than safely backed by two of the chief concert, music, radio and entertainment monopolies, the Columbia Broadcasting System and the National Broadcasting Corporation. There is a persistent belief on Broadway, difficult to ground, that these are one and the same company, and their rivalry is on the same pattern as the Standard Oil Company of New Jersey's earnest competition with its arch-enemy the Standard Oil Company of New York. Maybe the same banks backed both at the beginning. In any case, the monopolies control so much money budgeted for direct and indirect advertising, that they do not mind setting aside what is for them a relatively small amount to be spent on a prestige build-up accruing from the exploitation of music or dance attractions. This money is not really risked, but rather administered by these managers who are allowed to place "their" attractions through the booking facilities of the monopolies.

It is a waste of time talking to people who, supposedly interested in the so-called Fine Arts, nevertheless refuse to soil themselves by understanding the basic economic background which conditions the very painting, architecture, theatre and dancing to which they pretend they are so passionately attached. No one who honestly cares about the dance can afford to be lazy-minded about the concert-management racket. I am not calling for an economic Holy-War at the moment, since I am a realist, but I do call for an elementary historical and economic comprehension on the part of our dance-loving audience. The position of the monopolistic dance-managers is exactly parallel to that of the men who "made" such great railroads as the Central Pacific. In the words of Louis Hacker: "They achieved great wealth not because they were mighty enterprisers, taking risks with their personal fortunes and hence gaining well-earned rewards, but because of the bounty and, incidentally, the cheating of the government." For "government" insert Broadcasting Companies. As far as "cheating" goes, the definition of this word will be left to the District Court. The fact that the concert-managers don't make as much as the quarter-billion Archer Huntington and Leland Stanford took, does not eliminate them from our suspicion or excuse them from our disdain. We may not assume that the Huntingtons or the Stanfords did nothing in return for their plunder. Tammany Hall served many poor New Yorkers very creditably as an agency for quick relief for some years. All I wish to imply is that the price paid for these services has been too high, so high, in fact, that it would be cheaper to find other agencies, even if we have to go to the trouble of creating a new one or limiting the old.

Last spring, only because he happened to be a close friend of a friend of mine, I was permitted to interview the general-director of the greatest of these monopolies. I told him somewhat more angrily what I am writing here. He listened courteously but without interest. He explained frankly that his whole concert-bureau division which controls the dance and music attractions for his organization, grossed no more than eight or ten million dollars a year. Hence, it was maintained more for the benefits of its incidental publicity prestige-value than to make much money directly. He even humorously admitted that he didn't know the names of the dance-managers who had arrangements to book their important attractions through his companies' large resources, the very well-known names in the trade, about whom I was complaining. I pleaded with him desperately for some encouragement for our young American artists, but he could scarcely be expected to be impressed. I withdrew, frightened and vengeful, but patently helpless. The grotesquery of the situation nevertheless continues to appal me. Here we have an important part of our cultural lives entirely, if indirectly dependent on radio-advertising. Its very existence is made possible only through booking-agencies sponsored as a mere side-line by radio and movie monopolies which are so large that their sole interest in the original music or dance attraction is to use it in the flesh as a purely incidental aid for selling radio-time to national advertisers of coffee or cigarettes.

Recently our Federal Government has instituted a civil anti-trust action, *United States of America* v. *Paramount Pictures Inc. et al.*, entered in the Federal District Court of Southern New York. The Government is attacking the eight major motion-picture producing companies, together with their numerous subsidiaries, as well as one hundred and thirty-two executives. This is a major effort to break the monopolistic control of every means of production, distribution and exhibition which prevents an independent film operator from making a tiny living. It is an attempt to curb or regulate the vicious practice of block-booking. The case will unquestionably be protracted, but it may eventually have serious repercussions in radio, and hence indirectly on the entire field of concert-management, where the principles of block-booking are equally poisonous. Perhaps, as the Broadway cynics say, the Government is, in reality, only trying to force Hollywood to "regulate" itself. The situation is very complex. There are reports that the independent operators themselves are worried over the effects of a possible Federal legal victory, since it would throw them into violent open competition with an enormous headstart, by virtue of their capitalization and past contacts, in the hands of the big companies, even should the Government force them to break up. Now, at least, they know from which tables the crumbs will fall. If the tables are turned anything might happen.

There was a letter recently published in the theatrical trade-paper *Variety*, dated August 11, 1938, which succinctly analyzes the entire situation from the point of view of films. But even if one substitutes *"dance-attractions"* for *"films,"* no other word need be altered. This letter was signed by Leo F. Wolcott, president of the Allied-Independent Theatre Owners of Iowa and Nebraska. That is, this letter represents the attitude of an ordinary provincial distributor on whom the very life cash of the great monopolies depend.

> Because of the many abusive and evil trade practices forced upon the inpendent exhibitors by the motion picture trust such as unreasonable film rentals, block-booking, percentages and designated time, threats and coercion in selling, circuit expansion with consequent protection or non-availability and many others, the independent exhibitor has his back squarely against the wall, fighting for his very business existence. *It has been proven time and again that the monopolists in this industry do not willingly or easily relinquish the grip they hold.* In view of this, it would be remarkable indeed, if anything short of the full success of the Government's projected anti-trust action could correct the present situation.
>
> We have seen round-table conferences before, resulting apparently only in greater monopoly and we are frankly skeptical that the lasting reforms so urgently needed in this industry can be accomplished without government action, or at least common consent decrees.

The italics are mine.

All this may be rather tiresome reading for the disinterested balletomane, who only occupies himself with the purer aspects of the developments of Massine's symphonic achievements. But if he is only a little distinterested, it shows he has really no serious interest at all, for the future of dancing in America may not be settled in a theatre in London or Monte Carlo, but in a District Court in New York.

There is no use inveighing against the system of radio sponsorship or monopoly in American business here, but to put it rather crudely, that is why some people favor both the Roosevelt's, Theodore's or Franklin's, trust-busting policies. The ramifications of the twin Broadcasting Companies, control directly or indirectly through their concert bureaus of the "Community" or "Civic" systems almost the entire musical and dance-life of millions of metropolitan and provincial Americans. For their economic convenience, "dance" is always considered a part of "music," just as one might consider a violin is the only stringed instrument in an orchestra. There seems to be room for only one *kind* of dance, just as only one *kind* of musical virtuoso is allowed on a "series." Dancing itself, which has as many categories as there are instruments in a band, is not deemed worthy of a series of its own which, if handled right, would pay as well or better than the *hors d'oeuvres* which are now stingily offered. This is a situation which has naturally arisen from our general competitive economy. I do not think it is of any interest to complain of it from an ethical point of view. But realistically speaking, the managers, due to the greedy necessity of quick returns on an investment which they themselves only risk on paper, have an inevitable tendency at first to exhaust, then presently to destroy public interest in each ballet attraction which they undertake to present. It may also be true that without the managers, provincial Americans would see little or nothing of foreign attractions; but the price they pay for this, over and above the price of their admission, is by way of being hardly ever permitted to choose what they prefer to hear or see from their own native attractions. The dance-managers will tell you that a metropolitan audience seldom and a provincial audience never, knows what it wants to hear or see. It serves their purposes to believe this, and if possible, they will always keep both selection committee and the audience itself in convenient ignorance.

The managers feed the provincial selection committees or local managers their clippings of the criticism of their attractions by the New York dance and music reviewers. Mainly on this basis are the provinces sold. Take for example, any small town in the Middle West. The Entertainment Committee of a local Woman's Club has signed up exclusively, as they usually must, with one or the other broadcasting company's booking divisions, for, let us say, six concerts during their season. The Club offers to their town the whole course at a figure lower than if one bought tickets for each individual concert. They will receive, perhaps, a soprano, a lecturer on world-affairs, a symphony orchestra, a virtuoso instrumentalist, a travel lecture, and a single dance-attraction. They will not receive any soprano, any violinist or dance-attraction other than the one owned and operated by the monopoly. This artist or other attraction must correspond in importance to the category of the size of the town requesting the attractions. If the committee should by some evil chance not exactly desire one or two of the attractions offered, but rather a third, or else one on some other list, they are told they won't be able to get any if they won't take the lame-duck; because the lame-duck has been awarded a contract in one of the manager's off-moments, and the unlucky contract must write itself off. If the small town should by some rash error request an artist handled by another monopoly, or by an independent manager, the least the committee is made to feel is as if an indiscretion had been committed which is something nice people (in the big city) just rather not think about.

The competition in "concert" management, the moral slugging and back-stabbing is vicious, bitter and relentless as it is in all other forms of our competitive monopolistic commerce. For an independent manager successfully to sell his one or two attractions in territory controlled by the two monopolies or their subordinates who will not hesitate on occasion to combine against him in order to share the preservation of their monopoly, this independent manager must be prepared to encounter every form of blackguarding and intimidation up to physical violence itself. And he does encounter it, every inch of his way. If on occasion, a big manager booking through one of the monopolies' resources smiles with favor on an independent operator by tossing him a few crumbs when one of their own dates has accidentally fallen through, it is only because this same independent manager may be counted upon to ripen certain attractions generally considered difficult or unfamiliar, taking all the risk for his pioneer work, but only so that in the end his attraction will be snatched up by the monopoly after sufficient time has passed to insure a reasonably safe success. The managers themselves actually assume next to no risk. Why should they? They easily operate on prestige funds set aside by the parent broadcasting corporations. Even a European attraction has to assume the guarantee for its own existence before it is ever brought to America; and it can hardly ever expect to be clear of this obligation, labelled advanced royalties, slapped on by the manager to pay the boat-fare. No use in complaining about the weather or because you happen to have blue eyes. These are facts faced by every American working in the dance in America today. It is a different, but not an easier story, for aliens. Without a doubly sure margin of capital put up by a new attraction either in work or cash, the monopolies will not touch a native product because the artistic monopoly of Russian ballet in America can still be further exploited; and it it easier to prolong this exploitation even until the companies are run straight into the ground, rather than to encourage a single American troupe whose future is dubious. Can you blame them? I can and do, not because I think they're heartless bullies, but only because they're bad business men.

Ethically, I am not perturbed, for from a casual point of view the managers are charming men, their morals no worse than the boss of the company who sells you cigarettes, electricity or automobiles. But economically and from an attitude of material realism, I consider them short-sighted.

Take the particular case of the Ballet Jooss, for example: When this talented German exile won the international choreographic prize awarded by Rolf de Maré at Paris in 1932, he had made himself a small repertory, the focus of which was *The Green Table*. Jooss was brought to America, shoved into a Broadway theatre with a stage that was hardly small enough for his troupe, and forced to play *The Green Table* for six weeks straight. When the Russian Ballet itself came for its first season its manager was bright enough to run it for only ten days. It was even hard to give away seats for Jooss after his first fortnight, which was scarcely a disgrace for the novelty of this kind of attraction; but the manager wanted to be able to sell Jooss to the sticks, on the slogan "Direct from six weeks on Broadway." Jooss' splendidly trained and rehearsed company naturally made warm friends all over America, and these friends, like Jooss himself, wanted to see a logical and normal extension of his work. Everyone wondered what would happen—one ballet, two ballets, three ballets *after* his first and only success, *The Green Table?* But his knowing managers decided that Jooss was to be claimed for *The Green Table* and for that alone. It was a convenient saleable tag. That was all there was to it. Jooss worked for six months preparing a new ballet, his *Prodigal Son.* I am not interested for the moment in the artistic merit of this particular piece. But after one look at it, the manager decided that was not the kind of ballet which audiences who had been taught to like *The Green Table* would like. Hence it was summarily withdrawn, after a single New York performance, before anyone including Jooss himself had a fair chance to know whether it was really a good ballet or a bad ballet. I saw this same eminent manager at the dress-rehearsal of Serge Lifar's ill-fated debut in New York City. He personally insisted on so many alterations not only in Lifar's choreography, but in the lighting, costuming and program arrangement, that it was surprising that a highly strung, self-respecting artist like Lifar could appear at all.

The manager's place should never be in a position of artistic censorship. The manager is not an artist, but a booking-agent. This is not a snobbish criticism. It is merely a logical acceptance of the rôle which he has chosen for himself and for which he is too well paid. Extensive creation of repertory, presentation of the artist for whatever he or she may be in their own unadulterated essential personality, is the only method of exploitation possible if any permanent test for an extended commercial success can be expected. Ask anyone what chance Jooss or Lifar has in America today. They will reply, "Yes, but we've seen *The Green Table,*" or "Yes, but everyone said Lifar's *première* was so badly done." Whatever else the monopolies may or may not be, they are not lazy. They work hard for their cash, and it is perhaps curious that in so many cases they should be willing to milk an attraction to death so quickly, purely on the strength of a convenient selling point.

The commercial handling of the Russian Ballet in America has been efficiently exploited from nearly every point of view. The technical difficulties of routing sixty people around this continent, with supplemen-

55

tary musicians to be picked up in every town, with any amount of scenery and wardrobe, with all the details of publicity and box-office, is no easy task. But in order to sell the *Russian* ballet, it has been ordained that all ballet on this continent should be *Russian,* or else it isn't really ballet at all. They feel they are vindicated in this policy by the success of such a "Russian" spectacle as Fokine's *Coq d'Or* last year. But few people outside of New York and all over America, realize that the size and complexity of this production prohibit it from ever being shown to the country at large. At best, ten big cities have a chance to see it. For the hundreds of small cities which make the bulk of time on tour, they can always sling them *Les Sylphides,* or *Petrouchka, Schéhérazade* or *Prince Igor.* The small cities are finally sick of being sold, tired of being treated more patronizingly, for example, by the Russian ballet than they are by Helen Hayes, whose performances of *Victoria Regina* in Topeka or Houston were identical to her appearances in Chicago or New York. It is difficult to give good performances of large dance works in towns that have small theatrical facilities, but the point is this: The productions of the Diaghilev ballets, and those built on the same formula, still in the Russian repertory, were designed to hang in such big houses as the Champs Elysées Theatre in Paris, or Covent Garden in London, where their initial reputation is made. The present technical mechanism, just as the present economic policy, and artistic attitude of the Russian ballet does not any longer apply to the general needs or practical uses of the American theatre. But the sticks are notoriously five or ten years behind New York, although unfortunately for the managers, movies, radio and the ballet tours themselves have taken a tuck in the lag.

Sooner or later, after all our hard ditch-work and pile-driving is done, the managers will turn to our American companies and try to assimilate them on their own conditions. If Russian ballet still can be made to hold together, yet if the available Russians happen to be all in Australia or South Africa at the moment, it will not be difficult to tack a couple of Russian names onto a pick-up American company. They will be able for some time to come to find someone who remembers enough echoes of the Imperial repertory to slap it on a stage. The Mordkin Ballet announces for the present (1938-39) season *Voices of Spring* (Strauss), *Lac des Cygnes* (Tchaikovsky) and *Trepak* (Tcherepnin). He further states "there will be also new leading dancers from Leonide Massine's Monte Carlo troupe, including Nina Stroganova, Vladimir Dokoudovsky, Kari Karnakovsky and Tania Dokoudovska." It is significant that the Mordkin Company is the only native American (sic) troupe to be handled by one of the two large concert-management monopolies. Although Mordkin has been in America for years, one does not think of him as yet caring to qualify as the head of an "American" ballet.

And there may be some money in Russo-American ballet companies, but not for long. I only hope that when the time comes for the monopolies to turn their attention to our stripling American troupes, we will have the popular support or else the good luck to be able to resist them. They will need us badly, and naturally we will always need them, at least for *our* lifetime. But if we can survive independently up to the point of our being over-hauled, we ought to be able to hold out enough longer to get as clever lawyers as they've got. We all know the hard history of ballet in America; we've been making it and we've been paying for it. We will be to blame, not the managers, if we can't name our own terms at that juncture. And ultimately speaking, which is all in our favor, the managers don't care. They'll be big about it if they can, without much risk, clean up on our dancing. What difference does it make, ultimately speaking, and even to them, whether it's an American or a Russian company? Shucks, if the boobs want American ballet, let 'em buy it.

And then a warm, nostalgic glow will gently suffuse them. They will bend back in their swivel-chairs and allow themselves vague and gentle reminiscences of all their contacts and all their contracts with dancers dead and gone. They will tell you how much they lost on Mordkin, on Isadora Duncan, Pavlova, on Shan-Kar, and on the Russian tours. They will point to the framed photographs (and "framed" is correct) of all the artists they have "managed" over the long decades, with affection and genial amusement. They will be talking out loud about the artists, but they will be thinking inside about convenient bankruptcies, broken contracts, legal "reorganizations," artists snatched from their lists and artists they've been able to seduce from their rivals. And they will smile, partly to themselves. What the hell, it's not been such a bad game, after all. In their small way they have been art-patrons, too.

II. *PORTRAIT OF THE PATRON*

IS NOT A PATRON, MY LORD, ONE WHO LOOKS WITH UN-CONCERN ON A MAN STRUGGLING FOR LIFE IN THE WATER, AND WHEN HE HAS REACHED GROUND ENCUMBERS HIM WITH HELP? *Samuel Johnson: 1755*

Patronage of the arts either by states or individuals, once meant the provision of money towards certain creative ends. The Roman Catholic Church, the Medicis, Louis XIV, the Esterhazys, Ida Rubenstein, derived pleasure in the productions of painting, sculpture, architecture, music or stage-works for which they paid, for a variety of public and private reasons. Some delighted in a product in which they themselves had no part except the capacious enjoyment of achieved beauty. Others preferred to participate, and still others to pay for a frame in which they could themselves shine, or could be illuminated by reflected glory. The patrons of Diaghilev included at various times: Baron Dimitri Guinzbourg, the Comtesses de Greffuhle, de Noailles, and Polignac; the Aga Khan, Otto Kahn, Sir Basil Zaharov, Lord Rothermere, Mesdames de Euphrussy, Chanel, Misia Sert, the Marchioness of Ripon and Etienne de Beaumont. Most of these influential but cultivated people genuinely loved the ballet. It was their opulent pleasure to permit Diaghilev to employ their money as he desired. There were few conditions attached. Frequently these patrons would detest the results which their money made possible. The givers were his devoted personal friends; the gifts, mostly genuine expressions of their affection or admiration.

Ballet-patronage continues with the Russian Ballet today, but in an altered form to fit the time. When Diaghilev was given money to stage opera or ballet, he spent it staging operas and ballets. He did not extract even a modest commission for their presentation, because he produced only what interested him to produce, and his pleasure demanded no surplus profit. He died bankrupt, and it is well known that Mme. Chanel even paid for his funeral. But in recent years ballet-patronage has operated differently.

For example, when *Union Pacific* was in consideration, that benevolent despot Colonel de Basil, implored a committee of American ladies to subvention this new ballet, which was to be *their* new ballet, as a private and personal enterprise. This was an efficient system used subsequently on other works. A sum was collected, just about enough to mount two large ballets of the same size. Yet to this date, neither the composer of the musical score nor the author of the libretto have been awarded their extremely modest royalties in full; although for three years the work must have been produced in America alone, some seventy-five or eighty times. The accident of the choice of the Baron d'Erlanger to write tepid music for *Les Cent Baisers* by Bronislava Nijinska, or for this season's *Cendrillon* by Fokine, is only explicable on the face of an elegant amateur's wanting to hear his music performed up to the point of being willing to pay for it. Diaghilev never accepted cash to produce works he did not deem worthy of production, even though he might have kept part of it to produce other works which interested him, any more than Fortune Magazine takes money for industrial surveys it considers news-worthy, from the corporations it chooses to describe. This kind of ingenious, if fragmentary, patronage by trifling amateurs to which de Basil assented, did little to enhance a growing repertory. Since it was based only on personal considerations of social prestige or economic convenience, the ideas in the dancing or artistic quality were inevitably secondary.

When the inevitable cracks became too apparent in the fabric of the contemporary Russian organizations for hiding even under its official veneer of glamor, when after seasons of bickering, threats and back-breaking tours of nightmare insecurity had culminated in a spectacular stabbing in Chicago, and a bigamy in Louisville; when even the cold sense of the dance-managers could no longer prevent an open split be-tween Leonide Massine, the chief artistic mover, and de Basil, the mo-tivating commercial energy, then came the call to auxiliary committees of American ladies who, fluttering on the fringes of Russian "first nights," had not been previously marshaled to their own best uses. A rear-guard of resident White Russian night-club colonels and a dapper composer left over from Diaghilev galvanized by the ballet-managers' busy press-agents, summoned thrilling emergency meetings at impor-tant homes to enlist the aid of one and all in the preservation for Amer-ica of the glorious tradition of Russian ballet, which seemed, heaven knows why, vaguely to be in some threatened condition.

The American female patron is an engaging specimen, young or old. She is utilized singly and in the herd as peripheral aid, on the one hand by the commercial-manager; on the other, by the ballet-organization it-self. She can be counted on for a certain amount of social-column space attendant upon her apparitions at *premières,* and she can always be ex-pected to know someone who knows someone who would be willing to ask someone who knows the president of General Telephones for a little cheque. She herself is a comparatively "poor" woman. She has given up her second car, and done without an extra man-servant. But she has a proprietary air about Ballet, "our" ballet, she calls it. Her father-in-law, or her uncle was a trustee of Juilliard Foundation, or of the Metropolitan Opera Association, or of the Philharmonic Society. She herself, has no longer time for music-lessons but a divine young Russian emigré, fright-fully attractive and talented, is coming or has just come to play his new score for her, which Massine absolutely must be made to do, and he in-sists, that to really understand it, she must take up her playing again. You can see even Massine's job is no cinch either.

Music indeed is very often the bait or link which lures or binds a female patron to a Russian ballet. Her training and experience in the arts has been mainly musical. From this one might have thought that

59

during the last five years she might have interested the Russian directorate in one single American composer. Yet who, with the exception of Hindemith, whom Diaghilev had approached ten years before, were even the new foreign composers: Jean Françaix (*Beach*), Vladimir Dukelsky (*Jardin Publique*), Nabokov (*Union Pacific*), Karol-Rathaus (*Le Lion Amoureux*), the Baron d'Erlanger (*Les Cent Baisers* and *Cendrillon*). In America, Catherine Littlefield had worked with David Guion, Ferdy Grofé and Herbert Kingsley; Ruth Page with Aaron Copland, Jerome Moross, W. G. Still, and Gershwin; the American Ballet with George Antheil, Kay Swift and Henry Brant; the Ballet Caravan with Paul Bowles, Elliott Carter, Copland, Robert McBride, Charles Naginski and Virgil Thomson. The female patron may be forgiven for not having heard among the names of all these younger American composers anyone save that of George Gershwin. Yet have the Europeans written scores intrinsically more significant or even more danceable than the Americans? They decidedly have not.

However, there are indications that the female patrons are weakening and may be in the market for an American or two. Last year Mr. Vladimir Dukelsky, in his dapper personality as "Vernon Duke" the Broadway songster, organized his *High-Low* Concerts, a tasty series at the St. Regis roof, which Muriel Draper promptly named the *New Low* (in Vulgarity). Duke attempted to veneer the younger American musicians with enough social glitter to make them passable to the international set by having "portraits" of well-known people set to a piano and oboe, or hiring a blues-singer to "swing" a few eighteenth-century songs. There is a special kind of Russian *hors d'oeuvre* which they make out of how-you-say? Indian sweet-corn and sour-cream. It must be about the only Russian *hors d'oeuvre* that isn't absolutely divine.

However, even though one pretty, idle, nervous woman may be unimpressive, an aggregation of idle, pretty, nervous women exert a certain furtive levy on retired bank-presidents, corporation lawyers, or indulgent husbands, and on an occasional unsuspecting but ambitious social-climber. The actual stake of the patrons is even less than the manager's, because these girls don't even work. But they do exert a kind of penumbral pressure, and serve a definitely useful function for the "Great Conspiracy." Their personal taste is no real taste, but merely a light preference for an amalgam of erroneous memories of the Golden Period of ballet, fashion-photos from the last two numbers of Harper's Bazaar, and whatever they can retain from the program-books of occasional Friday afternoon concerts in Carnegie Hall. To them snobbery in its fancier forms is no more alien than fleas to a dog. But congregated to back the

Ballet Exhibition, to buy boxes for the Ballet Benefit, to add their little ounce of obstructionist atmosphere to the general economic confusion, they are reliable enough. For them, New York is still a province of Paris, and the rest of America is its dirty back-yard. If they should be humanly sweet, or handsome, or well-meaning, or even for a moment or two genuinely and selflessly interested, then it is even harder for the serious artist to bear. For ultimately speaking, they are idle women, and we are occupied with work.

The plight of the ballet-patron, like the Policemen of Penzance, has not been, at least recently, a happy one. Due to the late unpleasantness in the world of Russian ballet, descent from Imperial days has been like the Greek Orthodox Church itself, split. But where is Rome, and where Byzantium now? There are the Montagues of the house of Colonel de Basil, and the Capulets of the house of Mr. Serge Denham. The managers (here, Hurok Attractions, Inc.) oscillated nervously, which was quite understandable, before finally passionately espousing the colors of the Capulets. There were a lot of Montagues who wouldn't mind being Capulets, and some Capulets weren't so damn sure, themselves. The managers and the Committee of Patrons arranged a desperate merger to fuse the family's interests, and at first they blandly operated without the consent of either Romeo or Juliet who, very much alive, resided together in the furious person of the artistic dictator, Leonide Massine. As far as dictators go, it is far more legitimate that Massine hold a whip-hand, than a hitherto obscure if agreeable Russian called Serge Denham, whose only claim to fame, aside from a decent reputation on Wall Street, is his recently expressed interest in dancing. Mr. Robert Pitney, America's number-one balletomane, is quoted as questioning, upon the mention of the unfamiliar name of this director of the bigger Ballet Russe: "Hum, Serge Denham? denim, serge? . . . Then it *must* be made up out of whole cloth."

The American female-patrons were treated to quite a gamut of hysteria following the daily developments of the great world-ballet serial-thriller, and the attendant publicity was not stinted. With one troupe at Drury Lane and another at Covent Garden, picture their confusion. Even today they resent any direct question as to whose colors they really sport—because they are not absolutely sure with whom Tania will be dancing, or where darling Baba's heart lies. But if de Basil is exiled today or Denham dethroned tomorrow, their hearts won't exactly break. Arnold Haskell, the manager's darling of the British tours, very recently was claiming de Basil as the unique figure fit to assume Diaghilev's cloak in the present distressing anarchy of ballet. His Cossack steel-eyed strength, his efficient use of the psychological knout was widely publicized as just what the doctor prescribed. Less than a year ago de Basil was the Stalin of ballet. Later, due to his regrettable but understandable misunderstanding of our so difficult, how-you-say, English language, de Basil accidentally disposed of the commercial rights of some of the more popular ballets in his repertory a couple of times to the different combines, which, as the English Courts of Law later decided, was an excess of efficiency. Yet this seems to me no worse than anything else de Basil did during his remarkable dictatorship, when one recalls he was only stopped by an hair-breadth from mounting Scriabine's *Le Poème d'Extase*, with an ecstatic libretto by the spurious mystic, Dimitri Merejekovski, and that he had never at any time any interest in dancing at all. Now, de Basil has been remanded to the caviar-industry, and Mr. Haskell is taking a reef in his Mosaic prophecies of the fulfilment of the contemporary Russian ballet's manifest destiny. Arnold Haskell is the Neville Chamberlain of ballet-spokesmanship. It will perhaps be a difficult yet not insurmountable task to explain the inevitable and necessary return from his Elba of the redoubtable Cossack Colonel. Judging, however, from the models of the "realistic" notes recently issued by Downing Street on Spain or Czechoslovakia, we can be confident of the logical and tactful formulation of Haskell's policy.

The Managers have, through their busy press-agents, developed quite an agile technique for catering to the American female-patron. Ballet-balls, ballet-teas, and matinee ballet club-specials with Russian-salad plates are sagely scheduled. Cards are issued for "open" dress-rehearsals. The female-patron's professional advice is occasionally requested, *en passant,* during an entr'acte—"What would Madam like to see in repertory tomorrow? How did Madam think Tania looked last night?" What difference does it make to the managers as it is always the same repertory and Tania either looked tired or else she didn't? The stage-door is usually open to them, and the poor Russian dancers, lonely enough in their eternal vagrancy, are not averse to having an expensive shoulder on which to sob. For the female-patrons are genuinely sympathetic: "My dear, what that little dancer told me about her life, why Siberia—, escape, Shanghai, Monte Carlo—, why it was incredible! You never read anything in a novel so fascinating." As we know, they don't read much.

Seriously speaking, as for ballet-backing, private patronage in America is almost a thing of the past. Even though I know of two or three spectacular and devoted exceptions to this rule over the last few years, nevertheless, and for the immediate future here at least, the reliable patrons must be the anonymous mass-audience of ordinary people all over the country, who will not interest themselves in ballet for either acquired prestige or direct publicity, but because they love it as theatre and pay as much for it as they do for any other form of theatre. This unquestionably is the way it should be. Either the ballet must keep itself, as it did, for example, in Europe from 1830 to 1850, and pay brilliantly,—or as it has in England and America from 1934 to 1938, and pay (due only to the "Great Conspiracy") less well, or else it is not worth our time or trouble.

There is an increasing and definite economic connection between art forms and their popular reception. No private patronage can much help that reception if the dance form itself lacks inherent interest, nor can an idle and fragmentary private patronage long fetter the form with its own narrow restrictions of inertia or idleness. There is not much use talking about State patonage in America for a long time to come. The recent Fine Arts Bill offered in Congress was laughed out of the House of Representatives, when an anti-New Deal Congressman brought down the House when he gave a crude imitation of a toe-dancer. However, there may eventually be a source of theatrical patronage from a field which may at first seem surprising. Many of us would not be a bit surprised if, in the next five years, some of the large labor-unions would directly occupy themselves with presenting works of independent theatrical excellence. The activities of a great organization such as the International Ladies Garment Workers Union, with its enlightened social and cultural program, has already successfully made its debut on Broadway with the production of its phenomenal revue hit, *Pins and Needles*, of which at the present time, some three or four companies are simultaneously touring the United States. Our best labor unions are in an excellent position to take the place of the Medici. Organized working people have been taught by their unions something more than elementary economic defense tactics. They have been taught to respect the cultural monuments of the human spirit as standards of human behavior. The creative theatre is a weapon as well as a recreation. Dancing may be also discovered as not the least of its defenses.

III. *THE FUNCTION OF THE CRITIC*

EDGAR DEGAS SAID THAT THE MUSES NEVER DISPUTE ANYTHING AMONG THEMSELVES. THEY WORK ALL DAY, ENTIRELY APART. WHEN EVENING COMES AND THEIR TASKS ARE DONE, ON FINDING THEMSELVES AGAIN TOGETHER, THEY DANCE. *They do not speak.**

There are several ways of considering the function of an art critic, whether his field is paint, music or the dance. Some people would have him explain and clarify for his general public by a technical, historical or dialectical analysis, the work under discussion, which from its very particular or original values might seem temporarily difficult to appreciate, and then to enhance this appreciation as the essence of the work is clearly revealed. Others would have him simmer down the essence of the work of art to its diluted lowest-common-denominator, showing its superficial resemblance to the origins from which it had sprung, and then to offer the public a vulgarized secondary version which removes the obligation of having to make up one's mind about the fresh original. Both these attitudes presuppose that the critic is mildly interested in what he is criticizing, and that if he finds something that pleases him he will praise it and induce others to share his pleasure; or if not, he will attack it and illuminate its sterility. But we have a third sort, who actually dislikes what he writes about, and whose interest is, however active, entirely negative. This sounds like an anomaly until we realize that too many of the dance-critics in America are not by experience or by profession critics of dancing at all, but usually music-critics who have been ordered by their editors to cover a given dance-attraction as a scheduled "musical" assignment. Here is another sinister alliance in our "Great Conspiracy."

The music management-bureaus find it convenient to sell dance-attractions as *music*-attractions; hence, the indirect commercial uses of the music-critics who have continually to be primed. The ordinary music-critic has a tolerant contempt for dancing. He chooses to think of it as a secondary accompaniment or tertiary complement to music, with which he may or may not be familiar. If he knows the music he will not perhaps bother to learn as much about the dancing and will assume that the dancing is "not as good as" the music, since he has less information, instinctive or acquired, about it. The critic must at all costs maintain the superior prestige of the *music* as such, over and above any dancing whatever, in order to insure the superiority of his own position. Hence, the music-critic usually *hears* the dancing. He seldom if ever allows

*Degas, Danse. Dessin. p. 11 (Paul Valèry).

64

himself to *see* it. The mediocre orchestral presentation of the Russian ballets has only furthered his disdain, should he have been a conscientious musician. But even had they a good orchestra instead of a bad one, such thinly informed pen-pushers as Samuel Chotzinoff of the New York *Post,* having once half-humorously voiced their ignorant dislike for dancing, would still be necessarily contemptuous on principle. There have been a few startling exceptions to this, exceptions which set the general average only in a blacker light. Heinrich Heine's and Théophile Gautier's correspondence and daily reviews, Stendhal's notes on the dancer Salvatore Viganò, or Carl van Vechten's notes on the Diaghilev Golden Period are excellent models. One remembers with gratitude the late H. T. Parker of the old *Boston Evening Transcript;* Margaret Lloyd of the *Christian Science Monitor* is very able and informed, but far too kind and gentle, even to me. For me, as with Blake: "Damn braces, bless relaxes." I am grateful for three intelligent younger critics—Jerome Boehm on the New York *Herald-Tribune,* Walter Terry of the Boston *Herald,* and Edwin Denby of the quarterly, *Modern Music.* The last two have actually danced. Lucile Marsh of *Dance Digest* has for a long time courageously defended our American dancers. Ruth Howard of *The American Dancer* has been actively interested in sensible national legislation in favor of our dancers. Anatole Chujoy in *Dance* has caused Agripina Vaganova's important technical treatise to be run serially, and is an ardent advocate of choreography by Americans. He is also one of the few Americans who has a reading knowledge of Russian, and is a devoted visitor to all dance studios. Albertina Vitak of *The American Dancer* knows good dancing because she is a good dancer. Ann Barzel of Chicago writes occasional letters to dance magazines. Some newspaper should employ her permanently. Her taste is excellent, and her wit is acid and true. Chicago, indeed, is favored with more critics who have a real interest in American dancing than New York. Claudia Cassidy of the *Journal of Commerce,* Eugene Stinson of the *Daily News,* Ashton Stevens of the *Evening American,* and particularly Cecil Smith of the *Daily Tribune* are all worth reading. In Los Angeles Isabel Morse Jones of the *Times* maintains a consistently high standard. John Rosenfeld, Jr., of the Dallas *News* is my candidate for the ablest younger generation dance critic in the country. In Washington, Glenn Dillard Gunn of the *Herald* formerly of Chicago, and Ray Brown of the *Post* are both reliable. In Pittsburgh, Dr. Frederick Dorian of the *Gazette* is both a scholar and a journalist. In Hartford, Theodore Parker of the *Courant* is particularly friendly to American dancers. In Springfield (Mass.) A. L. S. Wood of the *Union* is articulate and accurate.

In the farthest flung towns, strangely enough, one frequently finds the best critics. Personally, I would prefer to be reviewed by any critic rather than those in the "big" cities. For example, in Lewiston, Maine, Charlotte Michaud stimulates communities who have little chance to enjoy stage dancing. Page Hosmer of the Tacoma *News Tribune*, Elizabeth Hylblom of the Colorado Springs *Gazette*, Ilmar Grondhal of the Portland Morning *Oregonian*, and J. W. Sayre of the Seattle *Post Intelligensia* all appreciate our native efforts. In San Francisco Alfred Frankenstein on the *Chronicle* and Alexander Fried on the *Examiner* are far more open-minded and intelligent than their colleagues on the *News* and the *Call Bulletin*.

And above them all, there is Ernest Newman, the distinguished music-critic of the London *Times*, whose style is as urbane, knowing, witty and generous as his analysis is profound and full of common-sense. Theatrical dancing does not frighten him, and dance-music does not seem to him an impure or a secondary form. Read for example, his notice of Paul Hindemith's score for *Nobilissima Visione* (St. Francis, July 24, 1938) and Massine's symphonic treatment in general.

1. *The Historians*

In the realm of writers about the dance as a special art-form, there are three main divisions; the historians, the appreciators, and the journalists. I personally prefer the historians. These are writers who may or may not have been professional dancers, but who all at least have had a direct participation with the dance-stage and with the dance-works they describe. They have written the history of their theatrical epoch from first hand observation, because for the most part they have collaborated in creating that history. One can reread Calvocaressi's *Memoirs of Opera and Ballet*; Prince Lieven's *Birth of Ballets Russes*, and Ninette de Valois' excellent practical book on her work for the British National Ballet. Cocteau's, Stravinsky's, Lifar's and Astruc's memoirs are invaluable marginalia. The composer, Constant Lambert's *Music Ho!* was the first realistic study, and remains almost the only clear-eyed British book on the policy and aesthetic of the Diaghilev Period. In a slightly different category are Cyril Beaumont's invaluable bibliographies. He is the eminent English book-seller and publisher, who has done more to dignify the historic literature of the dance than any man of his epoch, by issuing such works, for example, as translation of Théophile Gautier's collected criticism, Noverre's letters, André Levinson's *Taglioni*, besides a recent large and fascinating anthology of ballet libretti. In America, the Kamin

Bookstore exercises a similar highly useful function with its shop and publishing headquarters in New York City. From the work of all these writers and editors, specific information may be obtained as to definite facts and events concerning the actual production of dancing in theatres. They do not set up too many aesthetic or qualitative judgments. They have been busy with practical problems, and we turn to them for aid in the solution of our own theatrical needs rather than to know gossip or personal opinion about a certain contemporary dancer in a certain personal situation.

2. *The Appreciators*

Great Britain is particularly lush in the ballet-appreciators. Hardly a month passes when some new work of enthusiastic appreciation is not issued by writers who are also usually critics of paintings, or films, or of literature. The English seem to exult in an unreleased and self-indulgent enthusiasm for ballet-ballet, which is due in part to their physical insularity, to their traditional suspicion that Paris is always patronizing them from across that Channel. Yet the ballet in Paris, aside from Lifar's Mondays at the Opéra, is barely popular enough in France today to warrant a Russian season once a year. Nowhere in the Western world today is there such an avid audience for classic dancing as London, and it is surely most fortunate for their own young national movement of British Ballet. But the ballet-appreciators, no matter how well-educated they are, and they have a general literary and artistic background that puts nearly every American writer to shame, do little or nothing to make dancing simpler to see for ordinary people who would like it anyway after being exposed to it once or twice. Either the appreciator constructs *recherché* baroque verbal panoramas of beloved ballets, as Sacheverell Sitwell treated Diaghilev's production of *La Belle au Bois Dormant* in his *Dance of the Quick and the Dead*, or else they erect vague philosophic systems of personal esthetic values, an ample sort of ballet epistemology as Adrian Stokes does. Stokes' two little books, *Tonight the Ballet* and *Russian Ballets,* have many good things to say about dancing; but in general, his particular passion and correspondences are too apparent; he is *personally* so convinced of his unique definitions that his descriptions read as if he were recording his own spiritual and emotional progress. The succeeding ballets he has seen and described are almost epigraphs for an autobiography. However, the ordinary British blanket-acceptance of the Russian phenomena as an aspect of divine artistic revelation has been recently tempered by the suggestive studies of Rayner Heppenstall,

Caryl Brahms, and A. V. Coton. Contemporary English prose-style, as far as most dance-criticism goes, has unfortunate models. Instead of basing their statement on a Coleridge, a Matthew Arnold, or even an I. A. Richards, their paragraphs are predominantly pre-Raphaelite. Markova and Toumanova are framed in pearly periods which but for Walter Pater could never have appeared. Yet the appreciators are always doomed to lose out in the end. They try to paint with fatty words what happens in time on a clean stage. They make of their word-painting a competitive indoor-sport, like bridge or badminton. You feel them earnestly forcing their pens: "We'll make you *see* it: we'll *make* you see it." As a matter of fact, even their most detailed and rhapsodic appreciations are usually unintelligible unless you *have* already seen the ballet, and if you have already seen it, there is hardly any need more than an enjoyable if superficial corroboration, to read the libretto after you get home from the theatre. And as a matter of fact, they merely supplement the candid camera. But in combination they'll have to do for us until we're given actual films of complete ballets.

a. On Ballet Photographers

Recently the candid-camera has invaded the field of ballet document-tion. The candid-camera in the hands of most news-photographers and the average eager amateur, is the worst liar in the photographic family. Under the guise of an objective and frank reporter, the candid-camera distorts, alters, and ultimately destroys the very dances it pretends to document. In the first place, the candid operator has usually to stand in the wings, on one side of the stage. At best, if placed in a prompter's box, he is too near to include the whole stage-picture, and from his seat he is too far away. Hence, nearly every shot is an angle-shot to start with, snapped from a place where no one in the audience has ever seen the ballet, and from where the choreographer never intended it to have been seen. If a considerable number of candid shots could be reproduced in sequence, an approximation of a record of motion might possibly be obtained. By a considerable number I mean fifty, not twenty. But lacking this, the ballet snapshot is usually seized out of its legitimate context, to accentuate an accidental if spectacular leap, or some astonishing motion only effective in a camera print, but which has little or no connection with the ballet as it is seen by an audience in the intended procedure of its performance. There has been recently published in England an extremely expensive album of such photos called *Ballet in Action*, by Merlyn Severn. Its blurb assures us:

The vast majority of ballet photographs published are not, strictly speaking, ballet photographs at all. They are pictures of one or more dancers in pre-arranged poses which may even bear only a vague resemblance to the poses actually used in the ballet in question. They are consequently of little use in the serious study of choreography, none at all in analyzing the style of individual dancers.

This book changes all that. Miss Severn's photographs, which it is not too much to say have revolutionized the art of ballet photography, were all taken during actual performances by the ordinary stage lighting.

Now Miss Severn may have spent time and effort on stage and in dark room, but her published efforts are not worth a tenth of the sixteen dollars they cost in this country. Ordinary stage-lighting is wretched illumination even for a fast candid film. The lack of any range of color is rendered more miserable by the falsification of chromatic values in the coarse-screen grain of black and white snap-shot. Instead of receiving a representation of startling accuracy we have only a record of arrested physical strain. Compare, for example, any old "posed" photo of Nijinsky in *Le Spectre de la Rose* and Miss Severn's shot of a contemporary dancer in the same rôle, with his face constricted in an agony of effort like a runner collapsing at the end of a hundred-yard dash. We are not, as a matter of fact, nearly as conscious of this strain when watching him across the footlights as in looking at the candid shot. The very reverse of her blurb's boasts are true. Any posed, static picture of a ballet, if arranged by a sensitive photographic crafstman or the ballet's choreographer himself, tells far more of the spirit, atmosphere and essence than a casual and accidental performance picture. It makes very little difference if the actual poses are included in the ballet or not. In neither case is any movement actually transcribed. But, by careful lighting and conscious arrangement, a designed approximation of the essential movement can be achieved, impossible in the broken hurry and accidental angling of a candid close-up. Looking over Miss Severn's coarse-textured and blurred plates, one sees only the clipped mistakes in technique of her suddenly betrayed subjects. It is true that the leaps seem incredibly high, higher than they do on the stage itself, because they are shot from far below the audience's eye-level. But for the most part, we have a permanent record of lazy legs, sloppy arms, indeterminate gestures which are only preliminaries to an absolute climactic position. These climaxes which she never records, or at least never selects to print, are the honest salient foci in ballet design. All others are diminishing movements departing from the climaxes, or crescendant ones approaching them. If we take Miss Severn's surface records as basic fact, we find the ballet troupes she photographs have a technical equipment so loose, ill-rehearsed and awkward that we can scarcely recognize them.

The posed photos of the Golden Age of Russian ballet are often very fine. The prints of Walery, Gerschel, Fisher and Bert may seem superficially old-fashioned in their decorative accessories or pre-war framing, but these craftsmen and others of their generation in Warsaw, Paris and Petersburg, were careful to light and arrange Nijinsky, Karsavina, Pavlova and Fokine in positions which were the summation, the highest common denominator of a kinetic sequence. Baron Gayne de Meyer's brilliant sequences of *Le Pavillon de Armide, Carnaval, Faune* and *Spectre* are particularly impressive. Taken twenty years ago, they seem as fresh as done today. Man Ray's portraits of Lifar in *Apollon Musagète, Jack-in-the-Box,* and *Barabau,* however, "posed," give a true impression of these ballets' movement. George Hoynigen-Huené and Cecil Beaton in London have made some splendid still-groupings of the Monte Carlo repertory. In New York, George Platt Lynes' numerous plates of the artists and productions of the American Ballet and the Ballet Caravan serve as a magnificently lit and complete visual record of their work, and yet hardly a plate is a literal transcript of actual choreography. All of it was posed by photographer or choreographer against backgrounds representing but not reproducing stage conditions. Maurice Seymour of Chicago has done good static portraits of the contemporary Russians on their American tours. None of these are candid operators. The candid camera is a facile fibber. One has to question its eye just as much as one must perforce be cynical of the writings of most ballet journalists. Perhaps, if a candid-artist used his eye, instead of his trigger-finger, he could get some good selective shots. But it takes more than quick fingering. Barbara Morgan and Paul Hansen have done some fine shots of Martha Graham, and Richard Tucker of Boston demonstrates by his conscientious work that there is nothing the matter with the candid-camera itself, but only the ordinary uses to which it is put.

3. *The Journalists*

The journalistic critic of the ballet ·is the hardest for a worker in the dance to tolerate. He it is who, combining the functions of historian and appreciator issues stop-press reports for the benefit of an audience whose latent hysteria it is his task to incite. It is he who must report or invent the juicier details attendant upon the lives, fortunes and private honor of the ballet dancers, directors and other collaborators.

Arnold Haskell of the London *Daily Telegraph* knows the ballet well enough, and it is not so much the sense of all of what he says, as the way he says it, that makes most of his writing so invincibly exasperating. He has assumed, consecutively, since his early monographs on Trefilova and Karsavina, the attitude of devout neophyte, inspired crusader, tender lover, and evangelical guardian. Book after book from his facile hand appears and the illustrations and format become annually better and better. His letter-press couched in the stylized apology of a helplessly obsessed yet sympathetic family friend, reads like an elder brother's letter to a schoolgirl about the facts of dance-life. He has nary a real disapproval, and has mastered the subtleties of critical evasion to the point of fastidious diplomacy. One can never be quite certain which current ballerina is to be the recipient of his unimpeachable accolade as sole guardian of *true* "classicism." For years, with his quiet yet burrowing energy he has played his game of critical tag; now Toumanova, no—now Baronova; no,—now Danilova; no, now one of our own English dancers is *it*. Both his reader and his ballerina were kept in an agony of delicious indecision, rather like sophomores waiting to be tapped for a college sorority, as Haskell groomed his catalogue of allusive parallels to great dancers of the past, his current comparisons with our own.

His extended biographical study of Diaghilev stands in that most trying category of first-rate subjects treated in a second-rate fashion. Arnold Haskell was discreet when he should have been surgical; genteel when he might have been honest; at all times styleless and dull when he had an unparalleled opportunity to recreate brilliance, human complexity and tragic splendor. Think of what Marcel Proust, or lacking him, what André Gide, Levinson, or even Harold Nicolson might have done with the same material.

Yet Haskell's last book *Ballet* is a remarkable piece of publishing. By no means a small book, it can be bought in America for less than half a dollar. It is clearly written, well organized, has excellent pictures, and is in every way his best work. In it he shows traces of a comprehension of the economic structure of Russian dancing. He betrays an approach to a new (for him) realism, accentuated by his knowledge of the break-up of Russian ballet, and a new, very honest and admirable passion, his devotion to the young national British ballet. Yet he still accepts *Schéhérazade, Carnaval, Igor,* and the dreary rest of them, on their face value; for him Fokine is still a criterion, and the future is anticipated only in terms of the familiar past.

In America we have of course our ballet journalists, yet they are not necessarily much improvement over our British cousins. There is no one here, for example, who is as experienced, as educated in dancing, or who writes as popularly as Haskell himself. Our methods are a little more high-pressure. We want immediate results in terms not of books published, but in minutes on radio-stations, inches in gossip-columns, pictures in the Sunday Supplements. Irving Deakin is an American version of Arnold Haskell. But he has neither Haskell's information, taste, nor devotion. He has been pursuing one of the most curious crusades in the rococo history of recent ballet journalism. He has dedicated his pen to proving that Adolph Bolm, preëminent Russian character of the Golden Age, was responsible not only for Serge de Diaghilev's initial success, but for the present happy status of ballet in America as well. This curiosity is not clarified even when one reads on his blurbs that he is "incidentally" Bolm's son-in-law. In his books which are pasted-up riflings without acknowledgment from every other writer on the dance since Noverre, in his radio talks and in his articles, he is a past-master of ballet-cliché and theatrical vulgarism. He is our "Great Conspiracy's" greatest journalistic conspirator.

a. The Critic's Lexicon: John Martin

When Mr. John Martin addressed a sell-out audience on the night of "Modern" Dance, which followed the Evening of American Theatrical Dancing at the Center Theatre in New York, given under the auspices of Dance International 1900-1937, he blandly assured us that what we were about to see was not *theatrical*, its scenery was not really *decor,* its costumes were only vesture for motion, its music mere aural scenery. The "modern" concert dance was relegated to a level distinctly superior to that of simple theatre-stage framed by an ordinary gilded proscenium. By his inference dancing became not simply a diverting or evocative spectacle but rather an autobiographical rite celebrating the psychic impulses of its individual dancers. In a review of the New York première of the American-Wigman follower, Hanya Holm's composition, *Trend*, Mr. Martin praised Arch Lauterer's ingenious and massive constructivist setting as having "no smack of decor." Last summer (1937) Mr. Martin was alarmed by certain "decadent" (i.e., theatrical) overtones he sensed in young Anna Sokolow's anti-Fascist dance work. Last year (1936-37) he detected in Martha Graham's a "neo-classic" tendency, and this year (1937-38) he found her perilously "surrealist."

The technique of dance-criticism lies chiefly in the use of the critic's vocabulary. In the field of dance the critic's vocabulary has often to be borrowed from another art. In architecture we can talk in terms of structure, material and function, calling Georgia grey, Vermont or Indiana limestone, lally columns, t-beams or soil-pipes by their specific given names. That is, these terms mean the same thing to everyone. Similarly in painting and music. The theatre, however, employs for its own uses architecture, poetry and music. Hence, its critical language, while more amplified, is also more vague. The vocabulary of dance criticism borrows the idiom of fine arts and literature, but the problem is not simple even when one is armed with this combined ammunition, primarily be-cause the dance critic, like his colleagues the drama critic and the sports-writer refer to an event passed forever before anyone reads of it, an event largely interesting only to those who saw it at a certain already vanished performance, and much of whose interest depends on the qual-ity of that particular performance. To combine an analysis of subject intention with a factual description of what actually transpired in a broad enough frame to be something more than a mere news-report, calls for a technique which is very developed, a vocabulary, in other words, which is precise.

I wish to consider the vocabulary of John Martin, the well-known critic of the New York *Times*. By his energy and interest in dancing he has almost single-handed created a place for the dance-critic in New York, and hence, in America. His job has not been easy, for on the one hand he has been assailed by the ballet-managers for his contempt of ballet as a theatrical form, and on the other, by a large section of young dancers in this form who fear his influential opposition to the future of their art. He is incorruptible, and this is no idle homage, for in the last two years I knew very well at least one powerful ballet-manager and one ballet-patron have done their best to have him displaced from the posi-tion he has done so much to dignify. The maintenance of this position and personal attitude testifies to his editors' complete faith in him. I myself was forced to resign as ballet-critic from "The Dance Observer," an anti-ballet monthly, because I had written an attack on Martin which they refused to print. My bread and butter luckily didn't depend on it, but I was given a fair taste of what it feels like to be under fire, even in journalism. I have even heard of Martin's being proposed for a per-manent chair of the Dance at Harvard. His presence at a college might easily prove more useful than his expression of continual irritation at his necessity to report the activity of our unfolding theatrical dance. My dis-agreement with Mr. Martin is the sincerest form of flattery because there is hardly any other name in the American field which represents the expression of a conviction based on preference rather than on second-hand reading.

Looking over his several published works, I assume Mr. Martin opposes his use of the words "health" to "degeneracy," "degeneracy" to "decadence," "Neo-classicism" to "classicism," "classicism" to "romanticism," "naturalism" to "realism," "realism" to "surrealism," and "aristocracy" to "democracy" in his idiosyncratic system of values, and that he can tell you exactly what he means by each and every epithet as well as the next man. But lurking in these categories there has become more and more apparent an insidious alignment of chapter-heads which has assumed a censorious attitude which is less in the analytical structure of an Aristotle than in the ethical strictures of Saint Augustine. We discover on the negative side "decadent," "neo-classic," "surrealist," "theatrical," "aristocratic." Under "theatrical" we find "decor," "ballet," "ballet-audience," "ballet-impresario." On the positive side we find "impulse," "inspiration," "heroic type," "integration," "inevitable," "logical," "democratic." Yet there seems to be no hard and fast adherence to these perilously equilibrated lists. For example, Mr. Martin found Hanya Holm's *Trend* less closely related to mere "concert" dancing than it was to "theatre" (i.e., Greek tragedy). I mean, in short, that this anti-theatrical bias which I have long sorrowfully observed in Mr. Martin has now shifted its attack from the ballet even to include Mr. Martin's personal protegé, the "modern" dance, and in particular the creations of its greatest worker, Martha Graham, because he feels her work increasingly theatrical, in his terminology "decadent."

As long ago as 1933, Mr. Martin in his book "The Modern Dance," complained that all dance had meant in the past the *ballet*, and ballet had meant only the *ballet-d'action*. Yet Mr. Martin should have known very well that the *ballet-d'action* or ballet dominated by eighteenth century dramatic pantomime was a reference in common use only as long as J. G. Noverre's immediate influence was felt. The *pas d'action*, a pantomimic number in mid-nineteenth century ballet-form is something quite else. There is all the difference in the world between Noverre's *ballet d'action*, ca. 1780, Vigano's *choreodrame*, ca. 1820, Manzotti's *azione coregrafica*, ca. 1870, and Fokine's *choregraphie*, ca. 1910. Martin also stated (p. 4) that there weren't half a dozen artists who could employ the classic dance properly, although he has since had occasion to mention Massine, Danilova, Spessivitza, Markova, Semenova and even Paul Haakon, who were all performing at the time (1933). He stated (p. 38) that in the old ballets the floor-plan was the *only* consideration, when he must have meant that most of our exact information about steps danced in the old ballets are derived from engravings of floor-patterns. He forgets that the visual and musical synthesis in antique ballet was due to such costumers as Berain and Bouquet, and musicians like Lully, Rameau and Gluck; but it is true that this combination of the dance, music and decor does "smack," as he says, of theatre. It was in fact a theatrical synthesis. He states (p. 107) that music developed and dancing stood still for "hundreds of years," although he grudgingly admitted a little earlier that great dancers did successively enlarge their technique's idiom. No use to call his attention to Noverre, Gardel, Angiolini, Gioja, Blasis, Perrot, St. Leon, Stepanov, Ivanov, Petipa, the Taglionis, Elssler, Manzotti, Fokine, or the more recent Russians—a name of primary historical importance to each decade, if one wished to cite them. In Mr. Martin's two books, historical data was included only as a condemnatory resumé; facts were rearranged and selected to present an apparently objective case against theatrical dancing which almost rivals the ingenuity of the Third Reich's *Kulturkammer*.

By 1936 Martin's anti-theatrical bias was firmly developed. In *America Dancing* (p. 56) we learn that by our early nineteenth century, the poisonous infiltration of foreign theatrical-dancers managed "pretty thoroughly to supplant the simpler English style of theatre-dancing." Following this, the French, Italian and Slav dancing-masters accomplished their invasion. He continues:

It is interesting to note each of these influences was occasioned not by any demand from the American field, but by political conditions in the homeland.

That is, committees of Boston or Philadelphia society-folk did not send over their boats for dancing-teachers. Which is the same as to suggest that the "pure" Massachusetts Indians ought to have felt a deep intuitive impulse to invite the Puritan Fathers over for the sole purpose of giving exhibitions of Playford's Country Dances. Mr. Martin finds it convenient to forget the facts. There were theatrical-dancers in Williamsburg, Virginia, as early as there were stage-plays; there were ordinances against dancing in Boston as early as 1684. By 1794, in Charleston (S. C.), pantomimes in which dancing had important parts were more popular than the plays themselves. Nearly every well-known international dancer has appeared in America since before our revolution, playing before the same kind of American audiences which made theatrical-dancing in Europe a continuous popular form. In an article in the winter 1937-38 number of the *North American Review*, Mr. Martin concedes the fact that the de Basil ballet grossed a million dollars on its transcontinental tour, which in his context means that this enterprise had (strictly) commercial implications, which are alone responsible for its inexplicable success. Yet in another paragraph, we are confronted with a most perfect example of this critic's lexicon (p. 239) :

This is what is sometimes called the classic view as opposed to the romantic, the aristocratic as opposed to the democratic. On its basis kings and courtiers have maintained ballets for their diversion, and today wealthy men of this opinion, whose tastes do not run to the outdoor life, keep companies of dancers instead of polo ponies.

Here we have in full flower a priggish jeremiad tailored to a categorical prejudice. Qualitative distinctions are colored by blind personal irritation. There are few ballet companies "kept" by kings and courtiers today unless government subsidy of the Vic-Wells, the Paris and Bordeaux Operas, the Scala at Milan, the Bolshoi and Marinsky Theatres can be considered mere bureaucratic prostitution. Native American ballet companies in Chicago, New York, San Francisco and Philadelphia to a surprising degree manage to pay their own way, keeping many dancers under long-term contract, and traveling far more, for example, than the "modern" concert-dance groups. That wise-crack about the outdoor life and polo ponies is on the same level of fancy pet that makes Mr. Martin fill our ballet audiences with the "usual silver-haired dowagers with their bald-pated escorts" (p. 249). I don't like dowagers any better than Mr. Martin, but there aren't a million dollars' worth of diamonds alone to give the big Russian companies their annual forty weeks of work, worse luck for them. Mr. Martin must learn that New York is not America. People who like ballet in the United States today are, in cross-section, people who like the legitimate theatre. This Mr. Martin, even after the recent Center Theatre performances, the de Basil tours, the present high commercial value of foreign dance-attractions, refuses to admit. Mr. Martin recognizes, as I do, the degeneracy, decadence and snobbery which vitiates too much ballet today. But with this difference. From his consideration of the situation within the confines of Russian ballet, he arrives at the decision that *all* ballet is equally infected. Hence, he believes as he leads many other people in his audience to believe, that all ballet is Russian ballet, thus qualifying for charter membership in the Great Conspiracy. It is unjust to blame a large art form for its misuse. Does one attack architecture as a whole because people still build bad imitations of Gothic churches, or music, because students still turn out watered Brahms? Mr. Martin does not care to realize that classic ballet is an exact science of theatrical movement and gesture, created by masters down to their pupils for four centuries. The vocabulary of classic ballet has been formulated by trial and error, brilliant experiment and great personalities, just like the history of homeopathic medicine

There is a *materia choreografica* just as there is a *materia medica*.

I submit Mr. Martin is, and has been consciously naive, temperamentally prejudiced or baldly ignorant about theatrical dancing. That he detests the theatrical element in the dance is his privilege, that he continually attempts to wreck it, is his right; but in so much as dancing happens to take place (even today) in theatres, and is in the minds of most of its audiences a theatrical form, I feel he must find some new terms to cover his dislike. He is the chief critical name in this country whom provincial selection committees and dance-managers have respected, and his word has gone far in influencing students of theatrical dancing in America. At the present, theatrical values in the dance, whether in the developed classic ballet or in the "modern" dance, are dominant values, and increasingly so by every indication. The "modern" dance, for example, has in numerous recent programs begun to call itself "modern" ballet, and Martin a very parfyt knight of purity smells theatrical taint even among such schismatic Modernists. Mr. Martin is upholding the banner of an imaginary anti-theatrical purity, an ideal and not a true purity which, if it were analyzed, could be broken down into dance forms that have already outworn their sojourn in the antique categories of the "interpretive," and "expressionist," and "absolute" and the "abstract."

Many critics at a certain age in their active development, start to defend their initial or past enthusiasm with a conservative philosophical barrage which employs an *avant garde* vocabulary to blackjack the future. This is the conservative attitude of "Redder Than the Rose" or "More Royal Than the King." It permits Mr. Martin to boost dismally retardative productions such as Fokine's recent remounting of *Le Coq d'Or* as all that is best in contemporary ballet.

Le Coq d'Or was a pompous and successful gift-book spectacle. It was an exact evocation of taste and tendency, which first blossoming in the Golden Age of a quarter of a century ago, has been reappearing ever since in diluted forms via Russian tea rooms, White Russian Folke Crafte Shoppes, night-club peasant "numbers," etc. Fokine's production was slick with the syrup of opera-house pantomime in which a fat King comically pats his jelly-belly, whereupon a self-conscious chuckle of inane amusement flickers through the house. John Martin called it "fine, healthy, full-blooded art," and found it "expansive, lusty, colossally humorous." After this judas-kiss from such a canny critic, one is hardly surprised to find little or no dancing in *Le Coq d'Or*. We cannot carp at Fokine's perennial competence. But his false-naive spirit, the placid silliness of his pantomime, the rigid sterility of the symmetrical parades, the weakly balanced surprises, the warmed-up buffoonesque fragments we know so well from every one of his works since *Fire Bird, Islamey, Schéhérezade, Thamar, Prince Igor,* down to *Don Juan,* slung together to comprise a *Fokiniana*—these we hate. And we also hate the critical accolade which from prejudice or ignorance hid the historical background of such a work as *Le Coq d'Or.*

Rimsky's opera was for a considerable time banned in Russia. The police of Nicolas II were quick to understand the contemporary use of Poushkin's satire on a do-nothing czar. The basic Russian fable has life, and is a definite social comment. The Queen of Shemakhan, the Lady in Red was well known as the symbolic precursor of revolutionary change. Fokine pulled the teeth of the tale and made it an infantile bed-time story when in reality it was a wise fable for grown-ups. It was within the function of a dance critic to illuminate this discrepancy. But Martin, no doubt tired of protests from his continual bad notices of the ballet was relieved to find something which he could praise without risk. Hence his critical conscience could rest untroubled at the cost of a modicum of creative information.

Similarly, Martin praised Balanchine's archaistic *Le Baiser de la Fée* as what a contemporary ballet should best be; that is, old-fashioned by definition, confined to the expected familiarity of what he thought he recognized. But even here he was wrong, and probably more from ignorance than prejudice confused the stylistic frame of a late 19th century revival with that of a far earlier epoch. Recently, in his Sunday section of the New York *Times,* Martin devoted almost his entire column to Balanchine's creative work, the first time he has troubled to consider it since the choreographer came here five years ago. In that time he has mounted some half dozen new works besides as many more new versions of older ones not seen before in this country. Did Martin discuss or analyze any of these, even to condemn them? Not at all. Instead he chose to laud Balanchine's incidental dance-numbers for Broadway musical comedies. I am second to none in my admiration for George Balanchine; indeed, I was the original pretext for his coming to New York; but no one who loves him or his art can pretend that the numbers he turns out every year for an *On Your Toes,* a *Babes in Arms,* an *I Married an Angel,* or *The Boys from Syracuse* are much more than competent or agreeable time-filling. Nor does Mr. Martin actually believe otherwise. By complimenting a readily misunderstood artist on his hack-work, he patronizingly knifes him in the back, so that Balanchine may be permitted to merit no serious attention as a genuine creator in the contemporary dance. That very number in *I Married an Angel* which Mr. Martin found so inventive, witty and so gracious is an easily recognizable hash of fragments from *Errante, Le Baiser de la Fée, Mozartiana*, and other well-remembered Balanchine ballets, already presented in the "dream" sequence of *Babes in Arms*, only here whittled down to a vulgarization which Broadway, and I am forced to admit, Mr. Martin as well, can digest without cramps.

If Mr. Martin's prejudices against theatrical values in dancing were sifted down to their psychological origins perhaps the clinical results would read something like this. Mr. Martin started out by being an actor. Somewhat accidentally he found himself on a newspaper, not as a critic of theatre, which was his background, but instead as a dance critic at a time when dancing was hardly recognized as worthy of an independent reporter. Martin's courageous attempt to separate dance from theatre in the mind of his readers led to a confusion based on his justifiable attempt to separate dance criticism from theatrical criticism. It forced him, perhaps unconsciously, but after his first few steps with an increasing logic, to defend and further those elements in the dance which had the least connection with the "legitimate" theatre. Hence, we find him as the consistent defender of the ephemeral amateur, the lay dancer, the grand spawn of experimental "Modernists." Column after column has he awarded to serious discussions of young dancers, who after receiving the benison of his attention, have vanished from the scene, seldom to reappear. On the one hand he has always encouraged new "modern" dancers, and his encouragement has gone a long way to providing them with whatever security the subsidies of interested Foundations, Schools or Fellowships have been able to award. On the other hand, he has created a whole alumni of semi-professional dancers, who can only point to a couple of tentative solo-recitals and a long notice by John Martin as the sum of their claim to fame. By this encouragement they have come to consider themselves artists too important for mere subsidiary "group" work. They either attempt to form their own "group," or remain in expectant and ambiguous isolation, or else, knowing nothing better to do, they presume to "teach." This may be an encouragement on Martin's part, but I doubt if it is a service.

If the specific theatrical elements are analyzed which he most dislikes, we find that it is most of all "sentimentality." I have yet to find a definition of the word which means approximately the same thing to most people, and which is not a personal opinion. If it means indulgence in a specious emotion for its own sake, a mawkish projection of emotion when no emotion is called for, then it is hard to know what Martin is talking about. In reference to dancing he seems to mean any overt expression of physical emotion, directly expressed, not "abstractly" rendered, as "sentimental." That is, *sexuality* or its dancing transcript is "sentimental" as in Martha Graham's Puritan duet from her "American Document." But *sensuality*, as lavished in any given Fokine opus of the Golden Age, he finds not "sentimental" but "lusty," "vigorous" or "healthy." Remove a gesture from essential reality, disinfect it from the physical, robe it in rhetorical decoration, then it can pass Martin's antiseptic muster. The anti-theatrical basis is essentially an anti-physical bias. Martin like many others who deeply suspect the sources of physicality, is shy-eyed. It would be curious to discover that Martin is innocent of a conscious dislike of theatrical dancing, since he has a temperamental blindness to it, and hence has never seen it at all.

4. *The Technicians*

What dancing in America needs today and what it will certainly get when the art of ballet is permitted to develop, is a group of critics who are neither historians, appreciators, or journalists. We need the honorable craft of dance technicians. We need newspaper men, poets, or novelists who can look at physical movement on a stage and translate their objective impressions to print without irrelevant autobiographical comment, personal prejudice, or an eye on the advertiser.

In Russia there was a whole class of technical amateurs of ballets, at their worst retired soldiers or men about town, and at their best a number of accomplished and learned commentators, the well-known character-dancer Lopoukov, the classic ballerina Vaganova, Valerien Svetlov, the aged Muscovite enthusiast Volyinsky, the historian Pleschaev, and Prince Serge Wolkonsky, the last Intendant of the Imperial Theatres. Anything Fokine or Massine have committed to paper is nearly as valuable to us as Noverre's own writing, because anyone who has been responsible for creating a theatrical epoch knows certain valuable things about his own intentions which may not even appear in the finished work. Even Serge Lifar's growing bibliography holds elements of historical interest if you forgive his egomaniacal conviction that he, not Fokine or Massine, invented Diaghilev. Even so, he has done work for ten years in the medium on which he writes which is a qualification not shared by many more voluminous writers. Best of all Russian criticism are the albums of caricatures by the two dancers Serge and Nicolai Legat, realistic cartoons of excruciating detail, and tenderly vicious familiarity, which gives us an almost complete picture of the two chief lyric theatres in Russia around 1905. We recognize clinical portraits of many of the dancers of the Golden Age of ballet in Western Europe, as they emerged from the embryo of their school training. But there are others, equally great dancers in all the curious mannerisms of style and technique, who never left Russia, and there is also portrayed the entire staff of the opera-house organization down to the last major-domo, wig-maker, machinist, and conductor. André Levinson's ballet criticism, most of which remains untranslated into English except in the excellent publication of *Theatre Arts Monthly* and Cyril Beaumont's *Taglioni*, had a ferociously difficult vocabulary, but he meant what he said, he knew what he meant, and his information both historical and by his own visual experience was colossal. Levinson wrote French like a foreigner, which he was. His vocabulary was precise, even in its utmost flights of the recondite. But compare a page of his with one by Paul Valéry. In this great academician's recent work, *"Degas. Danse. Dessin',"* we are given in the simplest yet most eloquent prose many a profound, witty and surprising technical analysis on art in general, drawing and dancing in particular. Levinson was a technician for technicians or historians, Valéry for the general audience of poetry at large.

One of the very best small books on ballet in recent years is the all too little known *Russian Ballet Through Russian Eyes* by Vladimir Kameneff, published in London in 1935. The author is obviously a technician, but he is also a creative critic in terms of dancing. He has a gracious, almost courtly style appropriate to his epoch and his origin, which gently renders such angry pens as mine discourteous and gauche. But under his deliberate elegance are steel claws. His questions eviscerate not only the vitiated ballet of the period of de Basil, symphonic or otherwise, but his analyses of the English ballet critics are models of able counter-attack. I am somewhat younger than Mr. Kameneff and hence, not as agreeable. If any readers are displeased with the tone of this pamphlet let them consult his book, a study by a Russian of Russian ballet; a Russian of the old school who loves ballet better than his memories.

Most American sport-writers have a real love for the sports they report. They are not impressed by them as Sport with a capital "S," as some ballet-critics are eager to be dazzled by ballet as Russian-Ballet. Sport-writers do not sentimentally fear or distrust any game as an exhausting form of exotic exercise, although they may detest bad form or style in whatever sport: golf, tennis, yachting, boxing or polo. Yet many of our dance- and music-critics write as if they are afraid of the dance or music with which they are confronted. They do not allow themselves to regard the spectacle with clean eyes. Either they are ignorant or sloppy, or else they are too busy discovering outstanding, heretical differences in new expression from their rigid conception of the basic form as they were originally taught it, and as they have lazily decided it may as well always remain. Sport-writers can usually play the games they describe with some amount of efficiency. Paul Gallico let Jack Dempsey knock him out to learn what it felt like. Hence, their bodies as well as their brains feel from actual experience what they are writing about. Many dance-critics cannot play the piano or read a note of music. It would, of course, be too much to expect that most dance critics should dance. However, the great Russian analyst, Volyinsky, took up the technique at the age of seventy for his professional purposes. Haskell has worked at the *barre,* and others have attended classes enough to make up for lack of actual physical application.

One can no more expect ballet-critics to praise everything they see any more than sports-writers personally must like individual runners or teams of tennis-players whose performance they are assigned to describe. We need ballet-critics who write about dancing with the lack of preciosity which Ring Lardner described baseball, Paul Gallico boxing, or John Tunis reported tennis. In some paragraphs of Ernest Hemingway's "Death in the Afternoon" he approaches great technical dance-criticism. In the military histories of Captain John W. Thomason and Colonel Liddel Hart, notably the lives of J. E. B. Stuart and "T. E. Lawrence," there are descriptions of the movements of individuals and troops, men, horses and machines, which are models of vivid pictorial exposition without personal bias, but which create an intense emotional response.

The technical critic of any art is occupied with the net efficiency or practical beauty, which turns out to be almost the same, of various physical results needed to gain a desired visual or audible end. They can also, by their technical analysis, judge the quality of those means and resultant ends; they cannot help to do so justly, at least by inference, if the presentation of their picture is technically complete, and if their historical background roughly coincides with their own visual or aural experience.

IV. *OUR YOUNG DANCER'S IDEAL*

The most dangerous thing about the "Great Conspiracy" in the world of ballet, is not that there has been such a conspiracy, which was historically inevitable, but that it may still operate on our next dancing generation. The female patrons of the Russian ballet will disclose to you their plans to interest American, yes, actually my dear, *American* painters and musicians, by annual competitions for music and scenery, to start possibly as soon as 1940. When you ask about what use they have now for American dancers, or by a daft chance, American choreographers, their confusion is only equal to their uncertainty as to *which* Russian ballet they are now connected with. "Americans may have some painters and composers for Us; but dancers, well, no, not just yet."

Hence, the American dancers already assimilated into the Russian companies are usually obliged to change their names from Peterson to Petrovsky, from Billings to Bilinsky. In the Diaghilev troupe, for example, Patrick Kay became first Patrikieff, then Anton Dolin, Hilda Munnings was Sokolova, Alice Marks, Markova. Their public naturally expects a *Russian* ballet. And so our provincial Russian-American dancing teachers or their imitators instruct their pupils to be Russian dancers, or at least try to impose upon them their semblance of a Russian, or at least a continental style. I remember when in the first year I worked with the American Ballet, a boy from Maine, born of French origin, but whose family for generations had been called Carter, asked me to pronounce it *Cartier* because it was, as he said, "Not exactly more foreign but, well, you know, softer."

During the tours of the de Basil Russian Ballet across the United States, auditions have been held in many cities to acquire new members for the troupe. Not a few Americans have been chosen to appear with the Russians. Yet of necessity, the printed record in the program has had to have been appeased. Shirley Bridges of Rochester, New York, is still visible under the veneer of "Adrianova." "Nina Radova" is Vivian Smith of Cleveland. "Kyra Strakova" was known in St. Louis as Patty Thall. Marcel Leplat of Seattle is the excellent mime "Marc Platoff." The late "Mira Dimina" was Madeleine Parker of New York. The dancers appearing with David Lichine (née Lichtenstein) in his latest ballet *Protée*, labelled Lerina, Sabinova and Denisova (by any chance Leroy, Sabin, or Denis?) were reared by June Roper, a dancing-teacher of Vancouver. If these kids, born and bred on this continent are considered able enough to hold their own in a Russian organization, then they are good enough to appear dignified by the names with which their parents blessed them.

Lacking a consecutive native tradition of renowned artists, we have logically enough appropriated Russians for our models. But there is a definite limit to our necessity for so doing much longer. If we continue this imitation, our young dancers may soon find they lack an inherent local magnetism which their increasing audiences expect, from a familiarity with a parallel native style as developed in movies and musical-comedy.

If we would learn from the results of persistent adherence to an alien tradition in our arts, consider the parallel field of sculpture. The insistent maintenance of the so-called "Greek" ideal has blinded too many competent American sculptors to the real beauties of an American physique. The Greek athlete had proportions and animal qualities determined by his sun, air, land and sea, and by the variants of military and physical training he underwent some three thousand years ago. He was transcribed by his great sculptors into an heroic type so powerful that it came to serve as a universal model for all times and places; and yet, how very rarely does one feel that in any of our contemporary classic sculpture (I am not speaking of academic "modern" sculpture) is there anything more than a pastiche or a dilution of Athens, Rome or Florence. Our classic sculptors have been blinded by their first version of Hellas, or its reworking under the Rome Empire or in the Renaissance. Their eyes and hands have no longer any real creative elasticity. Yet the human body is as beautiful here as it was thirty centuries ago. They cannot seem to adapt their preconceived preference for the Greek plastique to the new requirements which the creation of a specifically American archtype requires. Even in athletics our own best bodies are less rhetorically heroic than those we see in sport-photos of athletes demonstrating in Scandinavia, Russia, or in the Czech *sokols*. Plastically, American bodies are more compact and cast an aura of a somewhat more familiar intimacy than the more baroque European physique. Our muscular development is not monstrous or bulgy. We are always more surprised by the brilliant efficiency of one of our swimmer's, runner's, or tennis-player's technique, than by his or her anatomical endowment or personal "beauty." Don Budge, Glenn Cunningham, and Jesse Owens have the motor style of champions, and yet, except in action, we hardly think of them as especially Phidian, or Michelangelesque, perhaps not even then. Their ranginess is no less *intrinsically* beautiful than the particular antique quality of the winner of the first Olympian game. Only, these American athletes have their own particular value, due perhaps to California climate and inter-state University tournaments. Sports and dancing, at least in matters of national style, have many common elements. Our rowing style, our running style, and even our boxing style have assumed definite local characteristics which indicate the direction which our developed dancing style must one day take as well.

If we would pursue this parallel closer to theatre let us investigate the influence of Constantin Stanislavsky's "method" on native-born American actors. This great Russian stage-scientist developed a technique for projecting an approximation of spontaneous emotion. Russian and American actors have utilized his researches and developed from them a "universal" system, best demonstrated in New York City by performances of plays by the Group Theatre. Stanislavsky created his attitude from the basis of collaborations with such realistic prerevolutionary playwrights as Tchekov and Gorki. This fragmentary "naturalism" seems to us today as accidental and stylized as the "unreal" cloak-and-sword dramas of Edmond Rostand. It was the tendency of a period in reaction against official theatrical taste of its particular epoch.

Yet this Russian formula has been appropriated by certain over-intellectual American stage directors who were dazzled by a first vision of the Moscow Art Theatre, as their blanket panacea. The principle of "breaking-down" any given actor by inducing essential emotional conflicts, so that private "suffering" is projected as public "sincerity" has its underlying, yet deceptive logic. Stanislavsky himself worked for a certain high-bourgeois strata of nervous, volatile, francophile slavs of a decade when the influence of Zola, Flaubert and Antoine's theatre were dominant among Muscovite students and amateurs.

When we go to a play by the Group in New York, based on the Stanislavsky method, we persistently recognize the identical stock characterizations: the kindly old character-actor (Jewish or Italian), the frustrated young man (boxer, medical student, revolutionary), the aging or adolescent young woman,—suicidal, maternal or resigned. The Bronx is close enough to Moscow as it is, without slipping into an easy double-exposure. Instead of the transplanted Russian method giving elasticity, which is hard enough to get in any repertory company, since the same actors have all to be found parts, it produces rather a rigid formularization. It is the same as in the Gilbert and Sullivan repertory, when Katisha of "The Mikado" is Buttercup in "Pinafore," Lady Jane in "Patience" and Mad Meg in "Ruddigore." What has all this to do with dancing, pray? Just this: The Stanislavsky technique is a specifically Muscovite method, applicable to the particular repertory of a particular epoch. Classic ballet training is an international technique, traditional and *not* epochal, whose most recent great period happened to reach its epopée first of all on Russian soil.

The fact of the matter is that no American can even pretend to be a Russian dancer, and few want to be. Surely no American dancer can get even to first-base in a Russian company. They are, it is true, able to swell the ranks of the corps de ballet, and every so often they are awarded a small solo. Remember the case of young Roland Guerard of Philadelphia, who had about the most faultless pure classic technique in the original Monte Carlo Company. His "Blue Bird" was a superlative academic accomplishment, and not like Lichine's, a flashy fluke. Yet Guerard has hardly ever been permitted to appear, except in the provinces where the ranking soloist was saving himself for the big cities.

The managers have spent too much money publicizing their three or four first-rank solo Russian names. Russian names aren't easy for strangers to remember, and no confusion will be risked by the addition of a Smith, Brown or Jones, no matter how well they may dance. At least not yet. Soon enough, probably, and perhaps too soon when the American ballet-drive starts in earnest, I can easily imagine that the managers will one day insist Lichine change his name to Little, Danilova to Daniels, and Massine to Mason. But that's perhaps not a grave threat at the present. Neither American dancers with Russian names, nor Russian dancers with American names will help much to create the American ballet for which we hope. That rests entirely with the developing invention of our native choreographers.

Every cultivated Russian choreographer feels Poushkin, Dostoyevsky or Gontcharov not as written literature, but as if they were chronicles of their own personal histories. They are *themselves* Onegin. They *are* Pierre Bezukhoi. They *are* Oblomov. They *are* Raskolnikov. The national monuments resident in the Skazki, Lomonossov, Poushkin, Tolstoi, Blok and the rest, utilized by Tchaikovsky, Moussorgsky, Rimsky, Borodin, Stravinsky, Shostakovich, Nabokov or Prokoviev, are their *essential* subject-matter, and if Russian choreographers aren't allowed to translate it into ballet terms with the national Russian background they breathe through, instead of a superimposed American background, we can have reason to expect Evgeni Onegin at the New Orleans' Mardi Gras, Ivan the Terrible at the Siege of the Alamo, and the Snegouroutchka by the shores of the Sky Blue Water. Massine's *Nobilissima Visione* (St. Francis), with Hindemith's great score and Tchelitchev's amazing decor may more than likely prove to be a revelation as the most fascinating danced work of this decade, but I want to see our American Gods and Heroes as we know them, canonized by our vision of them.

American dancers have earned the right to be *American* dancers. In the films, on ball-room floors, and on the musical-comedy stage, they are encouraged to be American, to develop freely in their own personal and national style. But in the realms of the "serious" dance they are not yet permitted to come of age. The old Russian names can still be worked, and it naturally pays better if the Russian monopoly is tightly held. When threatened by a new movement, the Monopolies will undoubtedly compromise by the inclusion of American dancers or ideas, as long as they can exert an ultimate control. And as long as they exert even the least taint of control there may be some slight chance for individual

Americans, but for the future of the best interests of American dancing, there will be no future at all.

Not that our immediate aspect is by any means hopeless. Quite the reverse. In the last few years, as the appendix to this pamphlet shows, the veritable American repertory has reached more than adolescent proportions. We may have to pay for an aggressively nationalistic period at present to offset the recent drag of Russian blackmail, but if so, it will be only a transient and healthy reaction. American folk-lore or historic atmosphere drawn from our national epos, from Pocahontas and Conestoga wagons, down to Harper's Ferry, Lindbergh and Corrigan, are rich veins to be mined for ballet-material. But there should be no reason why we will not be able eventually to present our American comment on England, France, Italy, or on Russia itself for that matter, just as the Russians have admirably done. But it will be *our* time's comment, a new comment, and a comment we only can achieve.

Parallel to the line of folk-lore or historical atmosphere, there will also emerge in our expanding American repertory a series of works to older music; works of a dominantly choreographic nature which will be used to develop and amplify our own ideas of the traditional classic dance. The literature of the dance-suite of the epoch of Bach and Händel are full of remarkable dancing-music, for these forms logically emerged from seventeenth and eighteenth century court and social-dances. Just because they have been for the last two centuries held sacrosanct for use in concert-halls alone, is nothing against their present or future legitimate employment as dance-music. Ernest Newman who is surely a music-critic for musicians, says "I have never been able, as a balletomane, to see anything sacrosanct either in the symphony or in Brahms and Beethoven. . . . The whole trouble has arisen because a few people insist on bringing their concert ears with them to the ballet theatre." The idiom of classic traditional dancing, the vocabulary of its movement and gesture has so enormously developed since the time of the music's composition, and particularly in the last thirty years, that the pieces can today receive a genuinely complementary and contemporary treatment, impossible if an attempt is made to present the music and dance archeologically in the strict period of their origin.

The Passacaglia, for example, offers superb chances for cohesive choreographic production with its melodic statement, developed variations, and eminently dramatic recapitulation. It has recently been used for an extended composition by the "modern" dancer and choreographer, Doris Humphrey. The so-called "modern" dance has among its four leading teachers no common basic technique except what John Martin calls a common "attitude," although through the teachings of Louis Horst, all of them share a considerable background in the basic dance-forms of the 17th century from which the sonata and the symphony were later developed. It is almost a paradox that so much of the formal compositional elements (apart from the idiosyncratic gesture) of the "modern" dance is almost academically rooted in these pre-classic dance forms. The architecture of their dancing is frequently well thought out. But just as often, due to too much respect for Sarabande, Pavane, Courante or whatever, they seem on the stage undramatic and flat. I have never understood the blanket acceptance by the "modern" faculty, of the pre-classic musical forms and their blanket rejection of the style of classic traditional gesture which was the close historic parallel of these very forms.

Music by Bach, Händel, Gluck and much more as late as Weber, Mendelsohn and Schubert, is, I feel, infinitely more suitable for contemporary stage-dancing than the large romantic symphonies which Massine has been recently appropriating. In the first place the older classic music is, if not actually written for dancing, then close in origin to basic dance-forms. The big bang-up symphonies with all their extra-musical prestige, their monumental literary history, their record of interpretations by famous conductors, will inevitably overbalance the dancing to compete with a visual production.

Personally, I have no ethical objection to Massine's use of any symphony he chooses to have played for his ballet-accompaniment. It saves him the trouble of collaborating with any living composer or commissioning a new score, and if the symphonic partition is reasonably familiar, the music-critics, at least, will immediately recognize the chief themes. They can hum them comfortably to themselves during the course of the dancing, and the harsh, fresh dash of unaccustomed vision will be made soothing and tolerable by one more hearing of the oft-heard noises. Only, and again only personally, I have not cared for extra-illustrated gift-books since my twelfth birthday. Even Gustave Doré's remarkable interpretations of Dante are superfluous, and Arthur Rackham's Shakespearean pixies are perfunctory. Massine's symphonic pictures are to me, at least, gratuitous illustrations, or vignettes, free fantasies on well-known themes. Anyone can shut his eyes during a performance of Beethoven's "Seventh," particularly if they have been only half listening to the sounds, and let moving tableaux form behind their eyelids. Perhaps you will see the first movement as the Creation of the world. Maybe, the second shows an Entombment; the third, the Marriage of the Earth and Sky; the fourth, the destruction of a Sodom or a Gomorrah. Why not? Your guess is as good as the next guy's. Except that the "Seventh" of all symphonies is a work of such consistent dance texture that these cheerful or lugubrious chromos seem an affront even tailored by such a dressmaker's edible talent as Bérard's. In any number of movies, it is very easy to have the sound-track dub in a recording of the Ride of the Valkyrs for a forest-fire, or the second theme of the first movement of the Cèsar Franck Symphony for a death-scene. Massine has a right to embellish the old music-masters, but it is scarcely a creative act when he does so. It is, pure and simple, an inferior act; the act of illustration.

But from a purely technical point of view, Beethoven's "Seventh Symphony" played by the required number of Union Local 802 musicians, is a possibility only in a dozen of the largest cities in this country. Otherwise the sacred "Seventh" is performed on a scale reduced to less than half the size of Beethoven's most ordinary demands. To this sort of sacrilege, our music-critics, otherwise vestal virgins of their muses' fire, discreetly wink. Arnold Haskell lays any criticism of Massine's symphonic treatment aside by blurting that whatever the legitimate objections may be, at least *Massine got away with it.* That is, if a Russian does it, it's all right. But catch an American or even an English choreographer (though God knows we don't want to) mounting a ballet to the César Franck, the Schubert "Unfinished," or the Sibelius Seventh (as nothing can probably stop Massine from doing) ! If one of our choreographers should do it, the critical howl would be unanimous, a field-day for the nifty music-boys: "Vulgarity, lack of due technical consideration; confusion of the media; no respect for musical values." Oh Yeah! Well, let them clean their eyes and ears, coldly watch Massine's version of Beethoven's Seventh, or Tchaikovsky's Fifth, when they see them for the next time, and then ask themselves a few cold questions.

But whatever one may think of Leonide Massine as a creative choreographer, there can be little question of his remarkakble personality in the execution of character rôles. He bridged the difficult gap between his youth and his maturity, so that he has never seemed an aging juvenile but always and only a mature male artist. Having danced so much in his life, it is impossible that he should not have acquired polish, presence, physical control. But he adds to the technique of experience a charming personal overtone, an idiosyncratic stamp of very strong flavor. Force and shyness, fire and tenderness which simultaneously mock each other in an exquisite theatrical urbanity, give a certain tragic or at the least an ironic quality to his vivid performances. It is almost as if he were making sober sport of his own interpretations while dancing them up to the hilt. It is almost as if he mocks or at least draws attention to the transient essence of dancing itself, and yet by his vivid activity demonstrates its mercurial permanence.

If, as I believe, an American ballet repertory will be built on the twin basis of native historic themes and contemporary traditional choreography to classic music, there will be unquestionably a third strain contributing much more to the technical development of classic dancing than to the ideas or subjects treated. This will be the two-fold contribution of choreographic elements *apart* from the traditional classic dance; on the one hand, from popular vaudeville, revue-dance, and popular jazz or swing music; that is what we could call American character dancing— our parallel to the national dances of Spain, Italy or Russia; and on the other, from certain aspects inherent in the "modern" concert dance. There is no American composer now writing who is in any way conscious of his time or place, who has not been affected by jazz. Hence, any serious music written as setting for contemporary themes will call for an understanding of basic contemporary dance-forms from the Two-Step, Tango, and Rhumba, to the Lindy Hop, Shag, or Suzy-Q, and their combined spontaneous use in the Big Apple or one of its variants, which are essentially a contemporary improvised Quadrille or square-dance. A salient feature of American style is the presence or at least the appearance of the presence of spontaneous improvisation. When a Russian accomplishes a difficult classic variation with their suave mastery of technique, one assumes they have done it hundreds of times before. When an American dances well one almost feels he or she is making it up as he goes along. Vaudeville training capitalized on this feature and made it one of the most attractive in the American theatrical idiom.

I have long been suspect as an enemy of the "modern" or "concert" dance, and with a single exception still vigorously am. I have always found to hate in most of it a persistent, arbitrary, priggish and doctrinaire avoidance of theatrical elements, a refusal to accept the traditional classic dance as a basic theatrical instrument. I have been irritated by its prejudiced rejection of the form of ballet as a decadent hangover of feudalism. I have been contemptuous of its general intellectualization and clannishness, divorced from the physical needs of our modern stage. But in the last two years I have been forced quite in spite of myself to recognize that there are some definite elements emerging from *one* "modern" dancer, which can be plastically important to all American classic dancers. I still feel, however, that these elements are largely useless without a profound groundwork of traditional ballet-training. I am not yet reconciled to dancers starting their professional training after the age of twenty-one. I do not think that a mere desire to dance is enough to make a dancer, or that six weeks at Bennington is a blanket diploma towards a professional stage-career.

Indeed last winter I talked to the charming directors of the Bennington School concerning their plans for establishing in New York a permanent Central School for the Modern Dance, extended along the lines of the six-week summer course they have so successfully conducted over the last five years in Vermont, and which they are transporting in its entirety to Mills College in California in July 1939. Although they knew perfectly well my attitude towards ballet training versus the "modern" dance, since my troupe had been invited twice to give performances and demonstrations at Bennington, nevertheless, they are very broad-minded women and we discussed the possibility of a Central School both on an ideal and a realistic basis. And I had only one really fundamental disagreement with them, which lay in the difficult problem of such a school's moral responsibility for the future professional employment of dancers which it undertakes to train. The ultimate obligation must rest with the dancers when they choose their school. While I realize no serious school can "guarantee" either professional standing or even a temporary job, nevertheless, the question of future employment inevitably enters in. A student with three or four years of ballet-training can reasonably expect to dance in half a dozen of the independent ballet troupes, in musical-comedy, in films, or at worst, in opera-ballet. A dancer with only "modern" training can merely attach herself or himself on a highly impermanent basis to one of the four or five "modern" teachers for occasional individual performances, or for infrequent tours which are rarely more than a month or two out of the twelve. It is perfectly true that able modern-dancers can find positions to *teach* the "modern" dance at State Universities, Physical Education Colleges, etc. I have always maintained the modern dance may be incidental physical training for laymen, but it is no pedagogy for the theatre. We discussed this problem for some time and at the end of the talk, one of the directors asked me: All right, but don't you think it would be better to have in *existence* such a central school rather than to have none at all? And I was forced to admit that even here, something was probably better than nothing, because in spite of the past, no one could tell what might happen in the future. Yet the problem remains. What chance of a *stage* career has the ordinary "modern" dancer?

One can almost forgive John Martin everything he has ever written or said, up to his remark on the Bennington School of the Dance, in his column of August 21st, 1938 (The New York *Times*). He says the School "must certainly have done much to break down the old notion that pro-

fessional and lay dancing are entirely different activities instead of merely different levels of the same subject." A dilettante, by this token, is some
one whose interest is not unlike, but only whose energy is unequal to
the rigors of a vulgar professionalism. It's all very well to have one
great big happy family in the "Modern" Dance, although its very lack
of professionalism up to date is just what has doomed it to a universal
popular failure.

As far as classic ballet goes—there are no *lay* ballet-dancers any more
than there are *lay* heart-specialists or *lay* plumbers. The trouble with
psycho-analysis is that there are still *lay*-analysts. One of the troubles of
the "modern" dance is that you never can tell who is a *lay* dancer. Ballet-
dancers are theatrical dance-specialists as well as artists. That is their
only dignity on which to base any self-respect or collective security.
An earnest will-to-dance or six jovial weeks in the lovely Vermont hills
are not enough guarantee either to make your living as a dancer, or to
be considered a serious artist. The Ballet is a serious art, craft and
science. Incidentally, it may also help a person to have a better body,
or at least a better educated body. But instruction in ballet has nothing
to do with Physical Education. Let the "modern" dance take care of
that. The "modern" dance may prove preferable to Swedish gymnastics.
It may educate a lay-audience to watch other "modern" dancers, but the
amateur spirit, outside of croquet and stamp-collecting, only induces
further amateurism on the stage, however healthy, vigorous, and good
for the nerves and digestion it might incidentally prove.

Nevertheless, particularly in the more recent work of Martha Graham,
I have been deeply impressed by a use of a lateral breadth in her leaps
and in her extended profile which is far more satisfactory for some athletic American dancers than a complete adherence to the perpendicular
stylistic rigidity of the Russo-Italian pedagogy. In Martha Graham's
finished work as in her strict professional classes, I can find nothing
inimical to the developed classic dance as expounded, for example, by
George Balanchine's *Apollon* (1927), in the second movement of Massine's *Choreartium* (1934), or even in Nijinska's *Les Noçes* (1922).
Graham does not use the virtuoso pirouette turn on half-toe or in the
air common to acrobatic ballet, nor do her girls wear toe-slippers. Yet
she has no root-prejudice against their use, and she admired Bronislava
Nijinska's *Les Noçes* as "modern" dance. Objections to turns, toe-work
and beats are mere decorative details in comparison to her recognition
of the essential five positions of the feet, the pelvic turn-out, and the complete linear extension which is the legible basis of good ballet-training.

Graham has developed an idiosyncratic gesture which is the reflection of a superb personal, feminine and native human quality. Her dancing vocabulary has moral and almost didactic overtones. Graham is a New England Purtian; there is something in her face and figure which recalls New Bedford sailing-ship figure-heads as well as the surface-finish, economy and suavity of Shaker architecture and wood-carving. Her philosophical links are with the Concord Revolutionary moralists, Emerson and Thoreau, with Whitman and the painter Albert Ryder, far more than with Mary Wigman, Nietzsche, or Richard Wagner. Graham has as little to do with Central European post-war dancing as Isadora Duncan with Michel Fokine. Any connection between them was independent and accidental, with the contact over-emphasized by superficial historians. Graham's contribution is unique and uniquely personal. I have always felt one of her most difficult characteristics was her frightening originality, her independence of *any* tradition whatsoever; but like Blake, she has had to create her "own system or be enslaved by another man's." In her intense effort to create and cleanse our native American dance idiom of its rhetoric and exoticism, its merely decorative accretions at the same time, and to find for it a way of its own, she has explored some dead-ends and has offered numerous manifestoes which she has later superseded, like any consistently creative artist. But recently her ideas have begun to be the equal of her technique, her impulse has been apparent in its theatrical fulfilment as in its intellectual inception. Virtuoso technique and decorative atmosphere to a remarkable degree the recent ballet has had, but ideas in general or particular have been almost completely lacking. Graham has ideas in plenty for the classic dancer as well as her own pupils. To a badly-trained, a part-trained, or to a self-indulgent or stupid classic dancer, Graham's method might prove disintegrating to the point of complete destruction. However, to an instinctive, clean, conscious or well-trained classic dancer, Martha Graham has much to offer. The personal frame her theatre makes is specifically her own, and cannot be appropriated undistilled by the ballet, which is a far more sophisticated, collective, complex and impersonal form. But her sense of a projected physicality, her spinal integration, her sense of controlled entrance, and the deep human color of her dancing style, is a purer and frequently deeper repository of essential classicism, even if it may be a narrower one than the easily accepted and much more superficial idiom of school-ballet.

PART THREE

Program and Manifesto

I. *BASIC PRINCIPLES*

THE ART OF LIVING IS MORE LIKE WRESTLING THAN DANCING.

MARCUS AURELIUS

What is there to be done in general, and indeed, what is there for us to do now? There is everything to be done. We must first of all, with the materials already in our hands, create a ballet repertory which will sufficiently interest a large public to support us on some more or less permanent basis, to permit us to continue without too much dictation from the dance-managers. We must create a repertory which will not only displace the existent Russian programs, but which can keep abreast of them in ideas and invention. To do this, we must not underestimate their very real powers. They are masters of the theatre, and past masters of dancing. Even in their decadence they have more knowledge of stage values in their toes than most of us have in our whole bodies. They have a basic experience from producing works with the collaboration of the best wits and talents of their generation, from their earliest youth. They have a discriminating taste which has been so dominant that we have come to think of it as infallible. The Russian dancers have their individual formula for effective stage-presence so well worked out that the assurance of a brilliant personal apparition has been frequently more than enough to save an otherwise boring ballet. They have, in fact, everything it takes to make great theatrical dancing except intellectual energy, moral stamina, and a reserve supply of native dancers.

These three desirable qualities might seem *sine qua non* for a healthy young movement, facing a future of vast possibility. But for a decadent old movement, reclining on its piled-up prestige, they are, realistically speaking, negligible. After the first opposition, the initial sales-resistance to a new idea or direction has been overcome, both seller and buyer are somewhat exhausted from their mutual struggle. The Russian Ballet as the seller, forced its unfamiliar wares on the Western World some thirty years ago. Within ten years these wares were fairly universally accepted, and the buyer, in the form of the audience, settled itself down to seeing what it expected to continue to be shown. A certain inertia pervaded both parties, and it was Diaghilev's great gift to pinch both buyer and seller

94

out of their tendency towards an imaginative apathy. But Diaghilev has been dead ten years, and apathy has finally prevailed. Of course, the automatic physical energy persists, but the recent split in the Russian Ballet's economic set-up as well as the signs of more imminent strain, show how shaky even that is. You can beat water till it foams, but even so it's never cream. The top is off the Russian Bottle. Now it's up to us to whip our own cream.

What can we do? A great deal. First of all, we can make ourselves conscious of the economic situation as it actually is. We can realistically marshal and inspect our own forces and feel our own power. For we have a lot. We must investigate recent history and the more remote past once and for all, to salvage from it whatever is immediately useful to us. We must consider every element which might go into the construction of great theatre in terms of dancing, and then construct a program for ourselves which although it must be elastic enough to include the unexpected, shall primarily be strong enough to stand the shock of our necessary experiment and our inevitable mistakes. We must be conscious of ourselves in the world in which we dance. The age of interior-decoration, even in ballet, is over. Period-rooms and period-ballets seem equally the tiresome and tricky left-overs of the nineteen-twenties. If we should mount works with an historic background, let them have a pressing connection with our present lives. Let this connection be more significant than the archeological reconstruction of correct costume or antique dance-pattern. Dance for the sake of Dance alone is no longer any more a tenable law for us than art for the sake of art. But certain dances, even without definite subject, can be more than merely agreeable divertissement. With the aid of great music and worthy gesture, they can always be a monumental testament to the powers of the human being expressed through his or her human body. A dancer actively released in his legible freedom, springing in space, is as satisfactory a witness to the irrepressible and indomitable instinct to human liberty as anyone can find. There are many ways to pay homage to liberty, equality and fraternity. Great dancing is not the least of them.

I am submitting first a program for our basic uses, and then a manifesto towards our immediate action. Neither is final, as I have worked entirely alone and only on a basis of personal experience. I invite comment, amplification and signatories, should they be forthcoming.

1. *The classic dance and American character-dancing.*

I submit an unalterable and fundamental basis for a national American ballet, training in the international classic traditional theatrical dance. If anything would render me more sure of the common-sense, collective usefulness and early instinctive preference for a professional attitude to be gained from a constant connection with classic dancing, it would be the spectacle of the last twenty years of experiment in the field of the "concert" or "modern" dance. The "concert" or "modern" dance was called into being to purge the theatrical tradition of ballet. From Duncan and Dalcroze to Wigman and the American "modernists," the net result has been education, not for dancers, but for the lay audience in elementary aesthetic principles, *away* from, not *towards* the theatre. Isadora's principle may have been far beyond mere roofed-in theatre, and Wigman had her extra-theatrical and ego-centric interests, but I am assuming from reader and audience an essential, immediate and constant interest in theatrical ends. That is, dance is done in theatres, is part of theatre, and is paid for as theatre. Towards theatrical ends I cannot recognize any means for a dancer less complete than whole-hearted training in the classic dance.

It is hardly necessary to indicate for dancers an historical background of traditional classic dance training. But for laymen, by "classic" dance, I mean a system of fundamental instruction for dancing comparable to an understanding of cadence, harmony and counterpoint in music; form, value and color in paint; structure, material and function in architecture. The roots of this instruction were first of all to be found in the social-dance books of Milanese dancing-masters of the late Renaissance. Their categories remain essentially the same today as, for example, the essential divisions in the anatomy of Vesalius, or the architecture of Vitruvius. Four centuries of work in France, Italy, Scandinavia, Poland and Russia have put flesh and muscle on the original bare skeletal structure. *Tradition* only means a *handing-down*. Great dancers, ballet-masters, musicians and costumers have each and everyone added their individual contributions, as in the brother dynasties of physicians, architects, and poets. There is, as I have said before, *materia choreographica* just as there is a *materia medica*.

In T. S. Eliot's remarkable essay "Tradition and the Individual Talent," he specifically spoke of English poetry and its relationship to criticism both French and English. Yet on a rereading its cogency is startling, turned on the field of another verse, the poetry of physical movement.

Tradition cannot be inherited, and if you want it you must obtain it by great labour. It involves, in the first place, the historical sense, which we may call nearly indispensable to anyone who would continue to be a poet beyond his twenty-fifth year; and the historical sense involves a perception, not only of the pastness of the past, but of its presence; the historical sense compels a man to write not merely with his own generation in his bones, but with a feeling that the whole literature of Europe from Homer and within it the whole of the literature of his own country has a simultaneous existence and composes a simultaneous order.

The experiment of cubism in painting has been loosely compared to experimental "modernism" in dancing. But cubism was a logical, traditional development, while the modern dance was "original." In the first place, no one any longer puts quotes around cubism, and yet because the exact degree or species of "modernity" in the dance is difficult to allocate under the general word "modernism," this term still remains an ism in quotation marks. The pictures of Nijinsky's *Le Sacre du Printemps* appearing in the *Illustrated London News* during the season of 1913 were labelled "cubist ballet." The superficial angularity of the gesture, even clothed in the pseudo-Scythian clothes of Prof. Roerich, seemed to the caption writers somehow related to Picasso's or Kandinsky's experiments. Yet had the *News* wished to be exact they might have called it a *Fauve* ballet, a ballet under the influence of the post-impressionist followers of Gauguin in the naiviste and exotic, ca. 1905. The "modern" dance has had little or nothing to do with cubism or abstract painting. The cubist method was an analytical method for breaking down representational rendering into shapes or forms which had a precise balance in their given frame. It was also an historical criticism of the vaguely composed, accidental snap-shots of the French Impressionists. It was a strong solvent which by way of Cezanne's previous researches reinvestigated the whole tradition of western pictorial composition. Cubism was a natural development in the classic tradition of French painting. Its validity was as much in its comment on impressionism, which had become a stuffy academy, as in its serving a new basis for subsequent painting for the neo-Romanticism and surrealism which followed it. And above all, we are left with some great individual cubist and abstract panels by Picasso, Braque and Mondrian.

The "modern" dance has left us, to begin with, not one notable composition to which one can refer like any of the half-dozen outstanding ballets of innovation in the Diaghilev repertory. Unlike cubism, the "modern" dance was not a traditional outgrowth of the rest of western classic theatrical dancing. It was a radical revolt from it, so violent at its outset that the base was rootless, or rather, only rooted in the idiosyncracies of the few leading personalities who professed this attitude. Nijinsky's gestures for *Le Sacre* seemed "original," yet they were really only the classic five positions adapted to their reversal. The turn-out was turned *in*. The classic dance was turned inside out. It was not thrown away. It was the reverse of the medal, not a different coin. As in politics, it is more legitimate and easier to affect party policy *within* the movement by a participating member, than to purge it from *outside* by however violent a criticism.

The aim of the "modern" dancer by and large has been to deny any traditional residual material whatsoever, to attempt to erect instead an *original* system which they felt might be more applicable to "our" time. They forgot that even "our" time is the cumulative result of other times, and has its connections with a continuous logical lineage. Nevertheless, the "moderns," on an idiosyncratic basis of personal preference and individual prejudice created as many "schools" of the "modern" dance as they were dance-teachers, having no more connection with each other than with their enemy, the theatrical dance, except in what John Martin called their "attitude." This attitude, reduced to its minimum verbosity, was quite simply a fundamental opposition to the tenets of classic ballet.

The reason for this fundamental opposition was not too hard to discover. None of the Modern Dancers had ever seen progressive ballet, as represented by the Silver Age of Diaghilev, until they were too fixed to alter their prejudice against it. This bias in the first place, had been gained from hearsay, and was then necessarily maintained out of a compensatory jealousy for their own considerable technical inadequacy. The dance- and music-training of Jacques Dalcroze, already formulated by 1910, towards making students and children conscious of audible rhythm and visible gesture, has more to teach us today than the entire results of the individual artists or choreographers he subsequently directly or indirectly affected. The Central-European dance, as represented by von Laban, Wigman, Bodenweiser, Trudi Schoop, their pupils in America, and even Jooss, has had a diminishing theatrical effect, not on the basis of its various individual ideologies but purely and simply on the basis of its lack of a comprehensible or consistent *technique*. Technically, the "modern" dance if taken in a pure dose does not offer a complete enough training for any serious theatrical dancer.

Take the case of Kurt Jooss, for example. He calls his choreographic works *Ballets*. But he makes an academic doctrine out of his avoidance of the culminating accents and emphasis of traditional classic ballet practice. He uses an aerial profile, a fluent extended silhouette, the gracious openness of plastic style which serves the basis of the academic dance, and which was founded among other influences, on the Italian baroque plastic arts—the *contraposto* or anatomical opposition of Giovanni di Bologna, Michelangelo and Bernini. But he stubbornly avoids the use of toe-shoes, air turns, brilliant beats, or acrobatic turns on the floor. Hence, his choreography, however magnificently rehearsed as it has had the unique good fortune of being able to afford, always seems muted, toned down, a simulacra; one is pleased by his smooth finish, yet one always expects something *more*. His own academic ideas are not significant enough to compensate for a lack, not of technical polish which his dancers surely have, but of the maintenance of theatrical tension or interest by technical virtuosity which his dancers surely have not. And why not? Partly because von Laban's early prejudice against the classic Russian training was a Prussian chauvinist hang-over that was transmitted blindly to Jooss, who later had to try to rationalize this inherited opposition. Partly because, purely by accident, Jooss does not have the patience to instruct up to the peak ultimate of classic method. Mostly because, as an "innovator" he has had to have some point of difference with the rest of the dance-world; so this has been it. His work has suffered for it very much over the last three years. Jooss has, through the patronage of Mrs. Elmhirst, enjoyed an unparalleled chance for creation. His own ideas, as testified at least by *The Green Table* (1933) are full of meaning to us. Yet why does nothing more come out of it? I think because Jooss has been fighting the chimera of traditional classic theatrical dancing. His opposition to the tradition has channeled his energies away from the full aims of dance-theatre.

A dancer must ideally be capable of everything. In Russia, where such things are valued more, dancers are speaking actors, sometimes singers, as well as acrobats. Why do people like dancing, anyway? Because they see in the flesh men and women with two arms and legs just like themselves, moving in air with the heightened, coördinated logic which represents for them their most-hoped-for possibilities, a denial of earthly gravity, an ultimate freedom of action, a super-human domination of flesh and earth. By definition, the dance is acrobatic. The dancer's only tool is in his or her proper human body. This tool is a universal instrument, capable of infinite articulate use. But all its uses must be theatrically legible. The bodies' activities must be able to be watched clearly by an audience seated at some distance from their actual moving. This is where theatricalism comes in. Classic ballet training provides first of all substructure for acrobatic brilliance, then the motor logic of a readable silhouette. By the trial and error of over four centuries stage-dancers have come to know the moving balance and axis of aerial and terrestrial excitement. By brilliance they create interest, tension, and accelerative excitement in their watchers. This information has become a strict science and an honorable craft. It can be taught. Our classic traditional dance training teaches it.

And the classic dance instructs us in something else which is even more necessary. This is a classic *style*. The frame, the outward glow, the final polish which it is impossible to superimpose on a structure anything less than solid, does, however, add the ultimate stamp which sets finished dancers in the aura of their accomplishment. The style may be a Russian style, which we have known, or an American style, which we may come to know; but in any case its importance cannot be overestimated. It is what the ignorant-eyed see first. It is what the knowing-eye sees first and last. It is what sells dancing to people all the time.

Parallel to the daily regimen of dancing exercises based on the five fundamental classic positions of hands and feet which are the equivalent of finger-exercises for a pianist or a singer's vocalized scales, the Russian pedagogy has developed a very complex instruction in character-dancing. The basic ethnic steps from Hungarian, Spanish, Polish, Italian or Cossack national forms were given a broader theatrical treatment for stage use. Simple turns became pirouettes. Leaps were filled out with foot-beats. The basic gesture founded on custom, earth and weather, were italicized for legibility in theatres. This whole department of the dance served as a "natural" and useful complement to the "artificial" academic classic tradition. The two lines crossed and recrossed. There was a whole intertwined genre of Italian, French and Russian operatic dancing known as the *demi-caractére*. "Spanish" hands or "Hungarian" heels were mixed with toe-work. Folk-influence enlivened the colder, purer, and more arbitrary foundation.

Americans have assimilated European character-dancing in the past and can learn it well. Arthur Mahoney's Spanish numbers have an astonishing authenticity and effectiveness. Paul Haakon's Russian sailor-dance from Glière's *Red Poppy* is a perfect example of character-dance for theatre. William Dollar's Czardas in Balanchine's *The Bat* had an ecstatic, almost desperate fire that came perhaps from the fact of his own Hungarian ancestry. But there is always the element of *tour de force* in an American dancing, however ably, authentic dances of other lands. Somehow the fact of the Russians having been born on earth shared by the rest of Europe makes their dancing of a *farucca* or a *tarantella* less strained.

It is only recently that Americans have discovered we also have our own character-dancing which can serve us theatrically better than any Russian or Spanish. And this is not the dance of the Sioux, the Hopi, or the Navaho, nor the square-dance of the Tennessee Mountaineers. Our character dancing is a vital contemporary manifestation, not an exotic left-over. Since the tradition of "eccentric" dancing descending from the days of buck-and-wing minstrel-shows vanished with four-a-day vaudeville, we have not been very aware of dancers employing "popular" dance - forms consciously. American character - dancing has stemmed from a double strain, one from vaudeville or musical-comedy, the other from social-dances in ball-rooms, barns, barracks, gyms or dance-halls. Buster West's American sailor number, Buddy Ebsen's hick fast flat feet, and of course such fine Negro teams as Buck and Bubbles have been continually paralleled by a "smoother" tradition stemming from Irene and Vernon Castle, Moss and Fontana, Veloz and Yolanda, and above all, Fred Astaire and Ginger Rogers. These "social-dancers," even though they frequently dance on ball-room floors instead of on a stage, take over from annual popular dance fads numerous new forms and tricky steps, and theatricalize them by adding specatcular lifts, or free fantasia on jazz steps with astonishing tap cadenzas, as Paul Draper does. The recent wide-spread interest in Charleston, Black-Bottom, Suzy-Q, Lindy Hop, Shag and Big Apple testifies to our inherent love for popular music and dancing on an intimate, or at least on a familiar basis. The ancestors of the Big Apple trace themselves back in an unbroken lineage to Bunny Hug, Turkey Trot and the Negro Cake-Walk. The complexity and ingenuity of "swing" band-music is equalled by the variety and invention of steps which the dancers create to accompany it. The Big Apple is a communal expression, recalling square-dances of the mid-nineteenth century which from the *contredanse* later developed into the *German* and *Cotillon*. The Big Apple is a kinetic *dance*, which the static, ordinary two-step of the 'twenties hardly ever was. Elements of rhumba and tango, fragments of negro, Mexican, Cuban and Argentine gesture and movement are embroidered into a consistent fabric of motion whose spontaneous flow fits the personal mood of the improvisor.

This material offers an American ballet-choreographer as rich material as *gopak, saltarello* or *bolero,* with the added advantage that our dancers have enjoyed these dances as part of their own experience from their earliest schooldays. They are able to perform stage versions of them with conviction, not as an imitation of a form they have seen done by Russians or Spaniards, but rather because the quality of their jazz and gesture is as familiar to them as the kids with whom they first danced at high-school prom, Saturday night socials, or in the summer-dances on the Mall in Central Park. These social-dances must necessarily be redesigned for the stage, and can be hung on a structure of classic technique for their greatest stage effect.

We are all of us familiar with the splendid stance, the proud spinal carriage of the Spanish gypsy. We easily recognize the jack-knife spring and release of Cossack knees. We have known the brilliant play of pantomimic flirtation in Italian peasant-dances. Let us also recognize our own native detachable snake-hips, our rangy legs, our educated feet. Our arms and fingers wave and snap in a special way. Our shoulders hang as no other people's shoulders hang. Our classic theatrical style will find an added authority and flavor from the essential qualities of American national dances.

2. *Ideas and Collaboration*

A ballet, no matter how rhetorical or how transparently atmospheric will, upon inspection, always be found to contain some substratum of *ideas*. This will be less upsetting to old-school balletomanes than at first appears. For them at least ideas may be all very well, in their place (in libraries possibly), but why drag them into dancing? Don't brush the gold-dust from the wings of the Sylphs. But take *Les Sylphides,* for example, a ballet in which it is usually assumed no idea has ever been permitted to penetrate. This suite of dances is framed as a decorative revery recalling the style and forms of Romantic Ballet in 1840. The corps de ballet float in the dreamy tarlatans of Taglioni's time. The single poetic young man represents, for the purposes of 1909 or 1939, the dance-maddened, or at least the dance-inflamed male dancer of the tradition of the romantic epoch, when the male dancer's position was anomalous. The ideas then in *Les Sylphides,* are decorative ideas about dancing itself, framing Fokine's stylized gesture which was his own invention, and except for final or accentual poses had probably very little to do with Romantic Ballet of the "forties," considered archeologically. I have always thought of ballets in the genre of *Les Sylphides* rather like still-life in painting. The French accurately term such work *nature-morte,* dead-nature. The still-lifes of Chardin, to take representatives of the greatest, are much more than formal arrangements of vegetables and kitchen-utensils. Aside from their dazzling display of the technique of the application of paint, the seemingly accidental choice of carrots or copper kettles patently testify to the homely domestic virtues, the peasant honesty and solid "human" values witnessing the rights of common-men at the period directly preceeding the first middle-class French Revolution. I mean that while there may be more apparent social *ideas* in a Chardin than there are in *Les Sylphides,* yet when you realize the choreographer Fokine was creating a work of art in the taste of the audience of the Imperial Russian Theatres, for retired generals, court chamberlains and visiting French and English diplomats, for the bureaucratic families all of whom were educated in a taste for the delicious charm of the epoch of their grandparents and the quaintness of the opera-houses of 1840, in fact, when you realize every ballet is thus a reflection of the concepts of the choreographer faced with the conditioning of his audience, then perhaps *Les Sylphides* can be thought to have its social implications too.

It is perhaps harder to find ideas, social or otherwise, in Russian-Russian ballets or in the oriental-Russian pseudo-exotic ballets. *Schéhérazade* and *Thamar* are pure exotic decoration, having little or nothing to do with genuine fantasy or fabulous invention. The emotion indicated is rhetorical and literary. If a memorable dancer's performance has been accidentally attached to the skeleton of the choreography, it is good luck, just as if some good dressmaker may have incidentally clothed the dancers. The ideas behind most of the ballets of Diaghilev's Golden Age are comparable to the extra-illustrated *editions de luxe* of Pierre Louys or Anatole France, which French booksellers in Paris and Petersburg tricked out with water-color pornography. The basic ideas reflected the delicate vacuity of the taste and education of Leon Bakst, for the Golden Period was dominantly pictorial. Bakst appropriated the style of any historic epoch he capriciously chose—romanticized it without respect for its inherent historical meaning, and served his riflings piping hot with a terrific palette of tomato-red, chrome yellow and sapphire high-pressure paint-guns borrowed from the methods of the French Impressionists.

It was Nijinsky, in *Jeux* (1913) who first permitted a little material from immediate life to penetrate into the Russian Ballet. A young artist, he was then feeling his way. He used only three dancers because he wanted the action to be clear of group helter-skelter or Fokine's pageantry. He was trying out a new *kind* of gesture and a new *kind* of subject-matter. Its decorative frame was a tennis-game. Its emotion was the three-angled love and play that Noel Coward popularized twenty years later. Sport, chic, the playful surface physicality of the twentieth-century received here its initial apotheosis. *Jeux* itself was not a popular success, in spite of Debussy's beautiful orchestral partition. Yet here the Russian Ballet for the first time stopped being not only Russian, but what was far more serious, it threatened to cease being exotic. It commenced to be slightly human.

Not until Jean Cocteau and Pablo Picasso entered Diaghilev's cabinet in 1917 did the ballet become human again. In *Parade*, Satie and Massine, with ideas inherited from Guillaume Apollinaire and the Cubist painters, faced the choreography with American rag-time, the infantile world of the modern "child," the fantasy of Chaplin films and the three-ring circus. Later came a series of "modern" ballets: *Les Biches*, Bronislava Nijinska's delightful houseparty, *Le Train Bleu*, *La Pastorale*, *Les Matelots*, etc. Even in the Monte Carlo Company there was Massine's *Beach* (1933) for a couple of seasons, a late rehash of all the old sport material. But very soon the contemporary subject-matter lost any claims to a human treatment. Instead, it became as decorative and exotic as any other period piece, Versailles, Poushkin, or Persia. Only this new "period" was, perforce, the present. Massine's *Le Pas d'Acier* was Diaghilev's *hommage aux Soviets* by way of Prokoviev. It may have shown an aristocrat's good-will toward the new Russia, but it was not very deeply felt. The material was a second-hand treatment from the early Eisenstein and Pudovkin films. It had a certain brash energy on first sight but it did not survive.

Decorative treatment of dance-material developed a succulent technique of presentation. Persia was no longer revived by way of Bakst's extra-illustrations. Now a gifted painter like Picasso, viewed an ancient Greece through his cubist spectacles; or he cast away cubism and saw Delphi through the decalcomania windows of a Paris suburb under the Third Republic, with overtones of Pompeii stencilled on the Rue de la Paix. This decorative attitude became a parlor-game of historical attribution. It served the dressmakers and fashion magazines well, because it had an immediate edible perfection of conglomerate taste which has always been and still persists as the strongest point of Russian Ballet.

Massine swung his attention on America in *Union Pacific*. He collaborated with an American poet and American designers—but his basic *ideas* were entirely decorative. He took over the material of building a transcontinental railway. It was surely epic, cinematic stuff, yet he cut it down to fit the familiar formula of Russian-ballet decoration. Any life his choreography had was in the vitality of its character-dancing. The dancers may have been costumed like children's picture-book Mexicans, Chinese coolies, Indians, or roving gamblers, but they danced nice Russian national dances, complete with Spanish arms, Hungarian feet and Russian boots. A decorative treatment of dancing ideas is of no use to us any longer. Audiences are too accustomed to the formula for further interest. It only attracts the surface eye which has already been surfeited.

During this season (1938-39) we will have a chance to inspect the works of a Russian ballet purged of the sinister coloration of Colonel de Basil. I do not think, however, there will be much alteration in its creative temperature. To be sure, we will get a chance at the ballets Fokine made some time ago for the René Blum troupe. Gluck's *Don Juan* contains considerable viscid pantomime in lush opera-house taste. Mozart's *L'Epreuve d'Amour* is one of the many pastiches which have been saved by the bell of André Derain's decorative taste. Massine gives us his latest symphony, now the Seventh of Beethoven, decor again by Bèrard, the whole thing rather *en série et sur commande*. Massine also produces his *Gaité Parisienne*, the last edition of *Le Beau Danube*, with his big character solo, this time clad in Peruvian dress. This is the same number we have loved since the Can-Can of *La Boutique Fantasque* (1919), the Mazurka of *Le Beau Danube* (1924), the Barman's dance of *Union Pacific* (1934), etc., etc. It is still a splendid number and it is proper that Massine should occasionally change its costume and scenery.

Bogatyri (Russian Heroes) to Borodin's symphony, has Gontcharova's decorations. Massine's story "is based on the brawling, fabulous heroes of Russian legend." All right, why not? As for *St. Francis (Visione Nobilissima)*, Hindemith's score and Tchelitchev's decor at least guarantees a provocative spectacle. The essence of Saint Francis might be a lovely point of departure for a vital lyric work. It will be interesting to discover whether or not Massine has created a human character and invented a mood, or has only designed decorative fragments from Byzantine or early North Italian painters. Lifar returns to New York in *Giselle*, his greatest rôle. Perhaps this reconstitution of the choreography will give us a clear museum headlight on the original romantic ballet for which *Les Sylphides* has been doing false service so long. His *Icare* with its much manifestoed percussion band, will hardly convince American audiences as a radical departure. Even before Mary Wigman came here, our "modernists" have been dancing to drum accompaniment for a decade.

No; I am afraid Massine's bigger and better Russian ballet is just the perennial *Ballet Russe*. One imagines working conditions may be happier, hence the morale of the troupe higher. But we want a new *idea;*

a new *use* of paint or music, a *feeling* in gesture you can't better derive from the actual paintings of Giotto, Constantin Guys, Christian Bérard, or Genia Berman. Neo-Romanticism is as collapsed as cubism. A Byzantine style is no substitute. *Le Martyre de Saint Sebastian* happened in 1911, and d'Annunzio died last year. Yet the application of a decorative *style,* any style, is the only formula left for them. Russian-ballet is still interior-decoration. The style of the Russian ballet is still pre-war and there is not much satisfaction in the fact that it shies before a second rather than tags after the first World War.

It is not that theatrical decoration, scenery and costume must necessarily be cancelled out, or that the ballet will take suddenly to a bare stage, like the Mercury Theatre's *Julius Caesar,* or Jed Harris's *Our Town.* Not at all. Scenery and costume will find a new and more interesting use if they are the *frame* and not the *excuse* for the dancing. Every theatrical idea has a superficial skin and an essential heart. The Russians for the last three decades have been anything but heart-specialists. They cannot afford to be. They have capitalized on the fact that due to their voluntary or involuntary exile they have either broken hearts or no hearts at all. The Russian Ballet long ago lost contact with a home-base. Instead they have been serving up decorative skin-treatment of whatever temporary home-base might serve them for the moment. This is matter for sympathy rather than for blame, but it merely shows why we who live in one place musn't imitate them.

Literal transcription of factual notions, incident, gesture or movement, is not for the dance any more than is interior decoration, in whatever epoch's style. Literalism in ballet is perhaps further from the essential lyric truth than even superficial decoration. It is for us to find an essential lyric truth in contemporary gesture grounded on our ideas, by study, research, taste and also our instinct. I can't tell any choreographer what he should do, but perhaps I can illuminate the general problem by telling a few things I have myself seen done.

When we were planning to mount a ballet on an every-day subject, which finally turned out to be "Filling Station," we first of all searched for a basic fable that would already be familiar to most of our prospective audiences, on which we could make our own comment. We couldn't find one ready-made. We looked into Aesop and La Fontaine, trying to reclaim an old fable with modern implications. No use. We had to make the whole thing up ourselves. It wasn't as if we didn't know what our ballet was about. We did. It was about work, today. It couldn't be put in a factory, on an open road or on a farm, because we didn't have enough dancers to suggest a mass of workers. Work-gestures and movements which in themselves may be beautiful in contact with actual machinery, if taken away from the machines and transcribed into literal pantomime, seem affected or naive.

We chose as locale a gasoline Filling Station. It was both cross-roads and way-station. It would be a logical place in which work could be done and where different kinds of people could meet. The locale once chosen, the hero was naturally the Filling Station Attendant. His name was Mac. He was both presiding genius, master of ceremonies, and first classic dancer. The character of the Filling Station Attendant was described by the virtuosity of his opening variation. His acrobatic brilliance showed him capable of treating any emergency that might come up, with brilliant resourcefulness. He was the type of self-reliant, agreeable and frank American working-man. His dancing was styled to announce him as such. I had wanted him to be interrupted by two little girls who lived like stray cats around the Filling Station and who were friends of his, but as the composer Virgil Thomson pointed out, these two had no real logic. They were useless decoration. The two truck-drivers, Roy and Ray, however, were not. They would be normally passing along the highway by Mac's station. It would be a natural place to stop off and break their haul. Lew Christensen saw them as tumblers and described them as if they had been vaudeville knockabout-comedians. Paul Cadmus clothed them in the zipper-front jacket that mechanics always wear in the open, but instead of ordinary canvas or leather, the work-clothes underwent a theatricalization into velvet, silk lastex and cellophane. He stencilled handprints in grease and oil on their trousers, and stuck a lilac in Roy's cap. It was soon apparent that the truck-drivers had come in for a definite reason. They were seeking refuge from the State-Trooper who was chasing them for speeding. After his warning and speedy departure, a family of ordinary motorists arrived on a dismal waltz of domestic life. The Husband, a combination of Caspar Milquetoast and Mutt, just as the Truck Drivers were paired as Mutt and Jeff, had already asked his way. His Wife, in green-blonde hair, summer slacks and sinister green-celluloid visor, chivied her little girl, who was a nightmare twin of Shirley Temple or Little Orphan Annie. Her toe-work was indicated as the prize-number of a spoiled child's dancing-class graduation exercises. To these representatives of the proletariat and the middle-class were added the Rich Boy and the Rich Girl, a drunken couple dropped in from the nearby Country Club. The number that described them was a pie-eyed classic adagio gravely built on a ball-room rhumba. The ensuing group-dance was a sublimated Big Apple. The *pas d'action* was the chase of the gangster who held up the station, based on movie-serial hurry-up music. The processional at the end was a reprise of the rhumba, *We won't get Home until Morning,* and *Hail, Hail.* At the end, the Attendant, Mac, was left in his empty station, turning on the radio, spreading his tabloid across his knee, waiting for the next thing to happen.

So, lacking a modern myth, we made one up, and discovered that it was already in existence since everyone immediately recognized it. Any success we may have had was due as much to our method as to our material. The handling of both was by a complete collaboration of painter, choreographer and musician. Each was of the same imaginative generation and provenance. Each respected the spine of classic dancing which was our language. Each knew as well as his own name the comic-strip, the movies, the manners of highway and suburb on which the pantomimic gesture was founded. The field of these ideas was like particles of energy waiting to be polarized into a specific channel. It was hard to say afterwards which of us had which idea first. We put to conscious use a set of corresponding concepts based on a tradition of American social humor with the tradition of international theatrical dancing. The traditional classic dance was grafted on American character-dancing. It may sound, written out here, doctrinaire, arbitrary and formularized. The element of fun, for example, which is present in the dancing, can't be indicated in a description either of the ballet as performed or as it was in preparation.

All sorts of collaborations are open to American ballets of the future. These collaborations will not be a mere haphazard juxtaposition of a convenient composer, a fashionable designer with any given ballet-master. Every talent has its close correspondent in the parallel fields. Certain designers have an essential sympathy with certain ideas which are best furthered by treatment with a particular personal selection of a musical gift. And first and last, the idea at the root of it all must be worthy of the most exhausting collaboration into which it can be plunged. Very often the selection of an idea is only an accidental choice of a ballet-master. Perhaps, due to the combination in an ensuing collaboration, it turns out to be a success, but very often and perhaps in spite of collaboration, it is a failure. The ballet-master cannot be expected to know or do everything. His or her particular job is the arrangement of dance pattern and gesture on the basis of a previously chosen plot. In the late Diaghilev ballet and in the early days of the Monte Carlo Company, Boris Kochno was the gag-man. Much of the atmospheric strangeness of Balanchine's *Cotillon* (1932), for example, can be traced to his pungent poetic talent, a poetry of ideas verbally rather than scripturally transcribed into terms of dance by way of the choreographer, rather into terms of verse by a poet. Jean Cocteau had this valuable and elusive gift, and perhaps to a lesser degree, Jean Louis Vaudoyer, who was responsible for the original idea of Fokine's enchanting *pas de deux, Le Spectre de la Rose.*

The poet of the written word can easily serve the ballet-master, not only as author of a written scenario, a vocal sound-track or a program-note, but during the actual rehearsals and production of the ballet. That is, if the poet can think in terms of theatrical dancing. Some poets and painters have a genuine gift for visual imagery which can be almost immediately transcribed into ballet incident. We remember how Lumley, the Director of the Queen's Theatre in London, had commissioned a ballet-scenario from Heinrich Heine, on whose work Théophile Gautier had based *La Sylphide.* Heine worked with erudition and enthusiasm. He produced *Der Doktor Faust, Ein Tanzpoem.* It was, due to a variety of reasons, never produced. Heine wrote from Paris in 1851:

The ballet master regarded it as a dangerous novelty that for once a poet had actually composed the libretto of a ballet, whereas up to that time, such products had always been delivered by dancing monkeys mimicking the poet's craft, in collaboration with any worthy literary hack.

Personally, I should welcome a working arrangement with young English and American poets of our persuasions. W. B. Yeats has always been absorbed by dancing, and has conceived several plays for dancers. His verse abounds in dance imagery. Christopher Isherwood and W. H. Auden have shown, from their verse plays, a clear lyrical sense of realistic fantasy and fabulous truth. Auden's "Dance of Death" was dedicated to its first dancer. Among our own writers I think of two. Muriel Rukeyser, author of "Theory of Flight" and "U. S. 1" can be of value to classic dancing. James Agee, author of "Permit Me Voyage" and a remarkable movie-scenario, "The House," published in "New Letters in America: 1937," could vitally aid contemporary choreographers. Glenway Wescott has composed an ingenious scenario based on the life and works of Audubon, the great American naturalist, which is too elaborate for most American companies to undertake, but which could make a fortune for the Russians. E. E. Cummings' published ballet scenario "Tom," based on the Harriet Beecher Stowe novel, is already equipped with a score by David Diamond, the gifted young American composer. I could even imagine Pare Lorenz, the instigator of the two fine U. S. Government films, "The Plough That Broke the Plains" and "The River" turning his eye to classic dancing. Anyone can "write" a ballet-scenario. But it takes a genuine poetic vein to be of any use as a collaborator in the theatre. A poet must be patient enough to be educated by the choreographer, and willing enough to conform to the stress and strain of the collective method.

II. *AN ORGANIZED AUDIENCE*

As has been indicated in this pamphlet, there is much at odds in the contemporary condition of our theatrical-dancing. I have presupposed the fact that my readers are to some degree interested in setting these odds to rights. But what is to be done? What can a mere individual do in the face of economic monopoly and entrenched commercial management? Hasn't the general situation always been virtually the same? Doesn't everything (dancing included) get done in spite of, rather than by aid of everything (or anything) else? After all, isn't our job rather watching the ballet than worrying about it.

Nevertheless, I am assuming, because my future depends on it, as well as the professional lives and artistic futures of certain dancers to whom I am personally attached, that in every city in America with a population of fifty thousand, there are at least half a dozen people interested in the presentation of American ballet in America. If they felt the same way about it, these might add up to quite an energetic force. To them I address a series of tentative suggestions which would materially benefit the development of ballet in America, not on a visionary but on a purely immediate and realistic basis. First I will briefly list them, then submit a plan whereby these suggestions, or others more feasible, can be put into effect.

1. The definite *separation* of dance-attractions from music-attractions on the commercial dance- and music-managers' seasonal block-booking schedule. That is, instead of listing a ballet-company in the same general category as a violinist, soprano, or symphony orchestra, they must list a ballet-company with perhaps a solo national-dancer, a "modern" dancer, or another ballet-company. This might even involve the coöperation of two or more managers from different bureaus.

2. The creation of a definite provincial American *circuit* for dance-attractions as such. This would take a little money for publicity. But if the program were worked out with a trace of care a contrast, and even a sense of competition could be created, with half the attractions remaining as foreign artists or troupes, and half from the native product, such as, for example, Mr. Joseph Mann's series at the Washington Irving

High School, and Mr. William Kolodney's at the New York Y.M.H.A. has done successfully for several years. This might easily depend on

3. *An annual or semi-annual season* of the American Ballet Companies in at least three centrally located large cities such as New York, Chicago, or San Francisco, in order that the provincial press and local section-managers could make use of the prestige of the reviews from the larger centralized capitals. This might easily depend on

4. *Coöperation with local symphony orchestras.* This season (1938-39) the Ballet Russe de Monte Carlo is appearing with at least eleven of our largest American orchestral organizations. It will unquestionably take some convincing their conductors that our American repertory is as musically distinguished as the Russian, which it is, or that Americans dance as well as the Russians, which they do. There are very few top-rank native-born conductors. The acceptance of the American repertory, in turn, might depend on

5. *The Commissioning* of American Ballet orchestral scores under the auspices of a local sponsorship, and with the interest of a local orchestral conductor. The more progressive sub-divisions of the big broadcasting companies have recently paid a number of our younger composers to write pieces specially for broadcasting orchestras. It would be possible for Women's Clubs, Garden Clubs or other local cultural groups, under a direction suggested immediately below, to occupy themselves with awards not only for music, but also for decor and costumes. If an orchestral conductor felt that there was a considerable interest in these commissions among individuals and groups who more than likely were also actively interested in the maintenance of the orchestra, there would be a new incentive to perform the works.

1. *Postscript for Conductors of Symphony Orchestras*

Aside from the organization of the Philadelphia Orchestra, which has so splendidly coöperated with the Littlefield Ballet, as well as other visiting companies, there has not been a great deal of interest on the part of our American conductors to play with any dancers except the Russians. Perhaps they scarcely realize that the American companies can serve them, that they already have in orchestral partitions which can be played tomorrow, a standard repertory of considerable musical distinction, entirely apart from contemporary works which the various ballet companies have commissioned for their own uses.

111

In chronological order of composition here are some two dozen works with choreography by only half a dozen American companies which should interest many orchestras to play, and their publics to see. Indeed, quite a few of them are at the present time in their current orchestral repertory.

Bach: Miss Littlefield has made a ballet to the first two Brandenburg Concerti. Adolph Bolm has used Bach, as well. William Christensen's company dances to the B Minor Suite. The Ballet Caravan dances to the Goldberg Variations, orchestrally arranged for them by Nicolas Nabokoff, Professor of Music at Wells College, Aurora, New York, as well as composer of *Ode* for Diaghilev, and *Union Pacific* for the Monte Carlo.

Mozart: Both the Mordkin Company and the American Ballet use the suite of dances arranged by Tchaikovsky for small orchestra and known as *Mozartiana.* The Ballet Caravan dances *Encounter* to the "Haffner" Serenade. The Christensen Ballet uses *Eine Kleine Nachtmusik.*

Chopin: The Littlefield Ballet in *Moment Romantique,* employs a set of dances which would be a welcome change to hear after the eternal *Les Sylphides.* William Christensen has composed a *Chopinade.* The American Ballet uses the F Minor Piano Concerto, with choreography by William Dollar.

Schubert: The American Ballet's *Errante* is his *Wanderer* fantasy magnificently orchestrated by Charles Koechlin, the distinguished master of the Paris Conservatoire. Ruth Page's *Love Song* is a series of short pieces chosen for their dancing quality, arranged by Wesley la Violette.

Tchaikovsky: The Littlefield Ballet employs most of "The Sleeping Beauty," perhaps the most brilliant theatrical dance music ever written. William Christensen has mounted the "Romeo and Juliet" overture with great success. The American Ballet's *Serenade* (for strings) was frequently performed at the Metropolitan.

Ravel: Both Ruth Page and Catherine Littlefield have employed the *Bolero,* each quite differently. The Ballet Caravan dances to *Les Valses Nobles et Sentimentales,* brilliantly orchestrated by the composer.

Stravinsky: Ruth Page danced *L'Histoire d'un Soldat;* Catherine Littlefield and Adolph Bolm, *Apollon Musagète;* and the American Ballet to *Apollon, Le Baiser de la Fée* and *Jeux des Cartes.*

This is only a small choice from the far larger repertory contained in my appendix, but any conductor can see that several interesting programs could be constructed on this basis alone. It is not perhaps easy to conduct for ballet. There is always likely to be a confusion between the choreographer and the orchestral conductor over the tempi, particularly if the composer of the score is not present. A pure orchestral treatment differs slightly from a choreographic one. With a ballet company, the conductor descends from his customary elevated place on the podium, and the orchestra itself shares the interest with the dancers, rather than with the conductor alone. Certain theatrical effects are demanded which the composer may or may not have indicated, but these differences can be resolved with a little patience. Nevertheless, the appearance of a ballet company with a symphony orchestra is a sure way to interest a larger public in the purely musical activities of its local organization.

III. *AN ALLIANCE OF AMERICAN BALLETS*

The suggestions proposed above depend entirely on our ballet companies and their audiences being organized into some active entity which can make their wishes realized. At present there is no similar organization in the dance field except the tacit alliance of dance-manager for utilizing their publics, and the promise of *The Ballet Guild, Inc.*, with headquarters in New York City, which, employing the services of the "patrons" I have recently indicated, will back the interests of Russian companies in America.

If every American Ballet Company could join in a strong combination with each other, much might be gained. The field of foreign attractions, due to the world situation, gets smaller every day. The management monopolies will soon turn to us, but they will only turn at the very last moment. In the meantime we can sink or swim. I propose we swim together. I propose we continue to get along *in spite of* the monopolies as we have so far done, even should they make proposals to us, as they are now beginning to do. I propose that the American Ballet Companies pool their resources and set up *their own* independent management office, which will be entirely occupied with furthering their particular interests, by building a national circuit and stimulating a national audience.

Every native local company could find backing for such a scheme. In every city exchange performances could be arranged, exhibition of prints, paintings and programs could be held, a national bulletin could be issued, and a national dance archives established. If the American Ballet managements could be organized into one powerful agency, the critics might be more respectful or at least more open-minded, and the patrons might think twice as to the object of their patronage.

Our audience awaits us. An alliance of American Ballets should have close connections with lay organizations on a broad basis. Whatever this base, let it be democratic, realistic and creative. Let the patronage be directed toward good lyric theatre, and let our dancers have the liberty, incentive and security to do what they best can do, and alone can do, which is to dance well on our stages.

THE REPERTORY OF THE PHILADELPHIA BALLET

All Choreography by CATHERINE LITTLEFIELD

BALLETS ON AMERICAN THEMES BY AMERICAN COMPOSERS

	Music	Designer of Scenery	Designer of Costumes	Date First Performance (All World Premieres)
*The Snow Queen	Murray Cutter	A. Jarin	P. T. Champs	Phila., Dec. 28, 1935
*Barn Dance	Folk tunes arranged by: John Powell, David Guion, L. M. Gottschalk	A. Pinto	S. Pinto	Phila., April 23, 1937
*Terminal	Herbert Kingsley	A. Pinto	S. Pinto	Paris, France, June 1, 1937
*Let the Righteous Be Glad	J. Donath (Arrangement of negro spirituals)	A. Pinto	S. Pinto	Phila., Dec. 13, 1937
*Parable in Blue	M. Gabowitz	George C. Jenkins	Lee Gainsborough	Phila., Dec. 22, 1937
*Ladies' Better Dresses	Herbert Kingsley	R. Starke	Joy Michael	Chicago, November, 1938
*Café Society	Ferdy Grofé	Carl Shaffer	Carl Shaffer	Chicago, November, 1938
*The Vacant Chair (The Meschianza)	Tibor Serly	(Not decided yet)	(Not decided yet)	Phila., March, 1939

* (Indicates the ballet is still in regular repertory)

BALLETS TO MUSIC OF FOREIGN COMPOSERS
(Philadelphia Ballet)

	Music	Designer of Scenery	Designer of Costumes	Date of 1st Performance
*Daphnis et Chloe (3 scenes)	M. Ravel	A. Jarin	J. Pascal	Phila., Mar. 31, 1936 (American premiere)
*The Sleeping Beauty (5 scenes)	Tchaikovsky	R. Deshays	Lee Gainsborough	Phila., Feb. 11, 1937 (American premiere)
*Bolero	M. Ravel	Lee Gainsborough	Lee Gainsborough	Phila., Aug. 3, 1936
*The Fairy Doll	J. Bayer	A. Jarin	P. T. Champs	Phila., Dec. 28, 1935
*Prince Igor (Polovetsian Dances)	Borodin	A. Jarin	(None)	Phila., Mar. 31, 1936
*Moment Romantique	F. Chopin	(None)	(None)	Phila., Aug. 3, 1936
*Viennese Waltz	J. Strauss	A. Jarin	P. T. Champs	Phila., May 13, 1936
*Classical Suite	J. S. Bach (Brandenberg Concerti, 1 and 2)	R. Deshays	P. T. Champs	Princeton, N. J., Nov. 6, 1937
*The Minstrel	Debussy (Menestrales)	A. Pinto	S. Pinto	Haverford, Pa., Oct. 25, 1935
*Poème	M. Ravel (Pavane)	(None)	(None)	Phila., Dec. 8, 1936
Aubade	F. Poulenc	R. Deshays	J. Pascal	Phila., Mar. 5, 1936
Fête Champêtre	Lully, Gretry & Rameau	A. Jarin	J. Pascal	Phila., Mar. 31, 1936
Romantic Variations	Saint Saens	(None)	J. Pascal	Phila., Dec. 8, 1936
The Prodigal Son	Cesar Franck	(None)	L. Galpern	Phila., Dec. 8, 1936
Home Life of the Gods	E. Satie (Mercure)	L. Galpern	L. Galpern	Phila., Dec. 8, 1936
*Fantasia	Johann Strauss (Perpetuum Mobile)	Mary Fales	Mary Fales	Chicago, November, 1938

THE REPERTORY OF THE RUTH PAGE BALLETS

All Choreography by RUTH PAGE

	Music	Designer	Auspices	First Performance
Frankie & Johnnie	Jerome Moross	Paul du Pont	Chicago Federal Theatre	June, 1938
American Pattern	Jerome Moross	Nicholas Remisoff	Chicago Opera	December, 1937
Americans in Paris	George Gershwin	Nicholas Remisoff	Cincinnati Opera	August, 1936
Love Song	Franz Schubert	Nicholas Remisoff	Chicago Opera	October, 1935
Hear Ye! Hear Ye!	Aaron Copland	Nicholas Remisoff	Chicago Opera	November, 1934
Gold Standard	Jacques Ibert	Nicholas Remisoff	Chicago Opera	November, 1934
La Guiablesse	William Grant Still	Nicholas Remisoff	Chicago (Century of Progress Exposition)	June, 1933
Iberian Monotone	Maurice Ravel	Nicholas Remisoff	Concert (Chicago)	April, 1932

117

THE REPERTORY OF THE BALLET CARAVAN

	Music	Costumes	Choreographer	First Performance
Ballets to Classic Music				
Encounter	W. A. Mozart ("*Haffner*" *Serenade*)	*after* J. G. von Schadow	Lew Christensen	Bennington, Vt., July, 1936
Harlequin for President	D. Scarlatti (*Sonatas*)	Keith Martin	Eugene Loring	Bennington, Vt., July, 1936
Folk Dance	Emmanuel Chabrier	Charles Rain	Douglas Coudy	Burlington, Vt., August, 1936
Promenade	M. Ravel (*Valses Nobles et Sentimentales*)	*after* Horace Vernet	William Dollar	Bennington, Vt., July, 1936
Variations	J. S. Bach (*The Goldberg Variations*)	Walter Gifford	William Dollar	Athens, Georgia, April, 1938
Ballets to American Music on Contemporary Themes				
Pocahontas	Elliott Carter, Jr.	Karl Free	Lew Christensen	Middlebury, Vt., August, 1936
Yankee-Clipper	Paul Bowles	Charles Rain	Eugene Loring	Saybrook, Conn., July, 1937
Show Piece	Robert McBride	Keith Martin	Erick Hawkins	Bar Harbor, Maine, August, 1937
Filling Station	Virgil Thomson	Paul Cadmus	Lew Christensen	Hartford, Conn., November, 1937
Billy the Kid	Aaron Copland	Jared French	Eugene Loring	Chicago, Ill., October, 1938
The Minotaur	Charles Naginski	Leslie Powell	Erick Hawkins	New York City, January, 1939

THE REPERTORY OF THE AMERICAN BALLET

All Choreography by GEORGE BALANCHINE

	Music	Costumes and Scenery	First Performance (All New York City)
Ballets to Classic Music			
Mozartiana	Mozart (Tchaikovsky)	Christian Bérard	March, 1935
Serenade	Tchaikovsky (*Serenade for Strings*)	Jean Lurçat	March, 1935
Errante	Schubert (Koechlin)	Pavel Tchelitchev	March, 1935
Transcendance	Liszt (*Mephisto Valse-Elegie*)	Franklin Watkins	March, 1935
Reminiscence	Godard (Brant)	Sergei Soudeikine	March, 1935
The Bat	Johann Strauss (*Fledermaus*)	Keith Martin	February, 1936
Concerto	Chopin (*F-Minor Piano Concerto*)	(Practice-tunics)	March, 1936
	(Choreography by William Dollar)		
Ballets to Contemporary Music			
Alma Mater	Kay Swift	John Held, Jr.	March, 1935
Dreams	George Antheil	André Derain	March, 1935
Apollon Musagète	Igor Stravinsky	Stewart Cheney	April, 1937
The Card Party	Igor Stravinsky	Irene Sharaff	April, 1937
The Fairy's Kiss	Igor Stravinsky	Alice Halicka	April, 1937
Opera Ballet			
Orpheus (complete)	Gluck	Pavel Tchelitchev	April, 1936

THE REPERTORY OF WILLIAM CHRISTENSEN

Choreographer of the San Francisco Opera Ballet

	Music	Costumes and Scenery	Auspices	First Performance
Ballets to Classic Music				
Chopinade	F. Chopin	J. C. Taylor		Seattle, Wash., July 28, 1935
Capriccio Espagnole	Rimsky-Korsakov (*Capriccio Espagnole*)	Harriette Meyers	Portland Symphony Orchestra	February, 1936
The Bartered Bride (*Three Dances*)	Smetana	J. C. Taylor	Portland Rose Festival	June 8, 1936
Coeur de Glace	W. A. Mozart (*Eine Kleine Nachtmusik*)	J. C. Taylor	Portland Symphony Orchestra	December, 1936
Sketches:				
Divertissement	Gounod	San Francisco Opera Company Costume Department	Santa Rosa Symphony	November 9, 1937
Rosamunde	Schubert			November 9, 1937
Dance Chinois	Tchaikovsky			November 9, 1937
Tarantella	Rossini-Resphigi			November 9, 1937
Romeo & Juliet	Tchaikovsky	Helen Green (Costumes) Armando Agnini (Scenery)	Sacramento Symphony	March 3, 1938
A Bach Suite	J. S. Bach (Suite No. 2: B-Minor)	Armando Agnini		San Francisco, Cal. April 20, 1938
In Vienna	Johann Strauss	Helen Green (Costumes) Armando Agnini (Scenery)		San Francisco, Cal., June 20, 1938
*A Midsummer Night's Dream	Mendelssohn	J. C. Taylor		Portland, Oregon, July, 1938
Ballets to Contemporary Music				
Rumanian Wedding	Georges Enesco (First Rhapsody)	J. C. Taylor	Portland Symphony Orchestra	February, 1936
Brides on Strike	Godfrey Turner			In Preparation

*Choreography of "A Midsummer Night's Dream" by Lew Christensen, with William Christensen's dancers.

120

II. GORDON CRAIG AND THE RUSSIAN BALLET

The great English stage designer Edward Gordon Craig, whose theatrical writing, suggestive designs and theatrical productions have so profoundly affected our "modern" theatre, was the only critic of eminence who, from the very start, held out against the Russian Ballet. In *The Mask* for October, 1911, was published an article signed by John Balance called "Kleptomania," on the Russian theatre. It was a cold-blooded analysis of the Russian dancing and stage decoration, and is unique in its realistic attitude. In 1937, I acquired through a London bookseller part of Craig's library. In a bound volume of the French illustrated theatrical revue *Commoedia Illustré,* for the early Russian Seasons of 1909 to 1914, Craig had written in pencil the following notes, ideas which were later organized in *The Mask* article. Anything from Craig's mind is of interest to the theatrical worker. These notes are doubly so from their historical and contemporary analysis. These penciled notes *were written in 1913.* There are later comments indicated.

1. *(In the front of the Volume.)*

1911 to 1913—Showing perhaps (better than) as well as, any other document exactly what was happening in the new movement as expressed by the following men and women:

Fokine, Nijinski, Karsavina, Mad. Fokina
Bakst, Roerich, Visconti*(?), Bolm
D'Annunzio (?), *Antoine,* Ida Rubenstein
Rheinhardt, Maria Carmi (Princess Matchabelli)
De Max
Jean Morax
Bernhardt (?), Tellegen.

(I question some of these as representing anything in the new movement. The names *italicized* are the principal figures.)

(Note how Meyerhold was overshadowed in these years—in Paris!)

E. G. C. 1935

Now we have at a glance more clear idea *how·much* of (and what class of thing) the new movement got into the great city of Paris.

We know that Isadora Duncan got in and left her mark but her presence was unable to prevent the pandemonium which a big city seems to crave for.

But there are some important people who did not go to Paris:

---

*Scenic designer: Designed decor for Fauré's opera *Penelope,* Monte Carlo. 1913.

Stanislavsky's company of actors
The Irish Players from Dublin
Dalcroze's company of dancers

Still, even all these as visitors would have amounted only to a passing fashion and made Parisians "rave" for a month or two.

But Appia, not a word of him, and he is the greatest scenic figure of the new movement. Of E. G. C. we do not hear either—not to be with D'Annunzio and Bakst in Paris is lucky. To be left with Appia and the others is a good sign.

This "new movement" amounts to nothing when you've considered carefully what (there) is in this volume.

Why nothing (?). I will tell you in two words.

It's a *new theatricalism* which the whole thing amounts to.
　—a new falsity
　—it is beliefless—

In this volume you can see what their method was.

They thought they could imitate so well as to deceive us into believing it was creation.

They went to see the Indian statue's pictures dancers and did an Indian affair.

They went to see the Egyptian statue's pictures dancers and did an Egyptian affair.

They went to see the Grecian statue's pictures dancers and did a Greek affair.

They went to see the Turkish statue's pictures dancers and did a Turkish affair.

They went to see the Italian statue's pictures dancers and did an (Italian) affair.

The list is as long as the list of nationalities.
They had no belief in themselves and in principles.
They put on and put off anyone elses' *belief*.
We will do it "like this" they said on Monday
We will do it "like that" they said on Tuesday

They could do it anyway.
They were not doubtful if they could manage it.
They were sure of themselves, very.
Very sure they could disguise anything.

How far were they successful(?)
They disguised everything and created nothing
We believe that is to have failed. (E.G.C.—May 1915.)

2. *Notes on illustrations in the text.*

On Bakst's costume design of Ida Rubenstein, martyred as Saint Sebastien. *Sickness.*

On Bakst's color sketches for Le Miracle de Saint Sebastien: *Compare photograph:*
  All is lost.

Costume is not dress (but only) a cover. Costumes is that which uncovers the Soul.

The flesh and bones are the costume of the Soul. Reveal them then—without exposing that which is mute and must remain so.   *E. G. C., 1911*

On four photos (Bert) of Nijinsky and Karsavina in *Le Spectre de la Rose:*

These four photos are charming indeed and represent all that is best in the Russian Ballet.

And yet Karsavina seems to be the very essence of insincerity and of vanity of a dull kind.

—but Nijinsky!!!

On a photo of Vera Fokina:

Possibly the best brains of the group. Her fat hands and whole person well under control and does not make mistakes.

On a photo of a Dancer designed by Leon Bakst for the Paquin (dressmaking) Pavilion at the Exposition of Turin 1911:

The awful effects of following the footsteps of Isadora Duncan.

The mixing of art-dressmakers-royalty-naked ladies-dancing and prostitution.

If pleasant things each in their own place how unpleasant when mixed in this friendly fashion.

All for commerce!

This kind of thing it is which makes us hate and wage war on commercialism. And this is only the fringe.

On a cover in color of *Commoedia Illustré* for June 1, 1912, showing Karsavina and Bolm in costume for *"Thamar"*:

Senseless if you will consider for a moment.

On Nijinsky's costumes for *Le Dieu Bleu* (Bakst):

Compare this first with the Indian plate 30 in Coomeraswamy. (The Mirror of gesture) after with the photographs facing (Nijinsky photographed in the finished costume).*

On a color plate for the decor of *Le Dieu Bleu* (Bakst):

The worms on the twig are rather unconvincing.
(The sketch) Not a bit like the result achieved. I saw it in 1912.   E. G. C.

On photos of dancers in costumes for *Le Dieu Bleu:*

Some good dresses.

On the dancer Baranovitch II:

Stupid woman, good dress.

On sketches by Roerich for *Le Sacre du Printemps:*

Roerich is the best of the Russians as decorators of painted scenes and costumes.

On the description with illustrations of *La Pisanelle* or *La Mort Parfumée,* words by D'Annunzio (Italian), music by da Parma (Italian), decor and costumes by Bakst (Russian), dances by Fokine (Russian), musical direction by Inghelbrecht (German)

And interesting this series of pictures, for it shows how much or how little the great Meyerhold could do without his own theatre, his own company and his liberty.   E. G. C., 1915

On a review by Louis Delluc of *La Pisanelle* (20 June, 1913)
"Is there nothing about Meyerhold?"

(The review had mentioned all the collaborators except the director-in-chief.)

---

*Craig's intention was to show how little the dead photo resembled the highly stylized sketch.

3. *Notes by E. G. C. in The Art of Nijinsky by Geoffrey Whitworth (1913), with Gordon Craig's bookplate. Florence 1913.*

On a quotation from the article on Ballet published in the Encyclopedia Brittanica (1910 page 1).

Only in an atmosphere of *ceremony, courtesy and chivalry* can the dance maintain itself in perfection. Right. (Italics of E. G. C.)

Page 9: The young Nijinsky soon *began to manifest the character of genius.* (Italics of E. G. C.)

and later on he blazed them by deserting the ranks of the Russian Ballet in Diaghilev's personal direction.

Page 17 and 18:

Nor must we forget the liberating force which sprang from the art of Isadora Duncan, whose heroic practice has done far more than any precepts of philosophy to widen our ideas as *to the intellectual and spiritual possibilities of the dance.* (Italics E. G. C.)

Not that—Isadora Duncan has not dealt with the dance intellectually, nor spiritually—but personally. The age saw to that!

III. *A LETTER TO* TIME

Mr. Glenway Wescott, the distinguished American novelist, wrote the following letter to TIME Magazine, after reading their review of the American Ballet's production of *Orpheus* at the Metropolitan Opera House in the spring of 1936. The letter was printed, with cuts. It is here reprinted entire.

May 30, 1936

To the Editors of TIME.

SIRS,

Though in an unhappy mood of revolt against the press, I think I know a good job of disapprobation when I see one. TIME is to be complimented upon its brisk descriptive damning of Balanchine's *Orpheus and Eurydice.* Critics of the daily papers indulged in obscure epithets, and bigotted defence of what they term tradition, in the ferocious diehard manner. TIME's policy, I believe, is to report the response of the public to such a performance in the spirit in which it reports the performance, as news; not to give individual opinion of its writers. In this case it failed to note the existence of two camps, two mutually exclusive views of the future of opera and ballet in New York. I submit what follows as information rather than resentful protest.

The present *Orpheus,* the only original undertaking of the opera association this season, gave as much pleasure to a certain public as offense to the critics. Readers of the various commentary up to date, including TIME's, could have had no inkling of this. Yet, attentive to the American Ballet's young reputation, and admiring Balanchine and Tchelitchew, we crowded the Metropolitan. By virtue of the strange new scenes and twentieth-century dances, I was more deeply moved by the ancient myth and 18th Century music than ever before. I know that some thirty or forty persons of my acquaintance also were not disappointed. To what extent the enthusiasts are in the minority, no one knows. Minority groups have in the past had powerful effect upon public taste in matters of art and entertainment. If our enthusiasm were to prove sufficiently contagious, the Metropolitan Opera Association would have to give us what we want, or fail. It seems to me that readers of TIME should be reminded of this possibility.

Alas, the guardians of tradition are suspicious as well as skeptical. Many of those who are paid to give opinions of such things as performances at the opera house evidently believe that mere citizens who pay for their seats are less inclined to be sincere than themselves. Therefore, since I speak of myself as fairly representative of a group or class, perhaps I should somewhat identify or characterize myself as an opera-goer. I am indeed what of late has been called by an ugly new name, *balletomane.* However, I am one who has believed that the Russian school of dancing has had its day: which has made me dubious of the effort of the company directed by Balanchine. Incidentally, working with these young Americans, he has adapted his imagination to make the best use of their native beauties and aptitudes; and this *Orpheus* is the only ballet I can think of that Isadora Duncan would have approved whole-heartedly. Balanchine is a very great man, I think. If I were to make a list of the dozen most exciting and inspiring things I have seen in the theatre, three of his choreographic works would be on it: *Apollon Musagéte* (Stravinski) and *The Prodigal Son* (Prokofieff) and *Errante,* revived at the Metropolitan this season. But by this general admiration I am not at all disposed to admire all that he does; quite the contrary. *The Bat,* for example, bores me. Need I add that I am not in anyone's pay? I did not receive complimentary tickets for *Orpheus,* nor do I know anyone who did. Now may I repeat that it gave me greater satisfaction and interested me more than any other art-event of the past season? I saw it both times it was given. I hope it will be given again. And I should like to see developed at the Metropolitan a new type of operatic art, uninhibited, unconventional, as suggested by it. I know that many people are of my opinion. Nothing has been done, and there has not even been time, for the curiosity of a great many more, who never set foot in the opera house at present, to be aroused. And I understand that it needs new patronage.

Perhaps I should admit that I and my friends have no great pious respect for the Metropolitan as a high place of operatic tradition, a temple, an academy. We go there for pleasure, nothing else. Also we have all heard that its vaunted tradition is no longer profitable. In the recent film, *Mr. Deeds Goes to Town,* the hero, asked to be chairman of the board of directors of an opera house, and informed of the deficit that he is expected to make up, remarks that evidently it is time for them to try some new kind of show. It would seem so. The banal repetition of nineteenth-century works amid tumbledown scenery, with no attempt at novelty except the expensive importation of phenomenal foreign singers, at a loss to the owners of the building, who annually campaign for funds as if operatic entertainment were a charity, cannot go on forever.

We honestly believe that—with its obvious faults corrected, given rehearsals that could not be provided for out of the spring budget, sung to a simple English libretto, under livelier orchestral direction—Balanchine's *Orpheus* would be a fine and sufficiently popular addition to the regular repertory. If Mr. Johnson and the deficit-ridden board of directors pay attention to the tradition-ridden critics, or even to TIME's anonymous impressionist, it may now be given up as a bad job; the money spent, the experiment only half-made. Perhaps the future of such public art as opera here is hopeless. It sometimes seems that we are a conventional, provincial people: in awe of artistic reputation built up abroad; credulous, docile; pathetically respectful of aged opinion. There is defeatism in the mere faithfulness to tradition. Advertisement is expensive. We have no aggressively young critics. It is hard to see how art can flourish without some form of free publicity. The older generation wins with a sneer its fruitless victory; the younger loses with a sigh.

The New York *Times'* Mr. Downes characterizes this production as impudent and pretentious and meddlesome. *Cavalleria Rusticana* was also given that night: indifferently sung, with the usual academic posturing, in old musical-comedy costumes, in glaring lighting, against a brightly daubed backdrop; and Mr. Downes praised this as competent, conventional, and comforting. His choice of adjectives, and the contrast between the two productions, makes the issue very clear.

In respect to art, when there is real difference of taste and a new division of opinion, it is not easy to be impartial. I am happy to admit

127

that I am not. TIME's reporter, for instance, says that the dance of the three principals together at the end of the opera suggests "a Japanese tumbling act." No doubt this comparison was scornfully intended. Yet it might be read as a compliment. For to those of us who find classic operatic pantomime ludicrous and of waning significance, the acts of acrobats often seem very fine. No doubt inadvertently, TIME has taken sides with the powerful old guard as against a merely potent young generation.

GLENWAY WESCOTT

BALLET ALPHABET

1939

BALLET ALPHABET

A PRIMER FOR LAYMEN BY

LINCOLN KIRSTEIN

DRAWINGS BY **PAUL CADMUS**

FOR
MY FATHER AND MOTHER
who sometimes pretend they don't
know what I am talking about.

FOREWORD

THIS book is intended to provide a foundation for the more common terms in the vocabulary of contemporary theatrical dancing. It is a practical reference work for laymen with few scholarly pretensions. While arranged in alphabetical order to be read piece-meal, it was conceived consecutively. Most readers will have some familiarity with the huge literature of the dance. For those who have not, the important definitions somehow manage to appear first, explaining and supplementing each other.

A general historical background is indicated, but space is too limited to render this either an encyclopedia or a biographical dictionary. Naturally, the opinions of a single author seem polemical when not strictly personal. The only polemics which may have crept in are the result of objective stage-experience, not of pedantic class-room prejudice.

The size of this book was limited by a desire to make it widely available. It is the author's intention one day to compile a more complete iconographic dictionary of the dance. As a visual art, its literature suffers grievously from having inadequate graphic representations for comparison. Ideally speaking, the only valid criticism of dancing would be motion-picture films taken from the dim past down into our own day. Lacking this, we must suffice with a few schematic diagrams.

The drawings by Paul Cadmus are generalized representations more to indicate the classic style than to serve as models for instruction. Absolute positions are only metaphysically absolute. Practically, they apply to the given bodies of particular dancers. These drawings seek an average, not alone of specific positions, but also of the various accepted academic canons and tastes.

Corrections, additions and suggestions for further headings in possible future editions would be appreciated.

LINCOLN KIRSTEIN

CONTENTS

Illustrations

A

ACADEMY: school, method or body of instruction which is also a standard of ideal excellence and residual practice of an art or science. Academies of dancing in Western Europe owed their origin to renaissance revivals of antique Greek precedent. Poets, scholars and artists banding together for professional purposes established the Academy of Saint Cecilia in Paris (1570) and the Accademia della Crusca in Florence (1582), which investigated music, prosody, diction and classic metric. In 1661, an impoverished poet called Perrin received letters-patent from Colbert, Louis XIV's minister, granting him privilege to plan a French Academy of Music and Poetry, based on Italian models. In the same year, a group of dancing-masters requested and received permission to establish an authorized Academy for (preponderantly social) Dancing in the Louvre. These last two ideas were the direct source of the Italian composer, J. B. Lully's Académie Royale de Musique, in which dancing had an important function as an aid to productions of ballet-opera. The *maître de ballet,* Beauchamps, was its first director from 1671 to 1687. The French academy, expanding throughout the eighteenth century, became a model for the world persisting today as *L'Académie Nationale de Musique et de la Danse.*

Only a little later, under German influence, a theatrical school was founded in the Kremlin. The first Russian theatre was built in 1703. In 1735 the Empress Anna Ivanovna ordered all her infantry cadets to be taught dancing, and this was the origin of the great Petersburg-Leningrad Academy. The school at Moscow, which has suffered a certain snobbish criticism at the hands of the Petersburgeois as a home for acrobats and vulgarians, was not founded until 1809, yet at present, seems to have surpassed its ancient rival. Both schools were instructed by aliens for many years. The descendants of the Italian, French, and Scandinavian masters are responsible for the great dancers of our own day. Russian masters did not start to instruct their own pupils until around 1890.

1

There was always a ballet school in Stockholm in the eighteenth century, but when Rolf de Maré was organizing his Swedish Ballet in 1920, he was obliged to include dancers from other countries. The Royal Danish Academy boasts a more ancient tradition. Galeotti, a follower of Angiolini and Noverre, headed this school from 1775 to 1815. The Bournonville family, Antoine and Auguste, were in control, off and on, from 1816 to 1877. The great "romantic" ballerina, Lucille Grahm, was trained in Copenhagen, and there are many charming photographs of Danish dancers as Valkyrs in *tutus*.

Individual Milanese dancing-masters had been renowned since the fifteenth century and schools were established by 1640. However, the permanent Imperial Dancing Academy connected with the Scala Theatre was not opened until 1812 under the impressario Benedetto Ricci, although the Scala itself had opened in 1778, producing five ballets in its first season. Its greatest efflorescence came with the intendancy of Carlo Blasis from 1837 on, throughout the greater part of the century. The Italian Academy was responsible for the greatest influences of the nineteenth century classic dance, just as the French had been in the eighteenth, and Russians in our own day.

An academy is the life-blood of ballet. It economically provides all materials necessary for a mastery of technique. It holds the accumulation of residual information of generations of pedagogues and practicing artists. It develops early habits of discipline, providing in its complementary training, actual apprentice performances, the practical basis for a stage career. It establishes a standard for style, proficiency and instruction. Usually situated in a capital, it feeds the provinces.

An academy, to be worthy of the name, must provide a complete education for its students in all attendant fields, and its connection with a working theatre must be elastic and secure. In London, the Vic-Wells Opera and Ballet established a school in alliance with its theatre in 1933. America, as yet, has no real academy. Schools connected with our opera houses have the advantage of some stage-practice in however debased a form, but the instruction provided is only commensurate to the possibilities of production which are inferior, and the length of the seasons which are short. Academic standards in private schools

2

are higher, but the results are difficult to gauge as few schools feed directly into permanent companies.

"The idea of an Academy is extremely important in the foundation of an national artistic tradition. In the beginning, a genuine aid and rallying point for creative energy, it often disintegrates into rigid bureaucracy. Then its standards are useful only insomuch as they precipitate against official rigidity, all youthful violence and ambition of talents, which usurping its authority, cause envy, contempt, and reform. A good academy is not by any means an anomaly, although recently there has not been much proof of this view."

In Paris, to become qualified, as a dancer at the Opéra, children start not much later than nine years. Students stay in the *classes supplementaires*, three years in the first and two in the second. At thirteen or fourteen they enter the *classes des quadrilles*, consisting of some fifteen boys and twenty girls. By yearly examinations the *corps de ballet* is chosen from the three groups.

At the present, the finest schools in the world are probably in Russia. Not only do they enjoy large state subsidy, economic security and work on a variety of stages, but also artists who are not suited for the large cities may find ready employment in numerous provincial theatres, not only as dancers but as teachers and choreographers. The Moscow State Choreographic Technicum is divided into the *Semeletka* (Preparatory High-School) and *Technicum* (University Technical Course). *Semeletka* is for seven years, *Technicum* for three. All courses are free at all times. Half the students qualify to receive pay as dancing-workers during the first or second year of instruction.

One hundred and ten persons are on the pedagogical staff, including eight instructors, in the various subjects, fifteen pianist accompanists, doctors, artists, costumers, etc. The Moscow State Academy is under the control of the Bolshoi Theatre, which is directly governed by the Central Commission of the All-Union Executive of the Socialist Soviet Republics.

In 1938, according to an article by W. G. Raffe in "The American Dancer" (September, 1939), 215 students were enrolled in the *Semeletka* and 20 in the *Technicum*. The elementary course has a large proportion of deserters who even go back to ordinary civil life, while the entrance to the technical course is extremely difficult.

Children from the age of nine are proposed by their parents or day-school instructors. All are annually examined by a special medical and psychological commission. There are seven courses, each of a year's duration in *Semeletka*. Eleven different subjects are taught in varying dispositions of time. The chief emphasis is naturally dance-practice, but languages, fine arts, anatomy, and history are also required. The standard and practical efficiency are equally very high.

In the *Technicum,* advanced students are taught as dancers and choreographers. Fencing, plastique, anatomy, piano, counterpoint and harmony are also mastered as well as political history, economic geography, art, literature, and Leninism. A trained dancer has an education equivalent of any other college-bred person, and the superior of almost any other stage artist in the world.

ADAGIO: From the Italian, *ad agio,* at ease or, at leisure. English teachers use *Adage,* the French adaptation, while Americans prefer the original Italian.

"A correct execution of an adagio is the *ne plus ultra* of our art; and I look on it as the touch-stone of the dancer." Carlo Blasis (1829).

1. Group name given to a series of ballet-exercises to slow music, calculated to develop sustaining power in a dancer, particularly by balance on one foot, and by held extensions of arms and legs.

2. Portions of a ballet in which girls perform, supported by male partners. The so-called "grand" adagio is the emotional climax of the classic dance, in which the ballerina, aided by her cavalier, achieves combinations of steps and positions of which she would be incapable alone. It was the function of the male partner of the early nineteenth century to display the ballerina to so great an advantage, even to effacing himself, that it resulted in his temporary disappearance from Western European stages from about 1845 until the Russians returned him in 1909. Even in the Grand Adagio of *Swan Lake* (Petipa: Ivanov, 1872), or *Aurora's Wedding* (Petipa: Sergeev, 1890-1921), the

4

male dancer is scarcely more than a mere *porteur*. He bears and braces. Yet even in such apparently insignificant rôles the male partner has his considerable theatrical responsibility. Much stage experience, as well as physical strength is demanded to carry a girl in those artificial leaps, by whose aid she seems to fly slowly over the stage at a single bound. A girl is often little enough aid, and either from ignorance or lack of consideration, frequently resists the man's upward thrust. Some good partners have an instinctive physical tact which enables them to gauge at once the girl's center of gravity. They know just where to hold, achieving an initial grasp without fumbling. Their grip has to be firm because they are holding, not solid flesh, but an exterior layer of costume which may slip in a shift of weight. Dancers, who, from habit or preference, have frequently danced together, come to have a sense of each other's physical presence, which translated into terms of dancing, is revealed to an audience as an exquisite mutual awareness or super-human courtesy. The big *adagio* of the classic Russian repertory may be considered as highly conventionalized love-scenes, in which the climax is not an actual embrace, but the most delicate support or adjustment of weight, which enables the ballerina to accomplish spectacular feats of sustained balance or elevation with the least *apparent* aid of her partner. The characteristic stage-gallantry of the male partner in adagio need not necessarily echo the feudal courtesies of European courts. Tenderness, playful solicitation, and a subtle, teasing flattery are the twentieth century equivalents for the devoted, dazzled, chivalric plume-sweeping behavior, of the nineteenth century *danseur noble*. Indeed, in certain Samoan tribes, the men sometimes make their gestures studiously clumsy and grotesque in order to accentuate a contrast with the fluidity of the woman dancers.

3. The term *Adagio* has been appropriated from the ballet stage by variety artists who perform acrobatic numbers. "Adagio" acts are sometimes strung on a series of dance steps, or consist of a team of tumblers who hurl themselves into the air to be caught by a partner or partners. Adagio dancers sometimes base their act on a dramatic pretext: a slave and her master, a snake charmer and his cobra, or the Moth and the Flame.

The man slings the girl by an arm or a leg in a series of vertiginous turns. The main difference between the Adagio dance of variety and the dancer of an Adagio in ballet is that the interest of the former is in a mechanical display for its own sake, while in the latter, acrobatic features merely enhance an expression of the dramatic relationship between the characters whom the dancers represent.

Supported Adagio of the ballet, as we see it today, did not come into existence until the last quarter of the eighteenth century, although men and women had appeared together professionally since the middle of the seventeenth. The ballet costume of the early eighteenth was a theatrical version of contemporary court-dress, except that both men and women wore higher heels, larger wigs, and fuller skirts. The stiff male skirt was called *tonnelet* (diminutive of the French *tonneau*: a cask), and while of knee-length was nevertheless calculated to immobilize the legs, even though it lent a kind of artificial monumentality to the figure as a whole. It was almost a physical impossibility for two wide-skirted dancers to clasp each other. Also, intimate physical contact did not suit the conventions of divinity with which the tradition of Court-Ballet endowed their chief protagonists.

Reforms in costume suggested by Noverre long before 1760, and only accomplished by the French Revolution, as well as the popularity of the waltz as a theatrical form borrowed from the ball-room (ca. 1800), laid the ground-work for our contemporary classic adagio. The waltz replaced the minuet, and other mincing or deliberate court-dances, for it involved rapidly moving couples more or less engaged in each other's arms. Weber's apotheosis of the Waltz,—the famous "Invitation to the Dance" (1815), has served for Fokine's inspired *pas de deux*— *Le Spectre de la Rose* (1910). *Spectre* is scarcely the conventional supported adagio but in the development of the genre, the more deliberate and dramatic duets, such as in *Swan Lake* (Petipa: Ivanov: 1872), could scarcely have come into existence without the presence of a more active idiom supported by such a swinging waltz.

A considerable impetus must have been given the department of Adagio by the tours of famous dancing couples in the

6

first third of the last century, though the dances executed were by no means all in slow time. A man and a woman was about the smallest touring unit around which a local *corps de ballet* could be rehearsed. The visiting pair, in all probability, had their own numbers which were offered purely as *divertissements,* or which might be adapted for insertion into a given dramatic repertory. The great Italian choreographer, Salvatore Vigano (1769-1821) traveled all over Europe with his wife, Maria Medina. The Neapolitan ballerina, Brugnoli (whose fiery execution was to influence Fanny Elssler), and her partner, Samingo; the French duo—M. Albert and Mlle. Heberlé, were followed later by Paul and Marie Taglioni, Perrot and Grisi, Cerrito and Saint-Léon.

Marie Taglioni's brother married a German dancer, Amélie Galster. They made their American debut in *La Sylphide* (F. Taglioni: 1832) in New York City in 1839. In our own day, our parents still recall the wonderful partnership of Pavlova and Mordkin in their *Autumn Bacchanal* (Fokine: ca. 1914). Every such personal collaboration unquestionably added new means of handling, balance, innovations in support and greater freedom in the purely danced sections of Adagio. Outstanding examples in our contemporary repertory are the variation of Apollo and Terpsichore (*Apollon Musagète:* Balanchine: 1927-37) and the meeting of Saint Francis with the Lady Poverty (*Nobilissima Visione:* Massine, 1938).

In the preface to "The Dance of Life" Havelock Ellis, who understood all dancing perhaps better than any other Englishman, apologized for his slowness in writing. He quoted the sculptor Rodin: "Slowness is Beauty." "Certainly it is the slowest dances that have been to me the most beautiful to see, while in the dance of life, the achievement of a civilization in beauty seems to be inversely to the rapidity of its pace."

AIR: While the dancer's natural element is always air, a specific reference to the aerial sphere suggests that the movement executed, to a greater part, is off the surface of the floor. Conquest of aerial space is our dancers' most spectacular problem. They have at their disposal a whole vocabulary of movement, *la* *danse d'élévation,* which applies to it; leaps, battery, *tours en l'air,* etc., symbolic testimony of the triumph over space.

From the earliest study of dancing as a science or conscious accomplishment, the two divisions of earth (floor) and air (*terre* and *air*) have been established. Guglielmo Ebreo, the Jewish dancing-master of Pesaro (ca. 1430-1500), called the third and fourth of his prerequisites, *Partire del terreno* and *Aiere.* A contemporary, Antonio Cornazano of Piacenza, refers to the former as *Compartimento di Terreno.* By this we understand the dancer's estimation of the limits of his floor. *Aiere* identifies the quality of dexterity or lightness as well as the rising and falling of his body. Dr. Otto Kinkeldey of Cornell, who is responsible for our knowledge of these matters, tells us the words *elevato movimento* and *dolcie et umanissimo relevamento* explain *aiere.* Here at last is the suggestion of elevation and even a hint of the classic ballet exercise, the *relevé,* which is so important as ground-work for the attack on space.

Thoinot Arbeau, the orchesographer (1588), reaffirmed the categorical distinction between the *basse danse,* in which feet were kept close to the floor, and the more active *haute danse.* Throughout the eighteenth century there was a gradual theatrical conquest of air paralleled in the field of science by the development of lighter-than-air craft. Indeed, the balloon ascension of Montgolfier (1783), with its ornamented sphere, and ceremonial inauguration, had elements of spectacle in it, and was the subject of a ballet by von Starzer and Asplmayr in Frankfurt a.M. during the same year.

The *danseur d'élévation* or aerialist has always captivated the public. It is Nijinsky's conquest of air (ca. 1910) that is recalled, not his individual characterizations or his choreographic innovations. He was compared to a bird, but arms are not wings, and the flight of a man is not aided by air pressure, but succeeds in spite of it.

ALLEGRO: A term encompassing all lively movement, or that portion of ballet-exercises in which such movements are stressed. The study of *allegro* is the foundation of a brilliant rapid manipulation of the body, particularly the feet. The most essential attendant quality is that of *ballon.*

ARABESQUE (see plate 2): A pose of the classic theatrical dance, taking its name from a style of renaissance leaflike ornament, in which the dancer's body is supported on one foot either straight (*tendu*) or half-bent (*demi-plié*) with the other in the air, extended at right angles to it, and the arms composed to further a harmonious horizontality, creating the longest possible line from toes to finger tips.

Marie Taglioni (1804-1884), the great sylphe of the nineteenth century, was noted for the purity of her *Arabesque,* which gave momentarily static impressions of her hanging in mid-flight. In our own day Anna Pavlova, in her extension on toe-point, supported the pose for what seemed an extraordinarily long time. When an *Arabesque* comes as a sudden colon, or semicolon in an *enchainement,* the dancer appears to be resting on a crest of motion or music, and is propelled in the minds of the audience off in further imagined flight. A feeling of effortless suspension can be gained by a dancer's final *Arabesque,* posed at the end of a variation, just before quitting the scene, a finality rendered breathlessly infinite.

Although Compan's Dictionary (1787) does not include a definition, the *Arabesque* is a more or less "natural" dance position and can be found in various approximations of contemporary academic correctness throughout the long history of dance iconography. In the twenty-fourth plate of Lambranzi's "New and Curious School of Theatrical Dancing" (1716), Scaramouche is revealed at the rise of the curtain, as a statue on a pedestal *en arabesque* more or less *plié,* and three plates on, very *tendu.*

The etymology of the term itself is derived by association through a genre of architectural decoration, to the Moors. Carlo Blasis (1829) writes "Nothing can be more agreeable to the eye than those charming positions which we call *Arabesques,* and which we have derived from antique basso relievos, from a few fragments of Greek paintings and from the paintings in fresco at the Vatican, executed after the beautiful designs of Raphael.

"*Arabica ornamenta,* as a term in painting means those ornaments, composed of plants, shrubs, light branches and flowers, with which the artist adorns pictures, compartments, frises, panels. The taste for this sort of an ornament was brought to us by the Moors and Arabs."

In "Letters on Dancing," by E. A. Théleur (1832), an interesting book, not sufficiently well known, there is this note: "I have not succeeded in discovering the authentic origin of the *arabesque* attitudes, but am inclined to think we borrow them from the Spaniards, who for the most part do their steps with the same arm and foot. They, I conjecture, copied them from the Moors who, in the eleventh century infested this country: this leads me to suppose that they derive their origin from the Arabians, and are thence called *arabesques*."

But Carlo Blasis, as usual, is probably right.

ARMS (see plate 4): Arms give meaning and emphasis to head and upper body. Yet few dancers possess "naturally beautiful" arms. By "naturally beautiful" is meant the capacity to instinctively establish a gracious angle of the arms in relation to the position of head and shoulders, this angle to be taken and locked without tentative readjustment. If an arm comes too close to the head, the space between tends to diminish, if seen from a distance, and the expressive separation of head and arm is lost in a confusing identity. The arm, of course, controls manual gesture, but it must be considered as a whole, not as a mere shaft onto which an expressive hand is attached. The upper arm and forearm are naturally broken by the elbow joint. In the pure classic dance, but not in character-dancing or "modern" plastique, this completely destroys its grand style.

Although there are traditional established *positions* for the arms, their designed movement or carriage (*ports de bras*) is only rigid in its adherence to a gracious or open style, and exercises achieving it are never arbitrary, but at the discretion of individual teachers. It is as true today as in 1760 when J. G. Noverre wrote that "The *port de bras* must be varied as the different sentiments which dancing can express; set rules become almost useless; they must be broken and set aside at each moment, or by following them exactly, the *port de bras* will be opposed to the movements of the soul, which cannot be limited to a fixed number of gestures."

The position, opposition and carriage of the arms are per-

10

haps the three most difficult things in dancing, as Carlo Blasis understood in 1829. "Few artists distinguish themselves by a good style of action in their arms, which deficiency generally proceeds either from the mediocrity of principle they receive from bad instructions or else it originates in their own negligence, believing as I have known many to do, that if they possess a brilliant mode of execution in their legs, they can do very well without the fine additional ornament of the arms. . . . When the arms accompany each movement of the body with exactitude, they may be compared to the frame that sets off a picture. . . . Take care to make your arms so encircling that the points of your elbows may be imperceptible. Beware lest they be jerked by the action and reaction of your legs."

ASSEMBLE: From the French for together. A step in which the feet are brought together, frequently finishing an *enchainement* of other steps. The *assemblé* is a kind of colon, semi-colon or period to a choreographic phrase. It serves to reunite after movement, the two feet, together, side by side.

ATTITUDE (see plate 3): From the Italian *attitudine,* a manner of holding the body.

This position was first demonstrated graphically by Carlo Blasis (Milan: 1820), who claimed he had invented a new dancing position from the famous renaissance bronze of the Flying Mercury by Giovanni da Bologna (1524-1608).

"On one occasion, performing the part of Mercury, I took, as I turned in my pirouette, the attitude of the statue of Mercury by J. Bologne. This fine position is very difficult to stand in. Unless a dancer is naturally arched he never can do it well, and the pirouette (*en attitude*) loses its effect. The body must lean forward, and the right arm develope (*sic*) itself almost entirely. The leg that is in attitude must be bent, and by its motion accompany the rounding contour of the position of the body. To render this attitude yet more graceful let the dancer stretch out his left arm, in which the *caduceus* is held; this takes off the angle at the elbows that it would otherwise present, and gives the pirouette much more elegance."

In a portrait by Jean Raoux in the Museum at Tours, Mlle.

11

Prévost is shown as a Bacchante, her outstretched arm holding grapes, on half toe, *en attitude*. It was she, who with Balon, mimed and danced *Les Horaces* for the Duchesse du Maine in the fêtes at Sceaux in 1708.

B

BALANCE: The *pas balancé* of eighteenth century social-dancing has come down in our ordinary class-room usage to be simply, *balancé*. It is an alternation of balance, or slight rocking from one foot to the other, usually in the same place.

BALLABILE: A group evolution of dancers usually employed as the end of a scene or grand finale of a ballet, in which members of the whole company lose their individual identities and are swept into mass formations. The term is derived from the Italian *ballare*, to dance. The plural is *ballabili* and was used, though not invented, by Carlo Blasis before 1830.

BALLERINA: Originally an Italian word meaning girl-dancer. It has come to signify in every western tongue an outstanding female soloist in a traveling company, a ranking principal in an opera-house, as well as a symbol for the whole art of classic dancing. There have been famous soloists ever since the foundation of Lully's Opéra (ca. 1670). A ballerina is created first by her own impetus and talent and is then fostered by commercial management which always needs prominent individuals on whom to focus publicity. It is necessary to canalize the generalized curiosity of the public to some degree with single personalities in a company. The ballerina is usually a not unwilling proxy. It is assumed that for these purposes she is more beautiful, more technically capable, and more exciting than any one else in the troupe. The possession of these qualities is frequently a myth, which can be upheld for a sufficient time to permit publicity to consolidate her official status. A ballerina with looks and *authority* need do little but appear.

The two greatest examples of the ballerina are Taglioni (active 1825-1840) and Pavlova (active 1909-1929). They resembled each other in their mineral remoteness, general ether-

12

eal super-human atmosphere and weakness in character rôles. They both dictated the dancing styles of their epoch, and both survived the efforts of choreographers to transform their individual personalities into expressions of dramatic power. Rival ballerinas gain reputations by specializing strictly in a chosen style. Taglioni was challenged by the fiery Elssler, who on occasion dared attack her faery rôles to suffer a prejudged failure at the hands of Taglioni hierophants.

It is said that a ballerina is born, and like a princess, can never rise from the ranks. Yet every mother assumes her dancing daughter is bred for it, and it is true that a child appearing as a prodigy has some advantage. This can be maintained only by discipline and judicious training which in our day of short-term commercial investment is more difficult than when Imperial subsidy established permanent theatrical security. Yet Alexandra Danilova, perhaps the most accomplished of Russian dancers today, while well known in the late Diaghilev repertory (1925-29), has only recently in the years of full maturity elevated herself into the rôle of a preëminent ballerina. She has gained this indisputable position by an accumulation of stage-experience so that in every successive season she appears more brilliant, sensitive and interesting. The careers of child-stars are frequently brief, and are in fact an extended decadence.

BALLET: From the Italian *ballare,* to dance.

Ballate were songs to accompany dancing in Tuscany of the thirteenth and fourteenth centuries. Not only minor poets, but even Dante and Boccaccio composed them. Later, in the high-renaissance, the Medici princes themselves wrote *canzon a ballo,* or dance-songs. *Balleti* is the diminutive, hence *ballet.* Dance-songs gradually acquired theatrical characteristics and so it is not surprising that when the Medici went to Paris in the middle of the sixteenth century, they took not only dancing-masters, but the term with them as well. The English *Ballet* (with a hard final *t*) refers to a short, rhythmical song, distinguished by Gastoldi and Thomas Morely (ca. 1590). The word *Ballad* is a cognate. Dr. Samuel Johnson stated in 1755 that a ballet is "an historical dance." Elsewhere he says, "History is a narration of fact."

Generally speaking, a *ballet* is a theatrical representation achieved through terms of dancing. Father Menestrier, writing in 1682, made this differentiation in speaking of certain Egyptian and Greek forms, "I refer to these dances as **Ballet,** because they are not simple dances like any other, but rather *ingenious representations,*" that is, dancing consciously contrived as spectacle.

Mark Perugini, the interesting author of "A Pageant of Dance and Ballet" (1935), makes his own definition which can stand for our time: "A ballet is a series of solo and concerted dances with mimetic actions accompanied by music and scenic accessories, all expressive of a poetic idea or series of ideas, or a dramatic story, provided by an author or choreographer."

What is commonly accepted as the first ballet in our understanding of the word is, *Le Ballet Comique de la Reine* (1581). In an introduction, its author, an Italian in the train of Catherine de Medici named Baltasarini, stated that "a ballet was a *geometric combination* of several persons dancing together."

John Weaver, in his "Essay Towards a History of Dancing" (1721), divided "Theatrical or Opera" dancing into three types, "the *serious,* the *grotesque,* the *scenical.* Serious dancing differs from the Common dancing usually taught in schools as Painting (House-painting) differs from Limning (Portraiture). For as the common dancing has a peculiar softness which would hardly be perceivable on the stage, so stage-dancing would have a rough and ridiculous air in a room when on the stage it would appear soft and delightful."

The Encyclopedia of Diderot and d'Alembert (ca. 1772) tells us that "Ballet is action explained by a dance." It goes on to trace the origin of dancing, repeating all earlier errors and confirming the confusion that persists into our own day that dance and ballet are identical. However, if we understand that the dancing is specifically *theatrical, spectacular* and done *to be seen,* the subsequent definition, probably by Cahusac, explains the eighteenth century conception. "A ballet is a picture, or, rather a series of pictures linked together by the action which makes the subject of the ballet. The stage is, as it were, the canvas on which the composer (choreographer) renders his ideas, the choice of music, scenery and costumes are his colors; the

14

choreographer is the painter." All action, however, is not dancing, and in recent years, the most important developments in ballet have been to transform mimed action or pantomime into dramatic dancing, eliminating dumb-show and elevating the ballet into an independent art form, completely expressive in its own terms.

BALLET-BLANC: A ballet whose girls are clad in white tarletan. Generally speaking this refers to contemporary ballets like *Les Sylphides* (Fokine: 1909), the various *Chopinianas,* in which the "Romantic" atmosphere of the epoch of Marie Taglioni (ca. 1830) is revived by eliminating male dancers save a single soloist, and equipping the ballerina and *corps de ballet* in long gauze skirts, satin bodice and butterly wings which Eugène Lami first provided for *La Sylphide* (P. Taglioni: 1830).

BALLETOMANE: Franco-Russian term. Literally, a ballet-maniac or enthusiast for theatrical dancing.

"In Imperial Russia," writes Rayner Heppenstall, a distinguished British sympathizer, "Balletomania was by way of being a definite polite career, alternative to the Army and Navy or Diplomacy. Such and such an emigré, wishing to account for his social worth, will tell you that his father was a great general, a great statesman or indifferently a great balletomane."

It is generally considered that rabid public balletomania is not so much the fault of the art as of the class of society whose idleness or frustrations affords them hysterical compensation. There is no doubt, however, that the consistent apparition of the maniacs at ballet performances tends to prejudice many laymen against dancing, who ignorantly identify it with such flagrant approbation.

BALLON: The dancer's balloon-like quality of lightness or bounciness; the suave rise and fall of knees and feet in a sequence of steps. *La danse ballonné* is a genre based on leaps and broad movements, in which considerable air and floor-space is covered. Marie Taglioni (1804-1884) was the exemplification of this style for her epoch. André Levinson, with the precocity of his unique precision, defines it as the *"legato* of

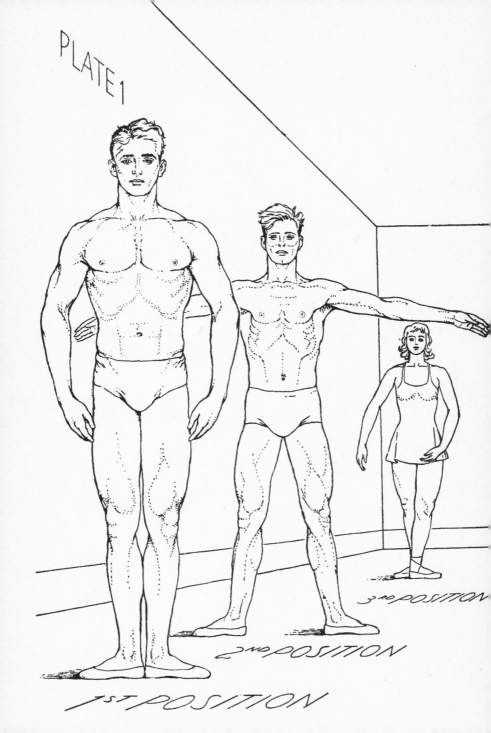

PLATE 1

3ʳᵈ POSITION

2ⁿᵈ POSITION

1ˢᵀ POSITION

4TH POSITION

4TH POSITION

5TH POSITION

great *paraboli* described in the air to a waltz movement, or the slow advancing of *developpées* in *adagio,* sustained by the singing of the (violinist's) bow." Carlo Blasis said in 1830: "Observe the *ballon:* nothing can be more delightful than to see you bouncing with graceful elasticity in your steps, scarcely touching the ground and seeming at every movement on the point of flying into the air."

BARRE (see plate 3): The bar, usually of wood, fixed opposite mirrors along the walls of ballet-practice rooms which students use in the first part of their daily lesson. This bar enables them to perform certain exercises with a maximum correctness, removing the need for sustained, unsupported balance. The bar thus provides an ideal criticism of faults, as well as aiding a weak dancer to become stronger.

BATTEMENT: Beating is the action of the extended or bent leg. There are *grands battements,* the straight lift of the leg to front, side and back which is a preparation for leaps. The *petits battements* are *battements degagés, frappés, relevés* or *tendus,*—separate or disengaged, full out from the knee, struck, raised on half-toe, or extended from a *plié.*

BATTERIE: "Generic term applied to all movements in which the feet beat together or one foot beats against the other. *Batterie* is divided into *grande batterie;* large battery; and *petite batterie;* small battery, according to the elevation, large or small. For instance: a *cabriole* is an example of *grande batterie* and *entrechat quatre* is an example of *petite batterie.*"

Cyril Beaumont's definition in his Franco-Italian Dictionary of classic dance terms (1931) can scarcely be improved.

A familiar demonstration of *batterie* is the sequence of *brisé volés* in the male section of the "Blue Bird" variation in *Aurora's Wedding* (Petipa: 1890). The *pas brisé volé* means the breaking step in flight. The swinging of the body in air from side to side suggests in the "Blue Bird" actual flying. Marie Taglioni (1804-1884) executed a new type of *brisé volé* in *La Sylphide* (P. Taglioni: 1830), which was later widely imitated and incorporated into classic idiom.

18

C

CABRIOLE: Derived from the Italian *capriola:* caper or goatish jump. In the seventeenth century, it referred to numerous jumps. It is now particularized. The dancer, raised off the floor while jumping, beats one foot against the extended length of the other. It can be executed to the side, back and front, while in each case the dancer's head faces the public to avoid an oblique angle, which would tend to diminish the full effect of the jump, although the actual visage may turn to the focus of action indicated by the dramatic expression of a given ballet.

CHOREOGRAPHY: Choregraphy, or as it is written today, choreography, meant in the time of its invention as a dance term (ca. 1700), the notation or stenographic record of dance steps. By corruption and association it has come to signify the design by a dance composer of dance patterns which comprise ballets.

It is the most important division of stage-dancing, since it regulates all that the dancers do. Its science is difficult to acquire and its practice, rare. There may be a hundred good dancers to a generation, and but half a dozen choreographers.

As in other arts, there are different levels of creation: choreography may be interpretative or decorative, or more importantly, inventive and creative. To "interpret" or illustrate music, or to decorate a stage with period revivals, however charming, is less interesting than the creation of lyric drama where dancing may not necessarily be a sole end in itself, but where it can be preëminently an arrangement of ideas particularly suitable to expression in dance terms.

CLASSIC BALLET: The classic dance is not merely a department of theatrical-dancing opposed to the "romantic," but rather a central line, or governing attitude which links the *purest* developments in traditional stage practice, whatever the epoch. To be sure, purity is comparative. In the vocabulary of step and gesture accumulated over the last five hundred years, there have been many "impure" influences, affecting the idiom from individual personalities, from exotic or national dances, from circus, music-hall and ball-room. But in the large residual body of expression, there is a basic-speech, founded on the five absolute *positions,* which demonstrate the human body on the stage in its grandest development by activity which is possible only in terms of dance, without reference to mimetic or associative gesture. As the residual information of medical practice is *materia medica,*—so in dancing it is *materia chore-ographica.* Its basic kinetic speech praises the body as free agent in air whose broadest extensions or highest leaps are its extreme lyric definition. The classic style is clean and open, grandiose without affectation, noble without pretension. Any idiosyncratic comment on it appears as offensive mannerism, which, however charming in a character-dance, destroys the linear purity of classicism.

"Classicism," wrote André Levinson, speaking of the ballerina Trefilova (ca. 1929), "tends towards geometric formula, but at the supreme moment, breaks and avoids it." Experiments in optics show that the line of least visual resistance is not necessarily the shortest distance between two points, but rather a long, easy curve which the eye may pursue with a gentle flow. This extended line is the property of every classic ballet position from *arabesque* and *attitude* to the more freely plastic *ports de bras.*

The classic dance may be rapid, but never brusque, jagged or broken. The classic line is sustained, serene and melodic, whose mercurial grace never disturbs its formal consistency unless it is dissolved on the metallic surface of technical incompetence or instinctive bad taste.

CORPS DE BALLET: A group of dancers used as chorus to project principal artists and to contrast by their mass evolutions, individual variations of soloists. In the classic repertory at least twice as many girls as boys are required and the men, except for their rôle of *porteurs* (in support), are usually restricted to the activity of the *premiers danseurs.* Although there is no fixed rule, even in our contemporary repertory, a general critical convention ignores the *corps de ballet.* It is snobbishly assumed they are ragged, badly trained, old, tired, partly as superficial proof of familiarity with the working mechanism of the profession, and partly because the *corps* of most traveling companies are too hard worked and under-rehearsed to be impressive.

In the subsidized state theatres, a formal hierarchy was recognized as iron-bound as the ranks of a peerage. The dancers farthest from the public performed their tasks almost anonymously, *près de l'eau* (near the fountain), since a jet of water was the familiar property of ballet back-drops. In Paris (ca. 1930) the company comprised forty *quadrilles*, twenty *coryphées*, seventeen *petits sujets*, sixteen *grands sujets*, three *premières danseuses*, three or four *étoiles*, and five *mimes*. The men were eighteen *messieurs du ballet*, three *premiers sujets*, three *grands sujets*, two *premier danseurs*, and four *mimes*.

Do soloists in large companies emerge from a *corps de ballet?* Infrequently. Soloists are usually "discovered" in school and elevated at once to positions of preëminence. To be sure, token emergence may occasionally prove that merit is rewarded. A *corps de ballet* somehow is usually a richer proving ground for boys and for girls.

A fair technical equipment is a prerequisite for a member of a *corps;* talent is not demanded, though experience may be gained. An ambitious chorus-member is a continual embarrassment to stage-managers, and a threat to principals. The work is no harder than in other jobs, and in large companies, at least, it has the advantage of a certain monotonous security.

Recently, particularly in the work of Diaghilev's choreographers, there has arisen the problem of the dissolution of the chorus, or at least the democratization of the *corps de ballet*. That is, drilled regimentation in the older repertory has been abandoned for a more broken background pattern. This naturally puts more responsibility for expression on individuals in the *corps*. The more disintegrated or specialized the choreographer, the greater the necessity for having a calibre of dancers who consider themselves more in the nature of soloists than of hacks.

The notion of having a troupe consisting entirely of soloists is a pleasant and democratic one. If it can be accomplished in practice without having the most advertised dancers desert, it may result in a competitive hysteria which even strong disciplinary measures will fail to correct. A horse once raced always wants to run. The fight back-stage is so bitter that the slightest chance to grasp a straw of prestige is not easily ceded, and a choreographer is faced with having ordinary dancers either refuse to learn certain rôles or else give so little coöperation that they may be almost useless.

CROISE (see plate 4): From the French *croiser,* to cross. A position of the body in which the dancer faces the body obliquely to the audience. The term also is used in connection with others, as *croisé en avant.* This means, the moving leg is nearest the footlights, opened to front *fourth* position, on the ground or in the air.

D

DANCE: *Dance,* the English word, is close to the French *danse;* deriving from the antique high-German *danson,* to drag, or stretch. In Middle English *danson* becomes *daunce* or *dawnce;* in Swiss and Dutch *dans;* in Danish, *dands;* in Spanish and Italian, *danza;* in Portuguese, *dansa;* in modern German, by the modification of Grimm's phonetic law, *tanz.* The Russian is close to German. The original Sanskrit root is *tan,* stretching; the Greek is *tenein,* and from the Latin *teneo* come tension, extend, intense, sustain, maintain, etc.

"But first," wrote John Weaver in 1721, "it will not be improper to explain what dancing is, and in what it consists. Dancing is an elegant, and regular movement, harmoniously composed of beautiful *Attitudes,* and contrasted graceful Posture of the Body, and parts thereof."

"Dancing according to the accepted definition of the word, is the art of composing steps with grace, precision and facility to the time and bars given in the music, just as music itself is simply the art of combining sounds and modulations so that they afford pleasure to the ear," wrote J. G. Noverre in 1760. Dancing as defined by Diderot and d'Alembert in the Encyclopedia (ca. 1772) is "Ordered movements of the body, leaps and measured steps made to the accompaniment of musical instruments or the voice." Desrat's Dictionary of Dancing (1895) says, "Dancing is the action of moving the body in harmony with a determined measure, and in allocating a given expression to the movements."

Perhaps the most complete contemporary definition is André Levinson's, quoted by Cyril Beaumont in his "Miscellany for Dancers" (1934). "Dancing is the continuous movement of the body traveling in a pre-determined space in accordance with a definite rhythm and a conscious mechanism." (*La Danse d'Aujourd'hui:* 1929.)

In a recent American radio program, *It's Up to You,* thousands of persons were polled to find out the twenty "happiest" words in our language. The first five were *healthy, laughter, home, love, peace.* The eleventh was *money,* the twentieth *dance.*

"Dancing," wrote Havelock Ellis in "The Dance of Life" (1923), "has forever been in existence as a spontaneous custom, a social discipline. Thus it is finally that dancing meets us not only as love, as religion, as art, but also as morals."

"All human work under natural conditions is a kind of dance. . . . Work differs from the dance not in kind but only in degree, since they are both essentially rhythmic. . . ."

"The dance lies at the beginning of art, and we find it also at the end. The first creators of civilization were making the dance, and the philosopher of a later age (Nietzsche), hovering over the dark abyss of insanity, with bleeding feet and muscles strained to the breaking point, still seems to himself to be weaving the maze of the dance."

DEVELOPPÉ: From the French, to develop or unfold. Ballet step and dance-exercise in which the leg employed is slowly raised and unfolded from its ordinary standing position to desired complete extension in the air.

DIVERTISSEMENT: A single number, or a suite of numbers calculated to display individuals or groups of dancers, through short dances, unrelated by a dramatic reason, which are sometimes hung on a plot pretext of festival or wedding. In classic ballets, such as *Coppelia* (Merante: 1870) or *La Belle au Bois Dormant* (M. Petipa: 1890), they occur as celebrations leading up to a finale. A kind of graduation exercise or vaudeville

23

atmosphere pervades the demonstration of address and personality by favorite artists in old favorites. Considerable technical skill is necessary to reclaim divertissements from the realm of band-concert taste.

The best known contemporary example is *Aurora's Wedding*, composed of fragments from the Diaghilev revival (1921) of Petipa's original *Sleeping Beauty*. It makes up in recognizable familiarity what it lacks in essential interest. The eyes of the audience hum it like the Blue Danube. Hence, if some of the soloists are proficient, or at least showy, this is the ballet in which the *corps de ballet* can relax from their labors and think about packing. A series of *divertissements* may, however, be worked out with some ingenuity if composed for special occasions, which is in the tradition of their origin. The Ballet comedies of Molière (ca. 1660-1670), with danced interludes as important parts of the plot, survive in revivals of *Les Facheux* (Nijinska: 1924) or *Le Bourgeois Gentilhomme* (Balanchine: 1932). Except here they have a logical connection with the whole dramatic structure as do even the divertissements of *Aurora's Wedding* in their original context.

The famous "Blue Bird" *pas de deux* is an excellent applause number. It is perennially useful because even the most resistant members of an audience can understand that its steps are intended to be difficult and hence can applaud with clear conscience if their execution happens to be negligible. An evening's otherwise tiresome program can be edited towards success by the judicious arrangement of divertissements as a climax, but if there is necessity to resort to this hypodermic it is only an index of the ill health of the rest of the repertory.

E

ECHAPPE: From the French, to slip or escape. A slipping movement, in which the body in *fifth* position, bends both knees equally and jumps, regaining the floor in *second* position. Feet retouch the ground toes first, heels last.

EFFACE (see plate 4): From the French *effacer,* to shade or diminish in plane. This term is generally applied to head and

24

shoulders when they are placed at angles to suggest greater plasticity. In dance lessons, *effacé* positions are used to elevate the chest and give a prouder carriage to the upper body. This raised position supports the expanded lungs, and hence aids breathing. Cyril Beaumont (1931) writes it is "A particular placing of the body, legs and head in which the dancer stands at an oblique angle to the audience so that a portion of the body is in shadow."

ELEVATION (see plate 3): Mastery of *la danse d'élévation* is a conquest of air. If one had to pick a single symbol with almost universal connotation for dancing in our century, it would be Vaslav Nijinsky's leap (active 1909-1917). How high that leap actually was is no longer of interest, although his Russian companions tell us that it was never seen at its peak in America, and to less advantage in Western Europe than in Russia. In legend it has become super-human. But since Nijinsky was human, and since other dancers have exceeded him (notably the Muscovite, Nicolas Petrovitch Damashov (ca. 1900), his is merely a kind of Olympic record for others to aim at.

There are at least two divisions of elevation: the *actual* defiance of gravity, and the rendering of an *appearance* of high-jumping. Exercises training dancers to leap are not in themselves particularly difficult. Indeed, if a dancer is naturally endowed for leaping, it is early shown, and may become a difficult fault to overcome. Exuberant natural jumpers sometimes ignore musical and dramatic expression for sheer height and easy applause. A dancer with little natural gift for jumps can often, by starting low and landing low, with a subtle recovery to full height, give the impression of considerable altitude conquered. The "secret" of Nijinsky's phenomenal leap has been frequently explained by his "double-preparation." With his lungs full of air to their capacity, he would leap. In mid-air he would still inhale breath to expend on his peak-effort, thereby giving the impression he remained momentarily suspended. The *danse d'élévation,* a preference for activity in the aerial province, is sometimes opposed to the *danse par terre,* or work on the floor. For a complete dancer, both are mastered, although some artists have fine legs which can be capi-

25

talized. A smooth spring, musically phrased, is frequently more satisfactory than a dancer's equivalent of a running high-jump or pole-vault.

ENCHAINEMENT: A combination of steps which may be a phrase in an extended theatrical dance pattern or simply a chain of harmonious movements strung on a fragment of music for use in the class-room. One can think of the contrivance of *enchainements* intended for stage use, as a melodic line. Some steps by their nature have a logic, or lack of it, when used in combination with others. A tactful juxtaposition of various constituent parts is like a smoothly forged chain, rather than a bumpy string of stones. A given *enchainement* may have its own individual climax which has been built up by steps calculated to frame an ultimate effect. A well-designed *enchainement* can have a gracious rhythmic and melodic sympathy, although by no means literally interpreting the largest melody in a musical accompaniment. Some *enchainements,* harmoniously conceived with a gracious curve of interest, may be accompanied by music which is little more than attenuated filler-in. An *enchainement* is only a choreographic phrase, the notes of which are *pas,* or steps. It can, however, be built up into a danced aria or *variation.*

ENTRECHAT: A step in which the feet braid back and forth in air.
The word has two traditional sources. The first (Compan: 1787) comes from *capriola intreciata* (Italian: a braiding jump). The second (Desrat: 1895) from *entrechas,* the French *châsse* (chassis), a piece of squared wood, framing metal work, combined with *entrelas,* twisted cords, interlacements or braiding,—hence *entrechat,* or interlacing of legs and feet as if they were restrained within the slots of a frame. This last ingenious if dubious etymology is traced to the Jesuit Menestrier's *Des Ballets Anciens et Modernes* (1682).
The shift of feet in mid-air, toes pointing straight down to earth, has a legible flash and twinkle which spells obvious brilliance to the public, since it requires some elevation to accomplish, for the higher the dancer jumps, the more beats can be

flashed, and since the combination of transverse movements of the feet with a perpendicular motion of the rest of the body seems to denote control of two actions at once.

Desrat explains *entrechat* as an appellation coming from the changings of feet operating between (*entre*) each of the dancer's jumps. This is better understood when we realize that in *entrechat trois, quatre,* or *six,* the feet beat three, four or six times during or in between (*entre*) each jump. *Entrechats* are divided into two general divisions; the even: that is to say, *deux, quatre, six, huit*—and the odd: *trois, cinq, sept.* The first terminate in a dancer regaining the ground on two feet; the second, in holding one foot off the ground. An *entrechat deux* is a simple *changement de pied;* with *entrechats quatre, six, huit,* the feet change completely back and forth, twice, three or four times while the dancer is raised in air during the jump. The toe always touches before the heel. In the odd *entrechats* the feet change three or five times while the dancer lands on one foot with the other kept *croisé* in front or back. It is absolutely necessary to make a preparation for the *entrechat* with both knees deeply bent, *grand plié,* to get enough push for a good jump.

A fresco on a wall in Egyptian Thebes, shows a dancer apparently executing a rudimentary *changement* in mid-air.

The step was used traditionally in antique *contredanses* and the *gavotte,* during the eighteenth century,—obviously in a non-theatrical form, at least for women, for it would not have been visible in their long skirts. Camargo (1710-1770) is popularly accredited with "inventing" the step in 1730, but Rameau in his "Dancing Master" had already described it in 1725. Camargo perfected it, however, so it frequently is associated with her name, although in 1750 Mademoiselle Lany is supposed to have executed *entrechat six* and even *huit.* From 1760 to 1800, the steps became an accepted part of the theatrical dancer's vocabulary. Contemporary myth tells us that Vaslav Nijinsky (active: 1909-1919) could execute his *entrechat dix,* but it is difficult to discover anyone who has counted them, personally.

Nicolas Legat, in his "Story of the Russian School" (1932) tells of the phenomenal dancer, N. P. Damashov (ca. 1900). He was generally unknown even in Russia, outside of Moscow.

27

Legat saw him execute an *entrechat huit* on his ascent;—then pause for a split second in mid-air and slowly descend with motionless legs. Then he reversed the process, executing the eight beats descending. Legat, who knew both dancers well, considered Nijinsky's marvels child-play beside those of Damashov.

ENTREE: The arrival by individuals or groups of dancers, usually in a ballet *divertissement.* The *entrée* originated from the epoch when ballets were masked balls at feudal courts, and arrivals entered in order of social rank, according to protocol. The entries in a masked ball, linked together by a single idea for costume pretext, might be the Queen of Night and her attendant owls, Fire and his Sparks, or Water and her mermaids and tritons. In a ballet Entry, the soloists arrive attended by dancers arranged to frame them, serving as a small individual *corps de ballet* background for a particular variation. Formal *entrées* arrive to a march time, or to a similar measure, such as a polonaise. The various *entrées* maintain their characteristic identities, and if they lose them in the *ballabile* or big finale, one may be sure to find them grouped again in character at the final curtain.

Compan's Dictionary of Dancing (1787) describes the arrangement of the usual mid-eighteenth century five-act ballet. "Each act consists of three, six, nine, and sometimes twelve entries. The term *entrée* is given to one or more bands of dancers, who by means of their steps, gestures, and attitudes express that portion of the whole theme which has been assigned to them."

J. G. Noverre wrote in his first letter (1760) that "Symmetrical figures from right to left are, in my opinion, only supportable in the *corps d'entrées,* which have no means of expression, and which, conveying nothing, are employed simply to give the premiers danseurs time to take breath."

We are all familiar with the formal entries in *Aurora's Wedding* (Petipa: Sergeev: 1890-1921) of Little Red Riding Hood and her Wolf, The Three Chinese, The Three Ivans, all of whom join hands with the rest in the Farandole. This is an academic nineteenth century Russian adaptation of the French eighteenth century form. But in a contemporary ballet, like

28

PLATE 2

FIRST
ARABESQUE
DEMI-
PLIÉ

SECOND
ARABESQUE
SUR
LA
DEMI-
POINTE

Petrouchka (Fokine: 1912), there are still *entrées,* only here the actual entrances are masked by the impressionist nature of Stravinsky's score. For example: there are entries of Nurse-maids, Coachmen, Gypsies, and the tipsy barin. Only they all emerge from the carnival crowd and are reabsorbed into it without that final apotheosized pose which might call attention to the fact that their *entrée* is concluded.

F

FEET: To the uninformed, it is frequently assumed that a dancer's most important individual equipment is the feet. J. G. Noverre, in 1760, already attacked those who "dance for the sake of dancing, imagining that all consists in the action of the legs." It would be impossible to dance without them, but they are not any more important than any other member. However, since we stand on them, and they are our immediate connection with the floor, we may be more immediately conscious of them. Classic dancers are frequently inclined not necessarily to over-train them, but at least to desert the canonical positions of arms, hands and head, as if these half-forgotten aids could take care of themselves. We jump from the feet, and since jumps are immediately spectacular (see *Elevation*), hours are spent cultivating *entrechats* (vide passim) while arms like tired car-rots dangle as they may. In boxing and running, the crux of a foot's structure is also in the metatarsal arch. Special exer-cises (*relevés*) are continually provided to strengthen this essen-tial bridge. A clean, snappy spring for beats and jumps is particularly effective. The toe must always be kept as much as possible straightly pointed down to continue indefinitely the extended direction of the body's action. Feet must not flap loosely like slapped fish. Since the feet receive the greatest impact at all times, they must be guarded against casual injury or careless fatigue. They support the weight of the whole body, not by a steady pressure, but by irregular jolting shocks. Vaslav Nijinsky (active: 1909-1919) is supposed to have had disarticu-lated bones in his feet caused by congenital mutation. His toes, assuming this to be accurate information, were almost evolved at birth to be like a bird's talons. The disarticulation of the

30

bones spread into a further cushion of expansion and received the extra shock of his phenomenal jump. He frequently burst his slippers from the swell of his powerful feet. Whether or not this is fact, it has a symbolic truth and happens to a lesser degree with all well-trained dancers.

FLOOR: Few except professional dancers realize how important is the surface on which they work. The floor can be considered almost as a dancer's violin. Bow and arm produce the vibration, but the wood reflects it, and renders it audible. As few theatres are designed specifically for dancing, floors are hardly ever tuned to the given need. Dancers accustom themselves to any floor; linoleum, hard-wood, canvas covered to hide dry-rot; or ideally, and if they are in luck, soft pine,—cheap yet unbeatable, unwaxed, unoiled and unvarnished. Elasticity, as well as a slight surface friction are desirable; a dancer is never, unfortunately, in a position to say they are essential. Soft pine with enough rosin powdered over it, gives a sense of security which can hearten a nervous dancer and exhilarate a phlegmatic one. Ballet dancers work in slippers or shoes, not in bare feet. Leather needs the slight lock of wood-fibre to create the minute frictional drag necessary to provide a spring-board balance. The good dancer imagines his feet as almost sucking the floor surface, pressing into it, as it were, for assurance and release when the pressure is removed.

On a fine stage which had been creosoted against dry-rot, in one of the newest and handsomest theatres in America, an experienced company of dancers was recently rendered almost impotent. Dancing upon such a surface was like hot roller-skating on ice. The audience instinctively felt the edge taken off the performance, but assumed it was the fault of the dancers. The management of many auditoriums prefer a handsome varnished expanse of hard maple, bright as a mirror, to the professional comfort of traveling artists. Unwaxed linoleum is not impossible and is excellent for bare-foot work, but even chipped pine and cracked joints are preferable to shiny varnish.

FOUETTE: From the French *fouet,* a whip. A step executed usually by girls on point, in which the free leg is whipped smartly up and around from fourth to second position and then into the knee. This step, often used in combination with a double turn on point, if kept up long enough, is a sure-fire applause net. For some time it served as a kind of graduation degree for the technically proficient ballerina.

Pierina Legnani, an Italian ballerina, as guest artist in Russia, is generally supposed to have first executed thirty-two *fouettés* in Tchaikovsky's Swan-Lake (Ivanov-Petipa: 1877-1895), creating a sensation. Rayner Heppenstall, in "Apology for Dancing" (1936), says this was in Petipa's *Zolushka,* ostensibly on information from Nicolas Legat, who had been Legnani's partner and who learned her secret to teach it to his fellow Russians. The Russian ballerina, quick to meet the challenge of a southern invasion, soon exceeded her.

Dancers today can easily execute many more. The *fouetté* remains a show step, although certain contemporary choreographers have contrived to endow it with a logical dramatic significance. The Top, in Massine's *Jeux d'Enfants* (1932), spins convincingly. The Finale of Balanchine's *Cotillon* (1932) permits the ballerina to commence her *fouettés* and by a large spiral design for the entrance of the rest of the troupe, she seems to whip the stage into a frenzied finish. In Balanchine's *Serenade* (1934) sixteen girls executed thirty-two *fouettés* without difficulty.

G

GESTURE: Literally understood, gesture is all voluntary or involuntary movement of the human body, the aim of which is to signify something. Cicero (*De Oratore*) considered "action" as the *external* part of oratory, hence gesture is corporal eloquence, or the language of the body, just as spoken words are the language of the vocal cords. The dance is generally silent. It may use gestures which normally enhance verbal speech and thereby have come to bear an associative reference, but necessarily in a heightened theatrical manner, suitable to stage use. Gesture is by no means a question of arms alone. Cicero included facial expression, as well as *Chironomia* (Delivery) or improperly, Elocution. All through classical literature, we find

32

works on gesture as compiled by rhetoricians and orators. These were restudied during the classic revival of the eighteenth century when an attempt was made to reduce everything to rigid canons based on antique precedent. Parliament, the Courts of Law, the pulpit itself, became places of entertainment due to the theatrical delivery of orators who aped Demosthenes.

Gesture can have literal associative reference or can be broadly suggestive. The narrative portion of dancing is composed of designed gesture. Gesture is the stuff, subdivision and working material of pantomime. If *enchainements* of dance steps comprise the *variation* or danced aria, then *enchainements* of gesture create pantomime or the danced recitative. But in ballet, gestures must not result in mere dumb-show but should be transferred into the more lyric terms of dancing.

As for academic gesture used by actors, orators and preachers, the Reverend Gilbert Austin, writing his great "Chironomia" in 1806, admitted that the English look to the French, the French to the Italians, and the Italians to the ancient Greeks as their masters. Each nation has a manual sign language accompanied by the rest of the body, which has erected over the centuries a corpus of associative reference. Stage-gesture cannot be wholly appropriated from oratory, because it is used in the accompaniment of speech not as complete explanation, but chiefly as attendant emphasis. It is necessary to have a particular style of gesture to construct a vocabulary of pantomime fitting not only the subject of a given ballet—but its music as well, which may be considered the words of the otherwise silent danced play.

Certain professional occupational gestures are familiar to all of us; the policeman directing traffic, the baseball pitcher winding up, the orchestral conductor building a climax. Of all the animals, said Buffon, man alone gesticulates, although some of the higher apes approximate it. This is due to the peculiar construction of the erect biped, who stands with dangling forearms. A man is not a four-foot. His arms give a direct significance to gestures supported by inclinations of the rest of the body. There is a different quality describing masculine and feminine gesture based on biological structure. Gesture is of the greatest human significance, not only in social intercourse,

33

but as a stage instrument and more recently even as a political manifestation, with the mass arm-movements of Fascist and Communist salutes. The Italians are traditionally endowed with the expressive language of arms and hand, from the salute of Caesar's legions to the silent pacification of the Neapolitan mob by King Ferdinand in 1821.

The classic study of gesture is formulated in Charles Darwin's "Expressions of Emotions in Man and Animals" (1872). His three basic principles are:

1. The principle of serviceable *associated* habits; spontaneous natural activity under given stress which has become habitual, whose reference we understand by association from the history of our race. If these are consciously controlled the muscles check them. This check creates characteristic reflex movements, equally recognizable.

2. The principle of antithesis or *opposites:* motions arise from a reaction to habitual ones (Principle 1) which are of no definite use, but assert themselves with involuntary strength and have the significance of contrast.

3. The principle of actions due to the *constitution* of the human system, independent of conscious direction, and to some degree of habit. The direct action of the nervous system under excitement produces an excess of nervous energy which is transmitted into various definite channels. The release of this energy into gesture is recognizable as *expressive*.

Students of the dance often despair that gesture cannot be learned in an academy like the classic ballet. There is a considerable literature on the subject both ancient and modern, from Cicero and Quintillian to Sir Charles Bell, the anatomist, and Mantegazza, the criminologist. However, for those seriously interested in practical results rather than historical curiosities, almost everything of value may be limited to studies attributed to François Delsarte. This remarkable man, who published nothing while alive, left sufficient material to provide a fundamental background for a universal academy of gesture. Famous as a teacher during his life, he enjoyed an even more remarkable posthumous reputation, particularly in America, from 1880 to 1900. However, lacking his presence to activate his theories, his system as promulgated by his heirs, fell under

34

the severe and just criticism of being purely mechanical and arbitrary. The apostolic fervor of his disciples may easily have been fanatic, but this does not excuse the disfavor and ridicule which has subsequently obscured his essentially important contribution. Almost the only reference to Delsarte in the repertory of the contemporary dance is a series of parodies worked out by the mime Angna Enters (ca. 1930), based on the naïve pictorial diagrams with which early editions of his system were illustrated.

To be sure, a few contemporary dramatic-teachers employ his underlying structure of expression, but its large system, which is in fact, an analysis and ordering of all effective gesture, is ignored or unknown by those very students of dancing, who, in search of a basic skeleton for pantomime, might need it most. Delsarte claimed no particular originality for his studies. They were practical results in research, not only through the classic rhetoricians but of comparative anatomy in clinics, morgues and hospitals. His reluctance to publish is perhaps significant. His contact was directly with his pupils. His generalizations were for their use, not as arbitrary formula for mechanical application, but as a kind of plastic geometry for universal correspondence. Delsarte did for gesture, and indirectly for dancing, what the other great formulators of the nineteenth century accomplished for their chosen fields. As Comte in exact science, Ruskin in aesthetics, Buckle, J. S. Mill, or even Marx, in historical analysis, and Carlo Blasis in the classic theatrical dance—so Delsarte provided an apparatus for the investigation and use of gesture. Unlike these others, Delsarte's theories received little subsequent amplification or challenge.

François Delsarte was born at Solesmes, November 11, 1811. His father, a doctor, abused his mother so that she fled to Paris with two small sons. Her early death was followed by that of Delsarte's brother, who expired of starvation in his arms. As a child of ten, he was kept by a rag-picker, and, developing a passion for music, invented his own system of musical notation to preserve songs of the beggars whom he daily encountered. At thirteen he was discovered in the gardens of the Tuilleries tracing his invented notes in the sand, by Bambini, a well-known music-teacher. Through his aid he entered the Conservatory.

Too original to receive official academic encouragement, he nevertheless finally received a contract to sing at the Opéra Comique. But the errors in his wretched conservatory training caused a complete failure of his voice in 1834, only four years after a successful debut. From that time he devoted himself to providing a more intelligent means of instructing students by methods of expression which would aid rather than destroy them. Combining a surgeon's science with an artist's passion, he became one of the most remarkable teachers of his day. Although among his pupils were Jenny Lind, Sontag, Macready, Rachel, and the great preachers: Père Hyacinthe and Lacordaire, he died comparatively unknown in 1871, under the shadow of the Franco-Prussian war. The American, Steele Mackaye, attended his pantomime classes and became an ardent disciple. Plans for bringing Delsarte to America for the establishment of a theatre and conservatory were prevented by his death.

Delsarte's system of expressive gesture is simple in essence, yet extremely complex in applied detail. It is founded on a *triune* division of the human organism, established by the triune conditioning of natural law. That is, the body restricted by space, time and motion, has correspondence in the physical, intellectual and emotional sources of its action. In every human, one of these three natures dominates, the degree of dominance causing the difference in personality. Delsarte separated the body into three grand divisions. The head represents the intellectual,—legs and arms the physical,—the trunk, the emotional nature. Each of these divisions is in turn subdivided and we have a trinity for each division. In the head, for example, he considered the eyes and forehead intellectual, the nose and cheeks emotional, the mouth and lips physical. In the torso, the region of the upper chest is intellectual, the central section (the heart) emotional, the lower abdomen, physical. As for arms and legs,—feet and hands are intellectual, forearms and lower legs are emotional, while upper arms and legs are physical. Still further subdivisions are made in the face, hands, legs, etc. But the application of the corresponding trinities is more significant than the formulation of further categories. In Delsarte's grand division, the arms and legs have the physical dominance. They disclose the most *apparent* strength and activity. In the zones of the leg, the thigh is designated as physically vital because the impulse of locomotion is first felt there. The lower leg as an emotional source is demonstrated by the use of knees in gestures of kneeling or subordination to another's will in supplication, request, reverence or obedience. The intellectuality of the foot is shown by the unconscious nervous tapping of impatience and the control by the feet as the sources of advance or retreat.

The mental zone is shown in the brain's effect on the shape and quality of head and its bony structure, the confirmation of visual expression. The emotional seat is in the diaphragm. As Lavatar, the author of a curious and influential work on Physiognomy (1772-83), has been quoted: "These three states of the Soul do not lodge in separate apartments of the body, but co-exist in every part, and form, by their combination, one whole; yet it is true that each of these principles has its particular place of residence in the body, where it is preference manifests and exerts itself."

With the sources of human movement thus consciously divided into a fabric of trinities, Delsarte proposes his nine laws of gesture.

1. The law of *Motion:* the center of his system. Motion is energy expending itself. Physical motion moves *outward* from a centered focus; intellectual motion moves *inward* towards this center; emotional motion appears in either concentric or eccentric forms, or by a poise or *balance* between the other two.

2. The law of *Velocity:* "The velocity of any agent is in proportion to the mass moved, and the energy moving. That is: serious ideas require deliberate gestures; lighter ones need shorter and more rapid ones."

3. The law of *Direction* and *Extension* (in ballet, the *Arabesque* and *Attitude*): All gestures have direction; physical gestures are projected forward or lengthwise; intellectual gestures above or below, emotional spread out laterally. The "extension" of gesture is in the intensity of its surrender to the dominant intellectual, physical or emotional source.

4. The law of *Reaction* (Darwin's Second Principle): "Every extreme of emotion tends to react to its opposite. Concentric

37

states tend to explosion; explosion to prostration (i.e., cessation)": The shift from physical activity to repose, from anger to tears, from tears to laughter, etc.

5. The law of *Form:* The exterior shape, or restraining figure by which matter is rendered visible. In gesture, all movements describe shapes or forms in air. Straight lines are said to be dominantly direct, hence physical; circular lines, emotional; while broken lines are considered the result of obstruction consciously conquered, and hence intellectual.

6. The law of *Personality:* Idiosyncratic characteristics conditioned by heredity, environment, and local culture.

7. The law of *Opposition* (see "Opposition"): "When two limbs follow the same direction, they cannot be simultaneous without injury to the law of opposition. Therefore, direct movements should be successive and opposite movements simultaneous." This law is based on the physical human mechanics of equilibrium and gravity.

8. The law of *Priority* or *Sequence:* The suite in which agents of expression act. "Impression always precedes expression; we must have before we can give, and give in the order of having." In general, Delsarte considered the physical nature asserts itself first, then the emotional, last the intellectual. But "The Will lends itself to which ever side of the being is in action." The eye reveals impressions first, the face responds, then follow the hands and other members. *Articulate speech is last.*

9. The law of *Rhythm:* "The vibration or swing of matter through equal spaces in equal times." The pulsation corresponding to the heart beat under given emotional tensions. In gesture, the consecutive inflections of the bodies' members from joint to joint.

With these nine laws presupposed, Delsarte proposed a series of "decomposing" exercises for freedom and relaxation, calculated to separate and analyze the sources of gesture in a conscious order for future *composition.* The decomposing exercises are intended as a complete, objective education of the many parts of the human body as an expressive agent, both in underlying detail and as a legible entity.

The above brief abstract has been compiled from a half-dozen available records of Delsarte which differ considerably in nomenclature, application, and even interpretation. However, the more one searches, the more one respects the critical wisdom, elastic logic and lack of arbitrary schematic thinking, of which Delsarte's superficial opponents have accused him. While not recommending either a particular book as an evangel, nor a particular series of exercises as fool-proof, any serious student can find more of value even in Delsarte's recorded shadow than in all the other "authorized" books on gesture and pantomime put together.

The reputation of Delsarte has suffered, not because the findings of his practical research have ever been seriously questioned, but largely because his literary remains were found to be full of a great mass of irrelevant, foggy philosophical drapery, parallels to Plotinus, the neo-platonists, the Hermetic doctrine, the Cabalists, the Christian mystics, and Oriental "secret" writings. He attempted to corroborate his essentially simple system with a testimony of universal and complete cosmic truth. No doubt the lasting part of his work partakes of that truth, but its particular revelation to its author took the form of an unending testimony of historic witnesses. Hence, posthumous critics have tended to spread their valid ridicule indiscriminately also over what was objectively sensible. Delsarte's misfortune lay in that he never superintended the publication of his own work, nor yet did Steele Mackaye, his most devoted pupil. In spite of a style which is no longer in vogue, the studies of Genevieve Stebbins are extremely well-arranged. It is she, who more emphatically than anyone else, stresses his greatest service,— the recreation for his own time (and for ours) of a system of correspondences. Delsarte did not exactly discover any original method. But by the *arrangement* of facts already known, he affected a structure of infinite correspondence. His great service was not so much to the small field of gesture, but to the broader science of *semantics*.

Semantics is the science of significance, or correspondence. "Correspondence is derived from three Latin words, *cor re spondeo;* it literally means to answer again, from the heart. We use the word in common speech to show that written communication has passed between two people. It is only complete when the one written to has replied; has spoken to the other again *from the heart.*"

Delsarte's *semantics,* his science of signs, is hence the science of the forms of human gesture. He categorized human beings into the dominantly constitutional (congenital or hereditary), the emotional, and the habitual, who are not so much bred as created by habit. The emotional type explains the habitual, and the habitual the hereditary or congenital. This is his complete analysis of people all of whom have essentially but three kinds of expressive gesture; the habitual bearing of the expressive agent (dancer, actor) which is the most permanent. The emotional attitudes are less so, and the various accidental inflections affecting the agent are only temporary.

It almost goes without saying that Delsarte's ideas have a particular reference to lyric theatre in Western Europe and America. There are of course numerous *oriental* academies of gesture, of which perhaps the most familiar is the "Mirror of Gesture" (or Expression), first edited in the West by Dr. Ananda Coomeraswamy (Harvard University Press, 1917), with a suggestive introduction. It was later more fully presented by Manomohan Ghosh (Calcutta, 1934). The system of gesture, and particularly of manual expression, presented in "The Mirror" is extraordinarily complex, arbitrary and traditional. Its use to Western actors or dancers, in spite of Dr. Coomeraswamy's good wishes, seems remote. The oriental actor-dancer has suffered a gradual thousand-year decadence, and even religious mandates governing dance technique have not prevented such contemporaries as the Javanese, Raden Mas Jodjana, and the East Indian, Uday Shankar, from appropriating the methods of European stage-presentation to aid their own presentation or personal adaptation of oriental classic dancing. The basic metaphysical principles of Eastern and Western art may both ultimately coincide to praise the life force, whatever it may be called,—but the specific use of Western dancing is for spectacle, not for praise. In the East, the great emphasis is on the gesture or the dance; in the West on the particular actor or dancer. Separate hierarchies of movement are repositories of meaning and may be read like a book, presupposing the audience's familiarity with Hindu folk-lore. In the Western tradi-

40

PLATE 3

EXERCISE AT
BARRE ON POINT

ELEVATION

ATTITUDE

tional classic dance, the human unit, the dancer, by his designed behavior, has a purely emotional reference to his audience, based on little more than association and direct sensuous appeal. In the East, the various static positions are ends in themselves, denoting final meaning; in the West, the named steps or stations are merely means to an end, which is the *enchainement* of gestures towards kinetic dramatic action. To be sure, Eastern gesture has been used as a "style" by Western choreographers.—*Sacountala* (L. Petipa: 1858), *Le Dieu Bleu* (Fokine: 1913), *Padmavâti* (Staats: 1923); but the actual effect is no more profound than the use of the sari a few years ago by Paris dressmakers, as an evening wrap. In spite of their respective beauties, Eastern and Western conceptions of individual action are too dissimilar to permit any practical interchange of much theatrical interest.

GRACE: The single most widely used noun applying to the dance. "Graceful" or "ungraceful" is a synonym in the minds of most people for the quality which renders a dancer easy or difficult to watch. What constitutes this quality is more difficult to define. The overlying ease by which a sequence of physical movements are flowingly accomplished is often applied to a very narrow range of activity. Yet a dancer can be graceful in an ungraceful position or dance. Grace is the binding element in a dancer's style, a mercurial fluid spreading invisibly over the body in an imperceptible film. It is an elastic endless chain of connections which link and at the same time contain separate movements in a supple net, never allowing one portion or motion of the body to become inconsistent with another, however outrageous the separate individual movements may be. Girls are assumed by virtue of their softness to be more graceful, but there are as few essentially graceful girls as boys. A boy is said to be graceful *for a boy,* or else *too* graceful, hence effeminate. Gracefulness is a quality covering all danced action, not a category applying to a certain ·aspect of free motion. This confusion arises from the antique philosophical concept that grace and beauty were identical, that the opposite of grace was any restrained or "ugly" action.

Despréaux, in his letter to Després (Journal de Paris, May 7,

1820), wrote:—"There are three kinds of grace; grace of form, grace of pose, grace of movement." His typically eighteenth century reasonable or rather rationalized argument tells us grace of form is a gift of nature,—and rare. Grace of poise is the ability to select a position of the body consonant with "good taste." Grace of movement is not merely the facility to pass from one pose to another in accordance with the rhythm of the music. It demands expression according to the character portrayed, particularly in the dance *terre à terre* (on the floor), which demands quite a different type needed for *la danse d'élévation* (in the air).

The Scotch philosopher, Henry Home, in his "Elements of Criticism" (1762), proposed that the quality of grace could be identified with physical movements of the human race, especially with the expressive, necessarily with the dignified. Herbert Spencer's essay on "Gracefulness" (1865) established that grace is present in all movements accomplished *with ease*. Behind this easy accomplishment must be *an economy of effort*. Such ease and economy arouse a *sympathy* in the spectator. To further paraphrase Spencer,—grace is physical action achieved in a manner to conserve muscular energy. Grace is animation calculated to demonstrate this economy. Grace of pose may be found in postures which are sustained while conserving the energy.

A further development of the theories of Home and Spencer may be studied in two large volumes of Raymond Bayer's, *L'Esthetique de la Grace* (1933). Bayer finds also that the ultimate base of grace is in an economy of effort, but only if such effort is concealed. He claims to have discovered the principle in grace for a *demonstration* of power, and an element of surprise or the *unexpected*.

Bayer divides the means of grace into the "natural" and the "artificial." The natural comprises a given person's hereditary endowment, his muscular structure, weight, instinctive mobility and capacity to coördinate. The artificial is a general interior control, regulation or counter-balance, the independence of the various members of the body and a certain softness, or rather elasticity. All of these combine to corroborate Spencer's principle of the concealment of effort. Bayer carefully

43

analyses the academic vocabulary of the classic dance, proposes definitions of equilibrium, static balance, and asymmetrical counterpoise as concomitants of grace.

J

JETE: From the French, *jeter*, to throw. A jump in which the body is thrown on to one foot, after the other has been raised, and is completed with the other foot at the side, or in front in third or fifth position. The term is also pronounced and even written *shtay* or even *stay*, a corruption of the phonetic French.

L

LESSON: The arrangement of exercises into daily periods to instruct a dancer in technique and to maintain technical proficiency during an active stage-career. The lesson consists of approximately the same movements from a pupil's first introduction to the *barre* down to the last year of his professional appearance. There is a natural difference bred by the ease of familiarity, but even the youngest student immediately tries to execute steps which will later be part of his accustomed vocabulary.

The class starts easily while progress is at first, by necessity, slow. Children without previous training, as well as accomplished dancers, commence with the *barre* and follow by work in the center of the floor, in a dry and rather invariable sequence. Soon, combinations of more complex movements are permitted at the *barre,* and then without its aid, in the center. The five fundamental positions, their variants in arms and'legs as well as principle of *opposition* and *plasticity* are mastered. An easy *adagio* combination is ventured to prepare for instruction in *balance*. The *adagio* becomes increasingly complex and difficult to sustain. Later on, new combinations are continually substituted for others. The student cannot afford to make any short cut. Everything follows inexorably from the simple sources: self-control, aplomb, balance, stamina, and limberness become the normal properties of a body which will finally be prepared to assume the more difficult department, *allegro*.

44

The slower exercises (*adagio*) coming first, warm up the muscular mechanism for its peak load of exertion.

Allegro cannot be undertaken until the feet are so correctly trained that their behavior is almost instinctive. The *turn-out* of the legs must be broad and effortless. The instep must be firm and well muscled. The exercises begin with simple jumps in which both feet are used to spring: *temps levé* and *changement de pied*. These are first practiced with the hands on the *barre*, the dancer facing the wall. Then comes the more complex *assemblé*. The *assemblé* correctly performed is a base for the rest of the division of *allegro*. The legs must coördinate into the rise and fall, and *yet* be turned-out in landing. There is no possibility of muscular laxity. Afterwards follow the *glissade*, *jeté, echappé, pas de basque,* and *balancé*. The last step cannot be learned until the muscles have been properly developed by single jumps. Having mastered the primary *jetés*, the lesson passes to jumps in which only one foot is used for a spring (the other resting *sur le coup de pied*, after the jump) and to the *sisonne ouverte* in various directions. More difficult jumps, as the *saut de basque,* come later, with *cabrioles* and the rest of *batterie*. *Allegro* is the basis of the rapid *enchainements* which constitute most of classic stage dancing. In advanced classes every one of these named steps is varied in execution by being practiced *en tournant*.

This is a rough outline for most of our standard "Russian" ballet classes, and does not apply to character-dancing, which has its own *barre* system, or to supported *adagio*, or to lessons for *pointes*. Agripina Vaganova, the author of the best modern work on the subject and academician of the Soviet Technicum for ballet in Leningrad, gives almost the same order. She wisely insists on no absolutely rigid rule for planning her class, recognizing that dancers are artists, not soldiers, and that theatrical life is variable. Fatigue must be taken into consideration as well as the individual progress of pupils.

Vaganova's daily exercises (except for the first-year pupils) follow. For advanced professionals it is naturally greatly amplified and rendered more complex and difficult to accommodate and enlarge their capacities.

1. *Barre; Plié* in the five absolute positions of the feet. (This is a period for warming up the muscles.)

Battements tendus, to accustom the legs to *turn-out* in an automatically perfect *fifth* position.

Ronds de jambe par terre, battements fondu and *frappé, ronds de jambe en l'air, petits battements, developpés* and *grand battement jeté.* All of these steps may be recombined and complicated at the discretion of the teacher.

2. *Centre-practice:* simple *adagio* with correct *porte de bras.*

Repetition of No. 1 without the aid of the *barre.*

Combinations of *allegro.* The lesson tapers off with *changements de pieds.*

LIBRETTO: In the classic French vocabulary, the plot of a ballet was referred to as the *prétexte* or *intrigue.* Ballets can be roughly classed in two groups, those with plots and those without. All ballets have a subject. *Les Sylphides* (Fokine: 1909), for example, has no plot, but its subject is the atmosphere of "romantic" theatrical dancing (ca. 1840). The plot of *Petrouchka* (Fokine: 1911), based on a folk-tale, is direct and narrative. The plot for *Choreartium* (Massine: 1934) is abstract and "epic." In *Petrouchka* the soloists possess human characteristics and act with conflict, climax and denouement. It is a dramatic scheme. In *Choreartium* the characters are symbols with generalized reference. They follow a logic dictated by the dramatic nature of the music (Brahms, Fourth Symphony). The libretto for *Choreartium* seems as if it were a rationalized description written to coincide with the dancing *after* it had been composed. Except in purely formal *divertissements,* the plot as an order of action, even in purely atmospherical work such as *Cotillon* (Balanchine: 1932) is important. It is the pretext which provides a possibility for an audience to suspend momentarily their natural expectation of logic, and accept the lyric super-logic of a ballet libretto. A good libretto, even an impressionist, double-exposed or portmanteaued one, follows most of the rules of simple dramaturgy. Balanchine once said the perfect type plot for a dramatic narrative ballet was the story of the Prodigal Son. Once there was a man who had everything, then he had nothing; finally he had everything

46

again. Here we have in persuasive causal logic a maximum dra-matic contrast. Complex plots which have to be explained by program notes, since the drama in the dancing is not in itself sufficiently legible, have more or less disappeared except for Massine's symphonic ballets and the elephantine Russian fairy stories such as *Le Coq d'Or* (Fokine: 1914) and *Bogatyri* (Massine: 1938). In the eighteenth and nineteenth century, however, ballet libretti were written by such well known poets as Gautier and Heine, to be printed and widely sold, just as are opera libretti today. At that time, people were accustomed to prepare themselves with a specific narrative background for what they were going to see. Today, we are either lazier or more sophisticated.

Unless the choreographer is a librettist himself, the problem of a contemporary ballet librettist is mostly one of tact. It is he who has the original idea which will be nursed into a ballet. It is his conviction about atmosphere, decorative incident, style and even the quality of music, which may dominate the chore-ographer and mould an ultimate production. Boris Kochno, Diaghilev's last secretary, was skillful in understanding how much plot a ballet could stand, the temper of its picturesque-ness and its just needs as to scenic investiture. Kochno also was conscious of various fashionable artistic and literary trends at work among the painters of the School of Paris (1924-1934). The heirs of Dada, the literary virtuosity of Jean Cocteau, the sad grandeurs of neo-classicism and neo-romanticism, dance-hall, music-hall, and film provided topical pretexts for the late Diaghilev repertory.

M

MAITRE DE BALLET: The classic French term is literally cor-rect. The equivalent English "Choreographer" means a sten-ographer of dance steps, while a composer of dance steps, to which this appellation has come to refer, is in truth Master of the Ballet. A *maître de ballet* is the single most important element in the complex organism of theatrical dancing. It is for him, that the Impressario arranges an instrument for crea-tion, for him the commercial manager books tours, for him

47

that dancers prove the results of their schooling. It goes without saying that a *maître de ballet* is himself something more than a dancer. Indeed J. G. Noverre, Carlo Blasis and Fokine urge him to be a scholar, poet, painter, sculptor, and, most important of all, geometer and musician. Primarily he must be a dancer and a good one. There have been no great choreographers who were not first-rate dancers as well. It is impossible for a dance-designer to imagine, devise or demonstrate steps which are not capable of arising from within his unique instrument, his own dancer's body. While it is metaphysically conceivable that a brain can envisage what a body cannot accomplish, it is nevertheless a working truth that unless a ballet-master is nearly all-capable, certain combinations of gestures will not occur to him, as he will have had no direct experience of them in practice.

MANNERISM: All dancers have mannerisms which are fragmentary unconscious expressions of their private characters. In personal life, these accumulated mannerisms are often endearing. If we love a person, we love their tricks of intonation, of turning their heads, or snapping their knuckles. On the stage, mannerisms can also be attractive. However, many merely spring from errors in training. An over-emphatic preparation for a *pirouette* by jogging madly on both points distinguishes a recently popular ballerina. Her actual turns were highly incorrect. Her body was never held rigid, nor her spine straight enough to prevent her from falling out of the spin. But by her preparatory attraction of notice to the difficulty of the evolution which she was about to perform, she knew that the audience's eye would be distracted from the execution of the step itself. Unfortunately, by the very authoritative ugliness of her mannerism, it was. She got away with it on a basis of blatant vanity. "This may look funny, but only because it is very difficult. It must look this way. You, the audience, are wrong. I am the criterion."

Mannerisms compensating for technical inadequacy can develop into almost pathological manifestations repeated like nervous *tics*. The best dancers consciously eliminate any mannerism to which their attention is drawn. The possession of a

48

clean instrument, devoid of any left-overs from other rôles or styles is the prerequisite of an artist who is occupied with giving maximum expressiveness to every part.. Each dancer has a personal manner as forever individual as his proper face or finger-prints. The intrusion of affectation is like a smudged face or hang-nails. In young dancers, affectations are, unfortunately, sedulously cultivated by imitating the stage-manners of admired dancers. The young dancer is not sure enough of himself to allow his own personality to make its slow emergence. He jumps the gun to acquire a set of idosyncrasies which are vanitous, arbitrary, more often than not inapplicable to a given rôle. The late Anna Pavlova, through no fault of her own, was responsible for a great crop of youngsters appropriating her swan's down, waxen fading-away, although these were her unique property. The Pavlovettes arranged their hair, their arms, their skirts in a perpetual death vigil and took on themselves aspects of taxidermists. Manner is personal expression of a given theatrical style, which is frequently a traditional accumulation of collective manners. Pavlova's manner, of course, recalled that of Taglioni, but she was accidentally close in spirit to the original sylph from the beginning. Mannerism is the dancer's conceited comment on his own individual personality as human being, not as dancing artist. By imitating the manners of other better dancers, they think to excuse an essential inadequacy. One hardly ever notices the mannerisms of character dancers, of an Argentina or an Escudero. Their idiom is compact of national mannerism, elevated into a classic idiom, so rigid that it requires only an intense execution, not a personal comment, to be effective.

N

NOTATION (Stenochoregraphy or Dance-Script): Of all forms of art, dancing alone still has no generally legible means of saving its literature. Music for the last five hundred years, literature for the last five thousand, have their preservative scripts. Painting, sculpture and architecture fend for themselves. Dancing, which in essence is the most transitory and ephemeral of the arts, if by no means the least intense, must depend for its survival on fragmentary graphic rendering, usually so transposed as to be only atmospherically suggestive, and on verbal description. Neither the film nor the still camera have much helped except to preserve more or less static poses, portraits or fragments of danced action seized out of context or taken under unfavorable circumstances.

To be sure, there have been innumerable systems of dance notations, yet the Egyptian, Greek, and Roman methods are almost as illegible as our most recent inventions. From Arbeau's essay in 1588, through Beauchamps, Pécour and Feuillet (ca. 1700), Magny (1765), Malpied (1770), Théleur (1831), Zorn (1840), Saint-Léon (1852) and Stepanov (1892), down to recent proposals of Nijinsky (1917-unpublished), von Laban (ca. (1914), and Meunier (1923), the ingenuity of dancers has been unquenchable.

A desire to avoid oblivion is the natural possession of any artist. It is intensified in the dancer, who is far more under the threat of time than others. The inventions of systems to preserve dance-steps have, since the early eighteenth century, shared a startling similarity. All the books contain interesting prefatory remarks on the structure of dancing. The graphs presented vary in fullness from the mere birds-eye scratch-track of Feuillet, to the more musical and inclusive stenochoreography of Saint-Léon and Stepanov, but all are logically conceived and invitingly rendered, each equipped with provocative diagrams calculated to fascinate the speculative processes of a chess-champion. And from a practical point of view, for work in determining the essential nature of old dances with any objective authority, they are equally useless. The systems, each of which may hold some slight improvement over its predecessor, are so difficult to decipher even to initial mastery of their alphabets, that when a student approaches the problem of putting the letters together, or finally fitting the phrases to music, he feels triumphant if he can decipher even a single short solo *enchainement*. An analysis of style is not attempted, and the problem of combining solo variations with a *corps de ballet* to provide a chart or an *entire* ballet movement reduces the complexity of the problem to the apoplectic. Yet every year, a new mutation of an old theory, or an invention of a new one

50

appears to perplex innocent students. The film is the only answer, not alone as record, seen head-on through the proscenium-arch but from all four sides, and from the flies as well. Who will pay for it is the historian's problem.

Assuming one could record dances by notation, except for the choreographer himself, it may not be a particularly valuable undertaking. The very essence of dance is evanescent. Arbitrary notation could be canonized into tyrannical rules by unimaginative dance theologians. A repertory, which is by nature changeable, might decline in an effort to maintain its "original" quality. Every style of dancing, as well as dress, has to be restudied for the special conditions of each epoch. Time passes; it does not stand still for scholars or aestheticians to delight in. The dance occurs primarily in time. An aesthetic historian may idly speculate on what Lully (ca. 1670) danced, as far as steps go, but he scarcely ever occupies himself with how Lully appeared dancing, since even he must recognize that a man's idiosyncratic manner dies with him. Always suspect a person occupied with dance notation as an unsuccessful choreographer, a disappointed dancer, or a person whose main relaxation is the kind of intellection which would be more profitably spent on symbolic logic or cross-word puzzles.

Before 1765, Giovanni Andrea Gallini wrote, in his "Critical Observations on the Art of Dancing," "Granted also that the enumeration of the motions and steps was possible which it unquestionably is not, considering the infinite variety of gestures and inflexion, concomitant to such motions as have received certain distinctive names; granted withal that such motions distinguished by names appropriated to them, may be specified by their respective characters, still there offers one invincible objection, and that is the nomenclature of those more complicated motions which mock all description, and which can only be comprehended by sight, so that like the most simple ones, they may have their peculiar character readily enough apprehensible by a master; they can be of no use in the world but to their master who does not need them. Nor even to him will that imaginary choreography preserve any dance, but some very plain ones. The written or engraved description by lines and characters, where there is anything

51

complicated, offers such an untoward medley of motions and figures that it is scarcely possible to decipher them. The plan has more the air of puzzling mathematical problems, or of figures in a conjuring book—than that of happy regularity and cleanness of which the notes of music are susceptible."

In the thirteenth of his "Letters on Dancing and Ballets" (1760), J. G. Noverre asserts, "I have learned choreography, sir, and I have forgotten it; if I think it useful for my progress, I shall learn it anew. The best dancers and most celebrated *maîtres de ballet* disdain it because it is of no real help to them." But he goes on to suggest a feasible if incomplete choreography in criticizing Cahusac's superficial article on the subject in Diderot's·and d'Alembert's Encyclopedia (1751-1772). He proposes that choreographers provide the track or floor plan which they alone know; that what they could not explain, should be described by the ablest theatrical journalists, and finally an artist like Boucher coupled with an engraver like Cochin would make renderings of essential groupings. However unwieldy this method may be, it is at least possible and had it been followed we might have a far clearer idea of how past ballets actually appeared than by attempting to decipher the ingenious devices of academic stenochoregraphers. In 1735, Kellom Tomlinson, a well-known English dancing-master, issued his "Art of Dancing" in two splendid volumes, anticipating the method suggested by Noverre. The finest representations of the Minuet to be found are rendered the more complete by a series of careful portrait engravings of dancers moving on the floor-track of a choreographic short-hand.

O

OPERA-BALLET: Opera-Ballet, as we know it, continues a nineteenth century institution. The elaborate ballet-divertissements of Lully (1632-1687) and the opera-ballet of Rameau (1683-1764) had been absorbed into purely atmospheric aids in such a work as Mozart's *Don Giovanni* (1787), where the famous minuet serves as background for the drama played by principals. Thus Verdi arranged the opening ballet for *Rigoletto* (1851). However, after the restoration of the official

Opéra under the Empire of Napoleon, ballet again resumed its more or less preposterous place as a decoration of the lyric repertory. Opera houses were maintained more as a sign of cultural prestige by rulers of European capitals than as entertainment for the general populace, who, incidentally, bought tickets, but whose support equalled only a fragment of government subsidies. Ballets for European operas had their own schools and professional hierarchies. They were maintained as a kind of perennial bait for a certain section of the almost professional audience of permanent opera-subscribers.

The *corps de ballet* on stage fluttered in ball-rooms, throne-rooms, at country-weddings, joyful celebrations, or as sprites or devils. Pretexts were provided by librettists for divertissements exhibiting a favorite soloist for seldom longer than ten minutes. This gave an opportunity for the evolution of a *corps de ballet,* variations by the ballerina, a duet with her partner, and the finale. Meanwhile, singers could rest their voices from the demands of *bel canto* and astronomical *fiorotura.* Opera-ballets, to be sure, danced in their own independent productions, but this note has special reference to ballet in operas.

Why ballets are inserted in Opera in 1939 is something of a mystery. They serve no practical purpose except to employ a limited number of dancers on a precarious basis. There is as little attempt to study the place of ballet in opera, as there is to study the *mise en scène* of opera as a whole. The victory scene in *Aida* as produced by the Metropolitan Opera Association in New York City, or at any other American house for that matter, is a case in point. The Ethiopian captives may indeed be negro supers, but they are followed by girls in black-face representing small negro boys in the tradition of the *travestie* (girls as boys) of the Paris Opéra. The *corps de ballet* evolves around an Italian ballerina on toe-point who does *cooch* gestures with "Egyptian" plastique. To omit the "ballet," however, would be to risk a circus without elephants. Hence opera-ballet is scrubbily maintained in its haphazard limbo, out of habit. It is more important to keep a shadow of dancing than abandon it entirely, since this might be interpreted as loss of face. Except for an unfortunately small fragment attaching to musical interest, the entire persistence of opera is purely a determination to maintain a certain social or economic prestige. Ballets in the opera are like the gardens of the Tuilleries. Even in war-time, they are tended to prove the country is still healthy.

A choreographer for opera-ballet must have by nature a character in which talents for compromise amount to an almost total lack of self-respect. Assistant stage-managers, the faithful serfs of starred singers, eliminate rehearsals for dancing, and simultaneously decrease space given to dance in. The conspiracy is furthered by the bland disregard of the wardrobe department, and the surrealist caprice of wigmakers, shoemakers, and property-men. For those who have a developed taste for taxidermy, a trip to the Metropolitan is fun. For such connoisseurs, the Bacchanale of *Tannhaüser* is rare cheese. Originally written for its Paris première in 1861, it had even then violated a protocol that opera did not introduce a French ballet until the members of the Jockey Club had finished their liqueurs, which was certainly not before the middle of a second act.

Wagner's indications for the choreography he desired are almost pornographic. The fulfillment of them, from Bayreuth to Petersburg, has been sterilized. To be sure, Isadora Duncan (ca. 1905) momentarily managed to clear away some ballet-skirts, but in revenge after her departure, the Bacchanale appeared in costumes which were a frantic corseted parody of the American Maenad herself.

One recalls the first words sung by the tenor representing Tannhaüser. The Minstrel lolling on the couch of Venus, passes his hand woozily before his eyes, avowing, "Heavens! This is unsupportable." There is a superstition backstage that he is referring to the preceding ballet.

OPPOSITION: A term denoting the means used to break the rigid, static and symmetrical position of a dancer's body. For example: when a dancer moves right arm and right leg together, it is less effective plastically than if the right arm moves against the action of the left leg. This opposition (Italian: *controposto*) creates an asymmetrical balance. It increases plasticity by a physical, though symbolic vivification of both sides of the whole body. Actually, the whole body is not affected. Symbol-

54

PLATE 4

CROISÉ DEVANT

BATTEMENT À LA SECONDE

PORT DE BRAS

EFFACÉ

ically, however, the right arm represents the movement of the entire upper half, the left leg that of the entire lower. If only the right arm and right leg were used it would appear that half the body were dead. Half a body is too great a proportion to be supported as dead weight, even by a completely alive other half. The actual impression given is that a body so shown is awkward and hence ineffective for all dancing purposes. The opposed balance of arms and legs, the alternation of head to shoulders, the counterpoise of the torso, twisted, faced front or back and then twisted again, showing to the public different aspects of the same body at once, suggests if it does not actually display, the difference between the muscularity of the chest and of the back. A parallel contemporary example may be found in the late double-image heads of Pablo Picasso, in which the front face masks a profile. This enhanced plasticity makes legible to an audience the dancers' existence in their element of air. It minimizes flatness, a hard, unresilient silhouette, a cold, inactive outline. J. G. Noverre and Salvatore Vigano carefully observed Hellenistic and Italian Baroque sculpture. Michelangelo, Giovanni da Bologna, Bernini, and the Imperial Romans indicated in static terms of bronze or stone peak positions of plastic expression suitable for climaxes of various *enchainements* which choreographers may be able consecutively to develop.

Carlo Blasis explained in 1829 that "In the Bacchanalian groups which I have composed, I have successfully introduced various attitudes, arabesques and groupings, the original idea of which was suggested to me during my journey to Naples and through Magna Graecia, on viewing the paintings, bronzes and sculptures, rescued from the Ruins of Herculaneum."

As Anna Morgan paraphrases the ideas of Delsarte ("An Hour With Delsarte": 1895): "The law of opposition in gesture has for its mechanical or physical basis, the laws of equilibrium and gravity. A vertical line directly through the body standing erect and perfectly poised, will mark the center of gravity. Any departure of the body from this right line, in any direction, must be compensated for by an equal portion of the body in the opposite direction, else equilibrium cannot be maintained. Equilibrium is one of the elements of physical grace, and, while there may be equilibrium without grace, there can be no grace without equilibrium, so in gesturing this law of compensation or balance must be preserved in the interests of grace. A gesture by one member of the body demands a compensating gesture by another member in opposition."

P

PAS: Theoretically, the *pas* is not a single but a combination of steps or movements of the feet. In classic ballet it also refers to a dance executed by a soloist (*pas seul*), a duet (*pas de deux*), or familiarly: *pas de trois, pas de quatre,* etc.

According to the Encyclopedia of Diderot and d'Alembert (ca. 1772), in an article based heavily on Rameau (1725), Cahusac (1754), and Noverre (1760) there were five types of steps. Steps in a *straight* line; slow, *spread-open* steps made as in walking, when one foot after the other describes a semi-circle; *struck* or beaten steps, in which one foot strikes in back or in front of the other before placing it on the floor; *turned* steps, in which the legs make a complete circle in the air or on the floor, and *twisted* steps.

Certain ballet movements have no other meaning than to display or praise the dancing organism through the mechanics of the human body. The vocabulary of active steps is considerable, and is based on the five absolute static *positions* of the feet. On this basis, choreographers and individual dancers for five hundred years have contributed to build on one another's work until we have been given the dancing practice of our contemporary stage. The two prime categories of *pas* govern the twin provinces of earth and air. Steps predominantly the gift of the seventeenth century demonstrated the resources of the plane stage-surface with adaptations of ball-room walk or march. By the middle of the eighteenth, new steps began to predicate the conquest of air. As time went on, greater subtlety, variety and plasticity evolved themselves into a fluid idiom. The nineteenth century provided a language accentuated by heel and toe beats borrowed from the characteristic national dance sources (polka, mazurka, cachucha, etc.), which gave color to the corpus of steps which had tended to become theatrically sterile. If the twentieth century has provided new steps, these have been appropriated from popular entertainments, public ball-rooms and music-halls. The steps of traditional social or ball-room dancing have always been amplified by theatrical gesture, but as for their execution from the minuet down to our two-step, it is more a question of tempi than of complex physical activity.

By a "step" in theatrical dancing, we usually refer to a combination of movements which has become popular enough to enjoy written definition or inclusion in dance manuals. The step thus defined becomes canonical, part of the material of dancing, which can be taught. But there are innumerable steps created by choreographers for their own private and transient uses, which may never bear a name.

Chefs invent new dishes in honor of persons or events. Dancers and choreographers are as ingenious. Sometimes the name sticks, and we have Pêche Melba or Spaghetti Caruso. When the great Italian teacher and dancer, Enrico Cecchetti (1850-1928), opened a new school in London, his *glissade de Mami* honored a black kitten mascot with which he had been presented. This was a *pas de chat*, indeed. There are steps named with reference to birds and animals, passing personalities and events.

PIROUETTE: From the Burgundian, *pirouelle:* spinning top (Littré): or from the French, *pied-roue,* foot-wheel (Frisch).

Cyril Beaumont (1928), in his excellent introduction to Lambranzi's "New and Curious School of Theatrical Dancing" (1716), has a paragraph on the German word *pirole,* which also appears as *piroleten* and *birollets. Pirouette* is a term for turning, in French and German, *pirouettd* in Italian; *pirueta* in Spanish. *Pirole* is Italian for peg or pin.

A *pirouette* is the complete spinning turn or whirl of the dancer's body in one place, usually in sequence of from two to eight or more. The effect of the well-executed pirouettes is to present the dancer's body in its full plasticity, front and back superimposed on one another, almost as in a double-exposure.

An audience necessarily remains stationary in its seat. If the seats could be imagined to revolve rapidly to enable spectators

58

to see back and front in a single frontal position, there might be no reason for pirouettes. In any case, it is one of the most brilliant steps in a classic dancer's vocabulary. A quick pirouette, performed high on the half toe, perfectly accompanies a run of notes in music. It can be accelerated in sequence, and a dancer cleanly stopping short after the swift spin produces a maximum contrast, complete immobility after intense mobility, in the same plane. *Pirouettes* on the floor are the basis for *tours en l'air.* Slow *pirouettes,* which few dancers execute well, can be as effective as fast ones. Instead of diminishing their already quiet pace, a good technician can perform slowly almost as many turns as he can quickly, producing thereby a remarkable display of controlled energy and reserve force. *Pirouettes* for girls are executed on toe point. They can be employed meaninglessly, or for their own sake as an irrelevant trick. Some unimaginative choreographers, when invention fails them, fill up gaps in design by a string of *pirouettes* which at least appear brilliant. The *pirouette à la seconde* is a turn with the leg extended and is a spectacular preparation for a final explosive twirl. (See plate 4.)

While the complete turn of the body must be among the oldest steps in the vocabulary of dancing, there is a tradition that the *pirouette* in its present theatrical form, arrived from Stuttgart in 1766. From that city came Mlle. Heinel and her young partner Ferville, to the Paris Opéra, where the subscribers were astonished by the multiplicity of the German debutante's *tours.* Both dancers supposedly executed the turn on *une seule pointe,* or as we would probably translate, on the high half-toe. The dancers Maximilien Gardel (1740-1787) and Gaetan Vestris (1729-1808) perfected the step until they were popularly thought to "shine like the sun" or "twinkle like a star." Serge Legat (ca. 1890) is said to have performed fourteen turns at a single time. Eight is still excellent for anyone. In our own day, Enrico Cecchetti (1850-1928) was known as *le roi des pirouettes,* or even sometimes *le diable des pirouettes,* but his typical Italian training limited him to turns in but a single direction. His pupil, Vaslav Nijinsky (active: 1909-1919), executed a series of renowned *pirouettes* at the end of his variation as Harlequin in *Carnival* (Fokine: 1909). Another Cecchetti pupil, Mascagno, who settled and taught in America, was partly responsible for the astonishing pirouettes of Lew Christensen, the brilliant young American dancer and choreographer. The slow pirouettes of André Eglevsky, with arms held arched over his head, are the despair of many of our best living dancers. In the summer of 1939, he is reported from Hollywood to have executed eighteen on a bet.

PLIE (see plate 2): "Dancing is no more than knowing how to bend (*plier*) the knees at the proper time." P. Rameau, *Le Maître à Danser* (1725).

The bending of the knees is perhaps the single most important foundation exercise in the classic academy. The index of a dancer's excellence can be recognized even at the barre by the depth, ease and steady rhythm of a *grand plié* from standing position, *demi plié*, deep down almost to the floor. The *plié* develops balance and muscularity, renders joints easy, and makes tendons strong and supple.

POINTES (see plate 3): The exact origin of dancing on toes is obscure. Throughout the eighteenth century, artists represented dancers supported on conventionalized bare toes to enhance an appearance of lightness, and long after toe-shoes were worn, draughtsmen still depicted dancers floating on bare pink feet. Sometime in the late eighteen-twenties or early thirties the heelless slipper with boxed toe made its entrance; the cardboard boxing of the toe, supported by stiff satin and thin sole-leather shank, added just sufficient extra support, while providing enough shock-absorption to enable girls to support their whole dancing weight on the tips of their toes. Drawings of Taglioni dated 1826 (Stuttgart) show her poised on point. The static position was soon abandoned for actual movement (such as the *pas de bourrée*) on the *pointes* themselves.

Toe-dancing requires considerable strengthening of the muscles involved, as so great a weight is not normally carried on that portion of the foot. Some Cossack tribesmen supposedly danced on their unsupported toes. But in western theatrical tradition men do not use points since it tends to suggest a finicking effeminacy. An exception was the Irish dancer, Anton

60

Dolin (Patrick Kay) in *Les Facheux* (Nijinska: 1925), where an approximation of seventeenth century atmosphere permitted it. Several contemporary American male-dancers are able to dance on toe, but do not in public.

Toe-dancing came into being, it is generally understood, as the logical outgrowth of the dancer's eagerness to quit the floor. A longing for the ethereal sphere (*élévation*) characterized the general idea behind these ballets based on French and German romantic literature as exemplified by Heine, Hoffman and Gautier, and as danced by Taglioni, Elssler, Cerrito and Grisi (1830-50). However, since this time, the use of points has been developed from a stylistic trick, into a useful, general attribute of classic dancing, far beyond the local expression of a limited literary and artistic tendency. It permits, by the use of a base smaller than the flat foot, more brilliance in turning (*pirouettes*). The extended toe-point when raised from the floor aids the continuous line of a dancing body, prolonging its direction, at least in the imaginations of the public, into infinity, rather than stopping it abruptly with the normal right angle of the walking foot. The sharp attack of the point on the floor can be accentually important. The arrow shape of the point gives the upper body an appearance of lightness and facile mobility. When the points sharply strike the floor it is called *la danse taqueté* (from *taquet:* peg). This staccato style was first so termed around 1834, to apply to Fanny Elssler's debut in *La Tempête* (Coralli). The effect of her feet was compared to golden arrows bouncing off a marble pavement, and contrasted with Taglioni's *danse ballonné*, one more example of the eternal duel between floor and air.

The artificiality of the convention of *pointes* removes the dragging banality of the association or identification of a stage-walk with a normal walk. Progress over the stage on points held more or less closely together is known as the *pas de bourrée*. It has little to do with the *Bourrée,* a quick eighteenth century dance-form, coming originally from the district of Auvergne. It was popularized for our time as the effortless locomotion of Anna Pavlova in *La Mort du Cygne* (Fokine: 1909), when she seemed to float over some impalpable yet polished surface. Movement on *pointes* effects an almost imperceptible advance

61

or retreat. There is scarcely any shift of weight and the bodies seem borne on stage, supported more on air than on legs.

Slippers which sheathe dancers' toes have become almost a totem or fetich of the dancing tribe. A conclave of Muscovite balletomanes, relates Alexander Pleschayev, having paid two hundred roubles for the ballet shoes of Marie Taglioni on the occasion of her leaving Russia in 1842, solemnly had them cooked with a special sauce and ate them. Those who saw the French film *Ballerina* (Jean Benoît-Lévy: 1937) recall the little *rat de l'Opéra* made an altar on the mantelpiece for the *chausson* of her adored god-mother.

One may hear violent arguments as to the respective merits of the Italian versus the French toe-shoe. Some dancers need a considerable strength in the cardboard or stiff satin box, others want little. Some learn to crochet a knotty protection in heavy pink silk to protect the tip of their shoes; others feel this dulls the sensitive contact with the floor.

The entry of the Journal of the Brothers de Goncourt for July 23, 1868, tells us that Théophile Gautier came down to their country place and talked about dancers at the Opéra. "He described their white (*sic*) satin ballet-slippers, saying that each slipper is re-enforced by a bit of wadding at the point where the dancer feels that her weight is concentrated; and that an expert could tell you,·from a glance at the wadding, the name of the dancer."

The wadding is still in use. It is usually made of lambs wool, to be bought at the drug-store. The ordinary slipper is traditionally pink, or flesh color, unless a costume designer orders otherwise.

POSE (see plates 2 and 3): A static position demonstrating the body in a fixed plastic design, such as *attitude* or *arabesque* in distinction to an active step (*pas*) or fundamental station (the *five positions*).

POSITIONS (see plate 1): The *positions* usually refer to five absolute positions of the feet which are the foundation of classic ballet exercises, and hence of western traditional theatrical dancing. Positions of the feet have their complements for head and arms, although these latter are frequently ignored, since in America, at least, our academic training is uncoördinated. The five positions of the feet permit no change, those of the head and arms have a less canonical rigidity based on less mechanical logic. Positions of the feet are founded on support of the spinal column, on the turn-out of pelvis, hips and thighs, and on locomotion. Text-book positions of head and arms have a secondary, decorative function which is frequently rendered more plastic and appealing by individual teachers. *Port de bras* (carriage of the arms) is largely a matter of taste, and positions of the head, framed by the arms, are determined by it.

The five absolute foot positions according to P. Rameau, "The Dancing Master" (1725) were established by the *maître de ballet,* Beauchamps, first director of the Académie Royale from 1671 to 1687. Rameau states that before his time the positions were "unknown." They were known, but not codified. In 1701 Feuillet, in his *Chorégraphie,* or "Art of Writing Dance Steps," stated that there were five types of steps (*pas*) to which the innumerable varieties could be reduced. They were the direct (straight ahead), open, round, twisted, and struck. Each is based on one of the five original positions of the two feet.

1. Heels together, toes turned completely out, so that the feet are in a straight line. In the time of Beauchamps (ca. 1670), when dancers wore high heeled shoes, the toes were turned out only to about 90°, but this gives far less mobility to the legs, stability after action, and support to the trunk than our contemporary extreme position.

2. Feet in parallel line, as in first position, weight evenly distributed on both, but separated by a distance of about twelve inches.

3. The heel of one foot locked against the instep of the other, weight equally distributed, with complete turn-out.

4. With weight divided equally, in complete turn-out, the fore foot is twelve inches in advance of the back.

5. In complete turn-out, the feet are locked, right heel to left toe, right toe to left heel.

Rameau gives many rules for "honours" (bows) and of particular positions of holding the arms in specific dances, of moving wrists, of doffing hats. Carlo Blasis (1820) established for the theatre (Rameau was occupied chiefly with social-dancing) various exercises for wrists and arms for stage-use. But his statement of absolute arm positions is vague. He tells us that in most cases a dancer should arrange them "as gracefully as possible."

Looking in a French text-book such as Meunier's *La Danse Classique* (1931), one finds considerable difference in the position of arms, head and of the body, from the Anglo-Italian method as demonstrated by *A Primer of Classical Ballet,* by Cyril Beaumont (1933). The Russian School, at least as instructed in the West, holds closer to the later (Cecchetti) method. In both French and Italian schools, there are more than a single station for many positions, since they can be executed high, low, or in front (*en haut, en bas,* or *en avant*). There are five canonical positions of arms and head. They complement the five positions of the feet. There are eight canonical positions of the body, but space is too limited to define each of them here.

The five positions of the feet bear a similar relation in the dance to the five staves of musical notation. Other systems of musical notation are possible, just as different systems of geometry besides the Euclidean may be invented. In dancing, also, particularly in forms invented by insurgent imitators, attempts to establish new positions are not unknown. However, they usually resolve themselves in arguments of nomenclature without establishing any new principle of mechanics.

E. A. Théleur, in his "Letter on Dancing" (1832), states reasons for dissenting with the accepted practice, insomuch as he claims to have found but *one* position, in the traditional sense, "the others, commonly known under that name, are nothing more than stations, their utility being to direct or determine us where we are to commence, change or finish our movements, while in the performance of an *enchainement,* the first and only position being that in which we should place the body, so as to be able to balance ourselves while performing any movements that may be required of us, as far as regards dancing." This is the *first* traditional position. Théleur's stations are divided into "ground," "half aerial," and "aerial" *stations,* and

64

he analyzes the classic dance according to his categories, which are logical enough, but of no more use than the ordinary.

The more one considers the five positions, the more absolute their logic seems. Simplicity itself, the underlying principle is based on our human anatomy, reduced to its essential capacities. It permits a five-note scale from which an infinitude of visual chords in innumerable keys may be rationally arranged. The five positions are a kind of net or comb through which dance movement must accommodate itself in its ceaseless shift.

R

RELEVE: From the French *relever:* to lift again. However, in ballet terminology it means raising the body in any position, by lifting the flat foot to half-toe, or with girls, to full point.

ROMANTIC BALLET: The term "romantic" as applied to ballet is a misnomer. Familiarly, it is a style of dancing as exemplified by revivals of *Giselle* (Coralli: 1841) or *Les Sylphides* (Fokine: 1909). Yet both ballets are familiarly labeled *ballets classiques,* although Fokine's is subtitled "a romantic revery" and is indeed an atmospheric pastiche of Taglioni's *La Sylphide* (P. Taglioni: 1830). In each case romanticism becomes not an opposition to, but a stylistic department of, classicism.

By "romantic" we generally understand an attitude in reaction to neo-classic Greek revivals of the late-eighteenth century and the republican Roman frigidity of Directory and Empire. Under Napoleon, dancers in Paris and Milan wore "Greek" tunics, not far from what Isadora Duncan would have considered "natural." But neo-classicism exhausted itself as a merely decorative style without reference to the life of its time. It was replaced by what came to be known as the "Gothick," but which was no more Gothic, as we understand it, than was its predecessor essentially antique. In philosophy, it was a shift from the finite, rational, orderly and demonstrable based on arbitrary archaeological precedent to the vague, atmospheric, warm, remote and infinite. The novels of Walter Scott and Monk Lewis, with their wild and loosely constructed plots, the tortured compositions of the painters Delacroix and Gericault, the verses of Byron and Victor Hugo, the dancing of Taglioni and Elssler on their elevated toe-points, were the facts of this revolution in action.

Taglioni embraced the colder aspect of romantic dancing, the marble maiden, the virgin lover, the human angel, the pure evanescent, ephemeral longed-for-eternal-feminine. Elssler embodied the warmer rôle; the exotic gypsy-hearted dashing earth-force of vague Central Europe, mysterious Spain, forbidding Scotland. National dances were the decorative frames for her characterizations. Romantic ballet did not forswear reality, since the neo-classic theatre itself had had little pretensions to realism. It merely denied logic, reason or formal design. Its principle was without ethic,—emotional and decorative. It disappeared (ca. 1850) because it could not survive the departure of its original exponents, and since it had even less connection with the life of its epoch than its predecessor, and was as well completely lacking in moral ideas. It had become instead of a comment on life through art, merely an outworn theatrical parody or pastiche of literature, painting and itself.

Hence the so-called Romantic ballet is not a department of the dance, but merely a localized theatrical echo of a transient influential literary and artistic movement.

ROND DE JAMBES: A movement in which the pointed toes describe circles on the floor (*à terre*) or in the air (*en l'air*) in both directions, while the body is supported on the other foot. It is used as an elementary class-room exercise to turn out the hips, feet and legs.

T

TOUR-EN-L'AIR: A *pirouette* (turn) executed not on the ground, but *in the air*. Desrat (1895) curiously enough speaks of this now familiar step as new to the vocabulary of the academic theatrical dance, having more reference to acrobatics than to classic ballet. The step to be brilliant is usually a *double* turn and perhaps it is the multiple *tour* to which Desrat refers. Spectacular dancers who claim triple air turns, in fact

66

usually accomplish at most two and a half, faking the complete frontal landing of the final *tour*.

Beauchamps, Louis XIV's choreographer, and first superintendent of his Académie Royale (ca. 1661-1675), was praised by La Bruyère, *"qu'il j'etait (jetait) les jambes en avant, et faisait un tour en l'air avant que de retomber a terre"* (for he leaped with his feet held in front, and made a turn before regaining the ground). *Un tour* must have referred to the single turn.

TURN-OUT: "In order to dance well, sir," wrote J. G. Noverre before 1760, "nothing is so important as the turning outwards of the thigh, and nothing is so natural to men as the contrary position." Turn-out of legs and thighs at a ninety degree angle, while always recognized as a fundamental for stage-dancing since the *first* and *fifth* positions were established (ca. 1700), received academic canonization somewhere between 1760 and 1780. Indeed, it was considered so important that a machine, the *tourne-hanche,* was invented to accomplish it all the quicker, and was in use as late as the middle of last century. In Albéric Second's *Les Petits Mystères de l'Opéra* (1844), so charmingly illustrated by Gavarni, a dancer complained, "Each morning the Master imprisoned my feet in a grooved box. There, heel to toe, and knees turned outward, my martyred feet became accustomed to remain in a parallel line. It is called 'turning oneself out' *(se tourner)*." Nearly a hundred years before, Noverre had warned that far from being efficacious "it cripples those who make use of it by forcing the waist to take on a much more disagreeable effect than the one it is desired to eliminate."

Carlo Blasis, in his "Code of Terpsichore" (1829), analyzed for our time, as well, this essential mechanical element in stage dance movement. "In the management of your legs, endeavor chiefly to acquire a facility of turning them (out) completely. To this end make yourself easy about your hips, that your thighs may move with freedom, and your knees turn well outwards. All the openings of your legs are thus rendered easy and graceful."

"Some young people are framed by nature with their limbs turning outwards; they possess, therefore, more facility, and succeed to greater advantage than those whose legs turn toward each other; a person of the latter kind indeed can cherish no hope of becoming a good dancer how diligent soever his labour and study be. Practice will do no more than turn his feet and bend his soles a little downwards, but his thighs and knees must remain always in their natural state. . . . The movement of the hip is a sort of guide to that of the knee and instep, as it is impossible for these last to move unless the hip acts first. In some steps the hips alone are set in motion, as in *entrechats, battements tendus,* etc."

TUTU: The familiar symbol of the ballet-girl is her many layered tarletan skirt. In comparison with the long history of theatrical dancing, it is a comparatively recent invention. All through the seventeenth and eighteenth centuries, dancers wore theatricalized versions of customary civil or court dress, no matter whether they portrayed a Greek god or a Roman emperor. Big skirts, wigs, and heeled shoes impeded free movement. Gradually, individual dancers protested by personal revolutions in their costume, which successively became accepted as academic practice. After the French Revolution, due to archaeological researches of the official painter, J. L. David (1748-1825), stage costume assumed a considerable historical accuracy. Neo-classicism attached itself to the name of the first Napoleon. When his dynasty fell, neo-classicism as a mode fell with it to be replaced by the "Romantic" revival,—an interest in Gothic architecture, dress and stories. Romanticism was at once reactionary and revolutionary. Antiquity was abandoned and Europe, however picturesque and unreal, was discovered as a more vital source of material. The court of Louis-Philippe undertook great balls, recalling the lost glories of Versailles and the *ancien regime.*

After the coronation of Charles the Tenth, the Duchesse de Berry became Madame; Le Pavillon de Marsan at the Louvre, her château; and its theatre Le Théatre de Madame. Her *Quadrille de Mary Stuart* was announced. for the second of March, 1829. More than six weeks were spent planning this stupendous fête, the costume and decor of which were scrupulously designed after monuments of the sixteenth century. There was not one, but many costume designers, each noble

68

participant choosing a particular painter: Lafitte, Lecomte, Isabey and even Fragonard. Eugène Lami recorded the ball *after* it took place, as well as designing dresses. The skirts were bell-shaped, full to the floor with square cut bodices, low across the bosom, and small puffed sleeves recalling subtly or else anticipating, the actual civil dress of the season of 1829-1830.

Taglioni appeared as *La Sylphide* at the Opéra on May 14, 1832, to become the lyric apotheosis of the Romantic Revolution. Her costumes were designed by Eugène Lami. Cyril Beaumont writes in his monumental "Complete Book of Ballets" (1937): "The dress consisted of a tight-fitting bodice, leaving the neck and shoulders bare, bell-shaped skirt reaching midway between the knee and the ankle, and pale pink tights and satin shoes; the only adornments were a pale blue ribbon about the waist, a pair of tiny wings between the shoulder-blades, a posy at the breast, a pearl necklace and bracelets, and a garland of convolvuli to frame the hair."

This costume was a transposition of the Stuart dress, adapted from ball-room to opera-house. Bodices, waist-line and skirt-shape were identical whether or not Lami consciously remembered his earlier fête. Taglioni's long arms were well-known to be the despair of her father. Some critics said the new skirt was intended to hide her long legs, but this was not true. In any event, the *Sylphide* costume was like a nun's uniform for ballet-dancers for almost thirty years, due to the persistent memory of the original sylph's prestige.

In 1887, the Italian ballerina Zucchi created a sensation in Petrograd by snipping her long tarletons to knee length in the already accepted Italian manner. In spite of Imperial interdict, Russian dancers followed suit, clipping theirs even shorter to give freer play to the feet. The short tutu skirt is now the badge of "classic" ballet, the long that of "romantic."

U

UNIONS: Dancers may consider themselves artists, but they are also workers, and need the mutual protection of other workers in their field against exploitation in wages, hours and against unemployment. Musicians, variety artists, and actors have been organized into unions for many years. Dancers in musical-comedy have fitted into a category under "actor" but now dancers are being unionized on an independent basis.

Before the musicians became welded into their present powerful units, it was possible for unscrupulous managers to hire foreign aggregations at low salaries for exploitation in the American concert market. This severely restricted the cultivation of native talent. The same situation now exists in the dance field and only strong dancers' unions can assure an artist that they will enjoy anything like even the precarious security of the permanent large white-Russian companies. Individual soloists and orchestral conductors are permitted to work here due to their unique artistic gifts, and the same could be arranged for dancers or choreographers. But for the rest, our own should have preference. If not, any attempt at maintaining an independent artistic ambition or standard will disappear at best into commercialism, at worst vanish completely.

V

VARIATION: A solo dance in a classic ballet, which, by association, has come to mean any portion of a ballet undertaken by individual dancers at which time the chief dramatic attention is focused upon them. The term undoubtedly is connected with the "variation" upon a given musical theme.

Y

YOUTH: The early years of a dancer's career are generally considered the most brilliant. Those who knew Nijinsky and Pavlova in Russia (ca. 1907) tell us they were never the same again. A brilliant debut can blot out the fame of subsequent seasons, and what might have been maturity turns into decadence. A dancer's instrument is his body, and, unlike a violin, it does not improve with age. The physical mechanism has an early prime, but it can be prolonged by strict attention for twenty years. The flash of agile energies, the exuberance of post-adolescent muscles are the most obvious attributes of a dancer, but it is important to remember that these are superficial beside intensity of expression or purity of line. These are not natural gifts, but come only with experience on and off stage. One recalls Nijinsky as a young dancer, yet he expected to dance until he was an old man, just as had his master, Cecchetti (1850-1928). Except, even as a young man, Nijinsky knew he would not perform the same rôles at fifty which he had created at twenty-five. The transition from a *jeune premier* into a mature *danseur noble* is as difficult to achieve in ballet as it is on the dramatic stage, where few juveniles become accomplished character actors. The juvenile remains young until he is old. The persistence of the rôle of youth disqualifies an artist from his final achievement. Exuberant dancers have at atmosphere of play, or sport, an ingenous exhibitionism which is touching because it is so transitory. The audiences know better than dancers how fast youth flies. A young dancer may look forward to a career of twenty or even thirty years, and afterwards to a score or more of teaching. Men tend to last longer than girls, but we recall Karsavina and Pavlova not as debutantes, but as distinguished women.

WHAT BALLET IS ABOUT

1959

WHAT BALLET IS ABOUT: An AMERICAN Glossary

by

Lincoln Kirstein

CONTENTS

Lincoln Kirstein

WHAT BALLET IS ABOUT:
An AMERICAN Glossary

for Wystan and Chester

Ballet dancing is a form of spectacle now popular to an extent which would have seemed improbable twenty-five years ago. Foreign companies make lucrative tours here. Our own, sponsored by plane-fares from the State Department, are dispatched all over the world as hopeful cultural ambassadors. Ballet at home commands a big and growing public. However, its art and craft are relatively new to the great audience, and ballet has now reached that point of historic development when it must have a popular audience to survive. There are those who, through vagueness or lack of curiosity, permit themselves prejudice against it which precise definition might alleviate. Much of the trouble is semantic. Many terms used to define elements of theatrical dancing overlap. Categories are superficially confusing. Hence, this short glossary for the American audience.

DANCE: Ordered bodily movement accompanied by a regulating percussive or rhythmic beat. A universal human act, it became theatrical or spectacular comparatively late in history. Originally, its designs sprang from rites; its end was social and religious. Its aim was to secure by mimetic action and gesture energy through the schedule of the seasons to gain Great Nature's bounty, conquer enemies, ward off evil, make babies, find food. On the most popular (dance-hall) level it is still communal or playful, done for fun rather than to be looked at, for pay.

BALLET: A codified language of exercise, movement and gesture designed for instruction, transmission and legibility; an ordering of formal patterns covering or filling a limited space. In the West, this is our opera-house stage floor, and for the efficiency of sight-lines, a triangular space, flat-surfaced under the scenery-grid and an area some ten feet above it. The ballet of India, South East Asia, China and Japan have even stricter vocabularies, older and more unchanging forms than Western dancing, calculated to be done in open air, temple or palace precincts rather than enclosed theaters with proscenium arches.

André Levinson says:

> The movement of the oriental dance is concentric. The knees almost instinctively come together and bend, the curved arms embrace the body. Everything is pulled together. Everything converges. The movement of the (western) classic dance, on the other hand, is excentric, the arms and the legs stretch out, freeing themselves from the torso, expanding the chest. The whole region of the dancer's being, body and soul, is dilated.

However, Western ballet, (our academic, traditional, classic theatrical dance), in the last fifty years has become an international language, comparable to that of the pianoforte keyboard, and is taught in approximately the same methodology everywhere. It derived from an analysis and codification of folk and social dances in North Italy during the early Renaissance. Steps were divided into fast and slow, high and low, to be done in the provinces of earth and air. Dominated at first by Milanese masters at the Medici court in the Louvre, it was subsequently developed, organized and amplified by French, Central European and Scandinavian dancers. Russians, Czarist and Soviet, have had hegemony for the last seventy-five years; before, ballet was Italian, French, Viennese and Danish. In our generation, in England and America, new crops of dancers testify annually to native independence. Our particular idiom of ballet in the West runs closely parallel to the development of Western music, from the sixteenth century dance-suite through the sonata, symphony and tone-poem, with powerful influences from folk-lore, and more recently from popular dance-music.

Our (Western) ballet is a clear if complex blending of human anatomy, solid geometry and acrobatics offered as a symbolic demonstration of manners—the morality of consideration for one human being moving *in time* with another. The visible projection of contact, support and release, of keeping step, shifting pace and weight is framed in styles of movement from the courtier's correctness to the athlete's competitive courtesy in obeying ground-rules. The formal bow (*révérence*), the curtsy (as in the minuet) are simple gestures from imperial protocol, based on mutual respect, expressed in legible physical terms.

The feudal ball-room turned itself into a theater by lifting a platform at one end. This stage, for so it became, was later raked towards footlights and structurally separated from the rest of the enclosure by a baroque picture-frame proscenium arch, locating the spectacle that it held as more elevated, different and apart from the social dancing that was conducted below on the flat parterre or orchestra-floor. A flashier extension of social dancing, ballet soon developed a rationale of readable movement, as well as dancers who were more than amateur performers. Its ultimate aim, building on each successive epoch, has been the most intense projection possible of the human silhouette in plastic action. Ballet has become a means for the extreme release of physical and mental capacity involving measure, melody, memory and money. Through the schooled elegance of skilled muscularity strictly ordered by music, there developed a drama of acrobatic excitement plus a melodrama of hazard dominated. The privy purse of king and courtier provided richness, and competitive ostentation had political employment.

The use of the trained body in field sports tends towards exhaustion in competition, mastering dangerous chances, breaking established records. The use of the dancer's body in ballet is an expression of spectacular skills, endlessly repeated for an unattainable perfection, non-competitive (except towards some metaphysical ideal) which must be coördinated with the behavior of all other performers, stars and soloists, on stage at the same time. It tends, however deviously, towards the state of ritual from which it remotely sprang.

THE BALLET: When people say that they love or they hate THE Ballet, they are usually speaking of a repertory of dance-compositions familiar to them over a five, or at most a twenty-five year period. This repertory is currently in performance of varying efficiency by

7

touring companies, showing combinations of music, scenic decoration, costume and movement, invested with life by dancing personalities.

THE Ballet is administered by organizations presenting a repertory which may or may not have been created for it, performed by dancers who may or may not have originally created the rôles in which they now appear. THE Russian Ballet, specifically the Diaghilev company, appearing in Western Europe from 1909 to 1929 and in the United States in 1916-17, meant THE Ballet for the first forty years of this century in our hemisphere. Its shadow, or rather the faded pattern of its policy, is still active, but its proper repertory as well as the analytical method which caused it to be born, and the historical necessities which framed it, are no longer vivid. Diaghilev himself was prodigal of novelty. His means were frequently more interesting as paint, poetry, music or personality than as dancing itself. After his departure from Russia by 1913, he was separated from the academic source of a dancer-pool and Western Europe, at that time, provided almost no executants of first quality. Western Europe did, however, provide the Paris School of painters, poets, musicians, dress-makers and an audience which made the city of light the capital of the world. Diaghilev was far less impressed by the importance and lasting powers of his novelties than his heirs; he, unlike them, was always able to find new combinations. His immediate successors chiefly preserved what they could of his. Attempts are now made to endow later revivals of his early repertory with sacrosanct prestige; they are presented with all the authority of a kept canon.

The difference between the ballets of Diaghilev and the accumulated repertory of his epigones was a unique personal predeliction in good taste and in bad taste, and his conviction for serious caprice. His successors had interests in a repertory that could be merchandised. They appropriated his repertory in desuetude as anchor, launching-pad and gilt-edged security. Whole troupes as far flung as Australia and Argentina lived for decades on works which were fresh in quite other circumstances, which did not improve in revival, nor in dilution, nor in a variety of pastiche which was evoked to show something as close as possible to an original without transparent plagiarism. Indeed, close imitation was a sort of abject flattery while here was a workable selling formula in making publics think they'd seen it all before.

A great number of new works equipped with scenery, costumes

and music to some sort of dancing have received first performances since Diaghilev's death in 1929. Three quarters of them have been attempts in one style or another to cash in on the fame of his innovation, but rarely with the focused taste or elevation of collaborative talent which he, for personal and historic reasons, commanded, not as dilletante or impresario, but as a powerful analytical intelligence, operating in the world of lyric theater, as amateur, craftsman, patron and prince.

CLASSIC BALLET: The books say this means ballet opposite to Romantic Ballet, the opposite of Classic Ballet. Romantic ballet is a period designation referring usually to works in a climate established under the influence of the poets Heine, Gautier and E. T. A. Hoffmann in the middle of the last century. It is loosely used to signify ballets in which dramatic pantomime or character-dancing predominated over the school-exercise academic vocabulary. Romantic Ballet today is a category which does not, like the developed classic dance, renew itself. Oddly enough, the archtypical Romantic works (*Giselle, Swan Lake, Coppelia*) are now considered The Classics, and serve as chief tests for the status of international star-style, in spite of an insistent presence of theatricalized folk-dancing and quasi-operatic pantomime.

It is easier to speak of classic style or even of 'classicism' than of Classic Ballet. A classic style may be recognized sooner than it can be defined. It is by no means, like classical sculpture or plastercasts, frigid, chaste, pure, serene or hard. It can also be warm, bright, soft and sharp, even gay. A true classic dancer is one whose instrument includes the mastery of traditional academic lessons to the degree that a pianist of mettle imposes his own ideas on a keyboard or a fine voice plays with coloratura. In addition to mechanical mastery, the classic dancer embodies a controlled energy towards a perfect delivery of the dance vocabulary, so concentrated, balanced and directed that new dimensions in the realization of steps and combinations of movement are manifest. Presupposing the instrument, an educated body, the distilled energy of the dancer's temperament colors his or her quality as pure pigment stains clear water. Control, concentration and balance in the self, both physical and psychic (control of the ego), combine into that final element which serves both as definition of personality and signature of an epoch. Whether we have ever seen them or not, we know by analeptic analysis that Taglioni means one date, Pavlova another, Spessiva another. Embodied classicism or peak performance in this kind of equilibrium seems even to repeat itself, identifying main dancers with each other so that there is a dynasty of dancers in being, a sequence of bodies born decades apart who may never have seen each other. What was the classic climate of the Romantic era of 1840 hinted of human loss, decline, wasting-away in waltzes; ethereal persistence of frail soul over proud flesh; love over death.

Our criterion, our classicism (in the American Century) a hundred years after Heine and Hoffmann, is the mastery of the human body over the machine, or the persistence of the body's possibility to move freely despite general dehumanization. Today the dancer's innate metric and musical accompaniment is no longer the sadly or the strongly flowing waltz. Rather, it is measured by syncopated, interrupted, discontinuous rhythms and serial forms; assonant melody and dissonant song. The shapes are abrupt, asymmetrical; movement can even be spastic. Accents are hit with unsuspected or even apparently unrelated emphasis; the correspondence is in their relative placement. Anything can happen, all over the floor or lifted off it, but it happens to an order—anything, that is, (in the classic dance) except the vanity of improvisation. Surprise is our substitute for solemnity, playfulness for fated purpose. Toes have a trip-hammer beat; the whole body finds a piston's pulsation. Sharp, clean, reiterant, hinting at irony even when the atmosphere is lyric, it is the impermanence of mortal performance alongside its chances for ephemeral perfection which is its own subject rather than a narrative explication of fading flowers or distraught innocence. While contemporary classicism, like all dancing, is haunted by the evanescence of energy and the delicate counterpoise in all extremes or opposites of action, it magnifies the meaning of liberty in disciplined dancing, almost while mocking it. The human machine can do as well as an invented machine, or even better, because while it automatically remembers to perform, it thinks during performance. While bodies sweat, machines rust. Balanchine said his *Agon* (Stravinsky, 1957) was a machine that thought; John Martin added that it also smiled.

In *The Trembling of the Veil,* Yeats wrote:

. . . . . Samuel Butler was the first Englishman to make the discovery, that it is possible to write with great effect without

10

music, without style, either good or bad, to eliminate from the mind all emotional implication and to prefer plain water to every vintage, so much metropolitan lead and solder to any tendril of the vine. Presently I had a nightmare that I was haunted by a sewing machine, that clicked and shone, but the incredible thing was that the machine smiled, smiled perpetually.

At Versailles, where the classic style as we recognize it in the West received its first framing, chiefly in ball-rooms that were pre-theatrical displays for propaganda purposes, partners were princes in their proud youth. These dancers would one day be kings and queens. On the apex of a social pyramid, dancers moved through the weather of majestic dominance, a gracious and graceful deliberate consideration symbolic of the sovereign's obligation to his realm. Just as imitations or mutations of Versailles appeared in the independent masterpieces of Potsdam, Schönbrunn and Peterhof, the Grand Style of classic court manners took over European operatic dancing. After the French Revolution, when kings started losing their crowns and large urban play-houses replaced intimate court-theaters, princes became disguised as peasant-lads who betrayed real peasant-lasses. The folk-dances of Central Europe and the Mediterranean countries widened the dancer's vocabulary lending freshness and frankness to the fusty court-style.

For our time, the first statement of a 'modern' classicism was presented by Diaghilev for Nijinsky, through a rediscovery of classic Greece, both archaic and Hellenistic, and then through sport (*Jeux*: Debussy-Bakst, 1913). On the eve of the first World War, tango and tennis replaced minuet and waltz and gave us our sportive manner, which has, nevertheless, taken the next forty years to be recognized as our one own really suitable style. Retardative repertories which, ironically enough, have attempted to freeze taste and style in the borrowed plumes of the earliest Diaghilev (who would have hated this more than anyone), try to make the audience believe that THE Ballet and the *Classic* Ballet are one and the same.

The new classicism is classless in essence, although its first expression symbolized a vaguely aristocratic, or at least detached leisure-class, which raced sports-cars and spent week-ends in big country houses or summers in the south of France. The music that was first heard on Petrouchka's barrel-organ developed into the *musiquette* of

11

, heirs, perforated rolls of the player-piano, mechanical rag-time, speakers and recorded jazz. Machine-music and even the music the Machine (*Le Pas d'Acier*: Prokoviev-Massine, 1927; *Iron undry*: Mossolov-Bolm, 1932) soon became domesticated as an accompaniment of the developed classic dance. As our century advanced, as elegance became more identified with the promise of leisure, sport and recreation through labor-saving machinery, rhythms from popular music took on a new lightness, heartlessness and nostalgia, a new classic irony and our proper classic chill. Just as IBM computers are housed in streamlined metal boxes, tastefully tailored with sharp stamping and a milky palette so the classic dance of today at its peak, (*Apollon-Agon*: 1926-1956, Stravinsky-Balanchine) takes its traditional feeling from necessities in history.

Dress-makers speak of classic clothes which persist or recur in a useful repertory of models, but the classic dresses of 1908, though quite reminiscent of the classic dresses of 1808 and 1958, are each recognizeable as representative of their own epoch.[1] So is our present high style in the academic dance. And nothing is less classical, or indeed less 'modern' than a lazy approximation of romantic classicism or the classic romanticism of a past epoch.

CHARACTER DANCING: This term was formerly used to designate the theatrical use of familiar folk-dances, heightened and intensified for performance in opera-houses. Long before there was a developed language of the academic classic ballet, the two chief provinces of Western dancing were High and Low, which meant that a rowdy peasantry jumped up off the ground when making merry in open air, while the gentry stuck to the floor when dancing in roofed ballrooms. The folk danced fast and high; the nobility grave and low. Later, folk-tunes were expropriated by courts and country-dances were adopted by palace people. When planned dances entered de-

---

1. "Those dance-critics who write as if dance criticism were penal servitude insist that the choreography of *Apollon* is pastiche, a parody of *Lac des Cygnes,* a transient echoing of 'Parisian smartness'. This last it certainly is, if one translates smartness not as smart-aleckness but as essential human elegance. *Apollon* has its chic; it partakes of the permanent international elegance characteristic of French thought, letters, painting, dress-making and cooking, upon which neither American industrialism nor military defeat has had the slightest effect. The dancers in *Apollon* were dressed by Mme. Chanel, who cinctured them with Charvet's striped cravats. They were Olympians of 1928; they remain Olympians in 1948. . . ." (L.K.: "Balanchine Musagète," *Theatre Arts Monthly,* November, 1947)

12

signed theaters, folk-dances from many remote provinces characterized the quality of racial or national geographical identity or difference. The nostalgia of distance made an international audience acquainted with rhythms from Spain, Italy, the Slavonic realms and Central Europe. What remained 'authentic' in these dances was their basic thematic material—melody, tempo and certain characteristic steps of jota, tarantella, mazurka, hopak, etc. Choreographers embroidered on the slight given groundwork and made solo-numbers or divertissements for opera-repertory, which was often placed in exotic national settings, and which also affected the independent ballet-repertory, itself. Impressive native soloists, with their troupes of fiery nationals started coming to Paris, capital of the world, fairly early in the last century. These were to include not alone Spanish and Russians, but also South East Asian and Japanese as well, frequently attracted by world-fairs. There was often an addition of purely classic school-steps too, in order that the natural or characteristic limitations of authentic steps could be rendered more interesting, indeed more legible, when seen in the alien air and huge spaces of opera-house plateaux. Waltz and cracoviak were performed on toe-point. These impure numbers were called *demi-caractère*; soloists in big institutions like the Paris Grand Opera or the Petersburg Marie Theater specialized in this genre.[2]

The chief use of character-dancing at the present is in divertissements traditionally required in nineteenth century opera-repertory,

2. In a lecture delivered under the auspices of the Dance Teachers Guild of New York City, June 22, 1958, Igor Moiseyev, master of Russian character-dancing said:

"If we analyze the movement of the dance of any nation we find that, in its basis, each system of folk dance possesses only a limited number of different movements. The movements upon which is based the entire system of the dance we call root movements. If we know a number of fundamental movements, a number of the roots of which the language of the dance is composed, and are familiar with the laws of connecting movements, our own fantasy will make it possible to add a number of new movements which would belong in the same system.

This is exactly like knowing a number of basic words in some language and wishing to express a certain thought or emotion. We could make ourselves understood in such an instance by combining the words we know even though we had never come across a complete sentence appropriate to the occasion.

As a rule, root movements are extraordinarily simple. Complexity begins with the combining and uniting of movements. It is important to recognize root movements and to realize how the people vary, embellish and complicate these movements, combining them with other movements." (As reported in *Dance News,* September 1958) or in revivals of romantic-classic ballets. There are still ex-dancers, chiefly of Russian or Slavic extraction, who teach these dances, but they no longer greatly interest the younger generation of North American performers. The sources, to say nothing of the actual statement, have all the vitality of habitat groups in the Museum of Natural History or photographs of Holland and Norway in the *National Geographic Magazine*.

Spanish dancing is, strictly speaking, hardly 'character-dancing' within the international theatrical vocabulary, since the Iberian peninsula still holds a very ancient and elaborate idiom of its own, just as the peoples of South East Asia and Japan have their own brands of an academic classic dance, remote from ours but scarcely less exact or complex. Spanish dancing has a large body of steps, song, music, costume, style and tradition in performance which demands as much authority in execution as any other expressive idiom. It is a coherent and classic school with overtones of oriental sensibility and mystery from contact with the Moors in Spain. Some foreigners learn to perform it fairly well, just as some strangers learn to fight bulls, but the fact that they are not native to the manner is more interesting than how well they manage it.

However, it can now be amply demonstrated that the United States, unlike any non-Mediterranean or Central European country, has a veritable character-dance style and language of its very own, born in the present century, based on popular musical materials of five decades, attending the development of social-dance band music from rag-time through jazz to rock'n roll. In describing the Newport Jazz Festival of 1958, fourth in a series devoted to the performance of live popular music, *The New Yorker,* July 19, 1958, reported:

> Marshall Stearns, a jazz historian, gave an informed and amusing rundown on jazz dancing, which was illustrated with two dozen interludes by two remarkable dancers, Leon James and Al Minns, who seemed in motion even while standing stock-still, and who did the Cakewalk, the Shake Dance, the Camel Walk, the Eagle Rock, the Shimmy, the Charleston (several variations), the Jig Walk, the Lindy Hop, Trucking, the Suzy-Q (the Arthur Murray version, as taught in 1936, and the legitimate version), the Shorty George, the Big Apple, and a good many more. During the Big Apple (1938), a dance with sixteen separate steps, Minns executed a section in exquisitely slow motion, moving his arms and legs in a series

14

of spare swoops and wide steps, which sustained, for perhaps a minute, a liquid tension that was extraordinarily poignant and graceful. This was balanced by a dance called the Shag (1938), which consists of extremely fast, short steps, delivered while the dancer—stiff as a ramrod, his arms at a forty-five degree angle over his head—moves directly up and down like a lightning pile driver, and by the Apple Jack (1945), a dance done to bebop—a music with peculiarly nervous, oblique rhythms and melodies. . . . . .

While these dances, in one form or another, have been utilized year after year in Broadway musicals, reflecting the season's fads in public dance-halls, and while the social dance-bands of the pre- and post World War I era have developed increasingly into an aural virtuoso phenomenon far more to be listened to than danced to, nevertheless a few choreographers have used our jazz vocabulary with arresting effect, most notably Jerome Robbins. His great gift in manipulating popular steps both in the commercial speculative theater and in ballet repertory derives from his classic academic training and innate gifts as a performing dancer. His jazz ballets remain in repertory because they possess a strong formal structure and show, over and above their employment of characteristic steps and combinations, a strong personal attitude. The nature of so much American popular music is its steady uninterrupted ground-base plugged with startling eruptions of improvised cadenzas. Robbins has made sinister games and drugged duets that contain the atmosphere of street-corners at night where teenagers are disguised as ballet dancers, and dancers are domesticated delinquents. He has proposed spasms approaching hypnotic or self-induced exhaustion with fierce bursts of fancy footwork, by no means always funny. Robbins' ballets were designed for particular bodies and qualities of dancers who moved to jazz from having been born into it, as a Balinese child hears the gamelan, and who have also benefitted by schooling in an academic dance. Robbins has made true character-ballets, defining much of the characteristics of his time (mid twentieth century) and place (urban society). It is no easier to make a good jazz ballet than any other kind; possibly it is more difficult, as few choreographers take the trouble to inform themselves in the chaotic vocabulary of steps which seem to wipe themselves out from year to year, where the very persistence of a dance form stamps it as worn-out. But the exuberance of invention

15

piles up its own accumulated vocabulary for future cultivation.[3]

While the atmosphere of sport has enhanced a new definition of classicism in the projection of the academic tradition, borrowings from ball-games and field-sports don't much help character-dancing. The Moiseyev company of character dancers had a delicious energy, exuberance and physical freshness in all their dances from Russian provinces, fast or slow, and even in a number based on the city social-dances of the epoch of Tchekov. But when they performed in a number inspired by soccer, they had to resort to stiff doses of not very notable pantomime to hold it together.[4] Newspaper photographs of basket-ball players, traffic cops and tennis players are often captioned with some reference to 'ballet', but the resemblance makes sense only through purely accidental slices of action. Most ball games and competitive sports are designed for the efficiency of pushing human muscular capacity to physiological extremity; this is incidentally spectacular, but a designed legibility would hamper the economy of movement which is necessary to win games and break records. It may be interesting to watch games, however hidden the actual strain of muscle, but a dancer's aims are different. Legibility

3. "By the fall of 1913 America had gone absolutely dance-mad. The whole nation seemed to be divided into two equal forces, those who were for it and those who were against it, and even the champions of the cause had to compromise to stay in business. When 'ragtime' swept the country the one-step came right along with it, killing off the waltz and the two-step. A list of the popular dances of the time reads like a table of contents for a zoo, with the turkey-trot, the grizzly bear, the bunny hug, the camel walk and the lame duck." (*Castles in the Air*, by Irene Castle, as told to Bob and Wanda Duncan, Doubleday, 1958)

4. Moiseyev reported in the Soviet Embassy magazine *USSR* (No. 8: 23): "I consider *West Side Story* by Jerome Robbins really good theater, done with beauty and great skill."

Moskovsky Komsomolets, the organ of the Moscow Young Communist League was reported on August 27, 1958 to say that a taste for jazz is a step towards murder. In reporting a trial of four youths held for murdering a policeman, the New York *Herald Tribune* said:

"The Newspaper attempted to explain by saying that the good influence of school and factory where they work was wasted on the four youths who were *stilyagi*. The epithet comes from the Russian word for style and is applied to youths who favor extremely narrow trousers, rainbow-colored shirts and long jackets with padded shoulders.

The paper said their ultra-fashionable clothes caused ironic smiles at the factory and mockery from Y.C.L. members. The youths began to hang out with other *stilyagi* dancing rock'n roll with girls and drinking cocktails instead of vodka.

The Newspaper said the boys next lost all interest in work and Communist ideology and began listening to the Voice of America. They turned to crime to get money for foreign clothes and bootleg jazz records made out of old x-ray plates."

is as important to him as maximum audibility for a musician. If he is not seen in all his possibility, he does not exist. If he is only partly seen, he does not entirely exist. Classic ballet, within the limits of the proscenium frame, by restrictions of theater-vision and a seated audience, has its maximum legibility. Character dancing has a blunted legibility; its roughness helps it characterize a particular place or epoch; if generalized, or rendered Olympian, its special aura is lost.

CHOREOGRAPHY: Space- and time-patterns in several dimensions, historic, geometric, literary and spiritual of what dancers do, not alone traced as an itinerary on stage-floors, but throughout all the air of their cubed area. It is a fluid contrapuntal and polyphonic architecture of groups and individuals, each unit of which bears other separate but corresponding counterpoint and harmony to the various moveable parts—head, neck, arms, trunk, legs down through fingers and toes, to their several working anatomies. And all this musculated apparatus is organized on a floor of rhythmic sonorities, clothed and orchestrated in light and color.

CHOREOGRAPHER: A dance-designer; one who composes dance movement to music, in a variety of styles, all governed by his own vision or commentary on historic periods, including his own. He must ultimately be judged by his personal capacity for stylistic and formal analysis. This determines his gifts as an individual inventor, just as a solo dancer becomes known for certain idiosyncratic talents projected in performance, distinct from the passive anonymity, however correct, of the corps de ballet.

YOUNG CHOREOGRAPHER: A term used to signify anyone under forty-five who designs dances. Young, in this designation, is an honorary token. After a dance-designer reaches the age of thirty and is still known as 'young' there has been little evidence that he has much to show for himself except the repeated promise in delayed maturity. Careers of 'young choreographers' have often announced themselves by flashy bits of ballet; this is infrequently followed by a succession of works embodying a coherent vision, primarily about movement to music, although even secondarily about gesture or pantomime. Young choreographers rarely consider themselves as carpenters or cabinet-makers of the dance. They want to stay young forever, so they may be forgiven ineptness and praised for possibility. One is most grateful when a choreographer of any age, boy, middle-aged or older makes a serviceable suite of dances which can survive in repertory five years, that will serve as faithfully as a kitchen table. Carpenters of the dance are as scarce as genuine ballet-masters.

Young choreographers, or dancers who decide they should compose dances, tend to lapse into the limbo of disputable success at about the age of thirty plus. If they have not done it by then, they are unlikely ever to do it. There is not much surprise or cumulative development in this field. Just as first-dancers or ballerinas are born heirs-apparent, and never need in a nice democratic way to climb the ladder of slow if merited advancement, a ballet-master is heralded at the outset by the unmistakeable clarion of his own gifts. Certainly, with a young choreographer, signs of newness are confusing; smart tricks and sexy shocks may momentarily mask an absence of analytical instinct.

Lack of opportunity for any dancer of energy to compose dances in America does not obtain at this epoch. Choreographer's workshops, studio chums, or just a couple of other dancers of good will are always at hand to let their bodies be borrowed to be worked on by ambitious characters, generally feeble performers. These should be educating themselves in the rules of musical form, or looking at any pictures or sculpture (except Abstract Art) or reading science, poetry and mythology, but they are licensed to waste the time of their technically more gifted colleagues purely by the promise of novelty. New ballets of value are so rare; ones that actually work and persist, so valuable, that any hint of a chance for a win is blown up by the infectious blackmail in expectation. As between an inventor of pure blood and a craftsman of proven capacity, there is no choice: take both. But as for the Young Choreographer, you tell me how many of them over the last three decades are even capable dance-designers, however old or young they may be in wicked years.

BALLET MASTER: A choreographer who has assimilated the language of the traditional, academic, classic theatrical dance to about the same degree that a Liberal Arts college student with an M. A., or an interne with his M. D., have mastered their materials. A ballet-master is capable of dancing creditably himself, of giving instruction, of reading at least a piano-score, and of dominating a troupe of pro-

18

fessional dancers so as not to waste their time nor that of the company-management's, which must always be budgeted on union scales per hour; time and a half, overtime. Ballet-masters are trained dancers with good memories who are sufficiently well organized to approximate the repertory in which they have been trained, and able to reproduce it for dancers unfamiliar with it. But they are not to be confused with the veritable and excessively rare,

DANCING MASTER (*Maître à danser*): A choreographer whose gifts or developed talents make him (seldom, if *ever,* her), capable of imposing upon the entire field of Western spectacular dancing an individual manner, so that the repertory he has been able to call into being defines a dominant taste for his time. He is an inventor, finder and amalgamator of dance-steps, gestures and movements, adopting and adapting what has been transmittable from past masters, so that his own combinations are transmogrified into apparent novelty either by reformation or deformation.[5] Often, with a brilliant youthful talent, deformation, a reversal or turning inside out of the expected leads to fresh syntheses of old and new. By the distillation of metrical action and musical mimicry he also enlarges the given language of the dance while elevating standards of capacity in actual performance. He heightens the receptivity of the combined eye-and-ear of the entire audience. Only a master of dancing creates masterpieces of the dance by which the repertory extends itself for survival and revival, constantly tickling a public always avid for the unfamiliar. On the average, through the last three centuries, there have been in all about two masters to a generation. And in each century there has been one master who made the period's durable output virtually his own.

TRADITION: Relative to ballet there are at least two meanings. There is a handing down of instruction, descending uninterruptedly for some three centuries, and a chain of performance of a more or less extant repertory applicable to the last twenty-five years. The tradition in instruction means that successive generations of aspirants learn a language of exercises, steps, movements and combined gesture in order that their stage-performance be accurate, legible and brilliant. The models for this teaching are five basic elementary positions, exer-

5. J.A.D. Ingres: "Le tâche n'est pas d'inventer, mais de continuer."

cises, fragments from past works, clad in a variety of styles, fitting many musics. Just as an inherited accumulation of gathered information swells the body of law, medicine, musical notation and poetic metric, so a descent of irreductible constants and accretions on these, form a method for transmitting lore. What is now danced in public is what has been found useful to teach in private, increasingly meaningful and exciting through the annual theater seasons of centuries. This uninterrupted and developed tradition, supported by the flowering of the symphonic band and the formal organization of musical composition is continuously amplified by shots in the arm from popular sources (for us, jazz), as it was for our great-grandfathers by theatricalized folk dancing (the later waltz, polka, mazurka, polonaise, etc.).

Tradition in performance is, unlike teaching, discontinuous, always interrupted, depending upon shifts in the social structure, manners, accidents of historic taste and revivals, tensions and treaties between nations, exiles of minorities, class wars and colonial settlement, reformations and revolutions. As understood today, particularly by Britain, bulwark of feudalism in decline, tradition means correctness in the restoration of an older repertory. The traumatic experience of the initial appearances of the Diaghilev company in Western Europe placed an almost insupportable weight on succeeding generations of producers and has precipitated them into a deep double dilemma. Any new ballet has its instant of dewy freshness and novel shock. This impact comes from a combination of the performances of those dancers who first appear in it, and from the fact that it has never, as a whole, been viewed before. If it enjoys success, it must be exploited. Then, eventually, soon or late, the moment arrives for retirement, having exhausted an immediate audience; finally, every audience has its limits. Hence the appeal of every new work, however triumphant, has limits too. If and when it is revived, as part of 'tradition' it often falls into the custody of a ballet-master whose only energy is memory. Assuming that memory is impeccable, complete and imaginative rather than partial and approximate, which is normal, the first flash of impact can never really be recaptured, recreated, nor a first cast re-assembled. As in recent revivals by the Royal Ballet of early Stravinsky works, the initial landmarks of the Diaghilev era (*Firebird, Petrouchka*) many still living collaborators associated with the original productions of pre-World War I were convened. But, first of all, Stravinsky's considered re-scoring and his revisions were ignored. His partition in its first performance had scaled theatrical heaven and was not to be tampered with, even by its own author. Portions disavowed both by Stravinsky and Diaghilev, who generally seem to have known what they were doing, were 'restored' making the revived version even more original than the original. Surprise was registered that the resuscitation fell short of the recorded effect of the debut, since music was the same, decor and costume were more than the same, and the choreography, at least in the steps of the chief dancers, was 'exactly' the 'same'. Three things were not the same and never could be: the dancers themselves (originally Nijinsky, Karsavina, Bolm); the taste of the public already long modified by Diaghilev and Stravinsky; the historical moment with its new necessities, interests and answers. Tradition invoked was correctness documented. Vain hope. Here is no lively continuum but an invidious attempt to repeat the unrepeatable.

The liveliest tradition of our ballet was that which Diaghilev came to introduce through annual seasons of Parisian novelty, coinciding with the showing of new salons, of automobiles, dress-making, painting and sculpture. Through the agency of international music and the plastic arts based on Paris, through an important connection with great dress-making (Poiret, Paquin, Lanvin, Chanel) and originally the chamberlain's wand of Jean Cocteau, Diaghilev translated the researches of painters and composers into a living tradition of focussed surprise. Cocteau's role in all this has been vastly underestimated, except by himself. When in 1909, Diaghilev commanded the adolescent flâneur: *Amaze me,* it was an imperial ukase. Diaghilev knew well that astonishment was not merely amusement. *Etonnemoi*: and that parade started which has not yet entirely stopped.[6] Cocteau, for half a century, has been the metaphysician of novelty. More than any other poet, except Stravinsky, with whose career he has had important contact, Cocteau has affected our lyric theater in drama, dance and film. Starting as an amateur court jester disguised as an harlequin (whose social background was not unlike Diaghilev's), he has had himself canonized as a respectably disreputable academician with a career that is paradoxically consistent. Only

6. "Le célèbre mot: 'Etonne-moi', qu'il me dit, place de la Concorde, résume sa soif marcopolesque d'inconnu." (Jean Cocteau: *Encyclopédie du Théâtre Contemporain, Paris,* 1957, Vol. I: 1850-1914.)

Cocteau could say: "The principle of novelty becomes very difficult to recognize when our age forces us to remove from it its usual attributes of strangeness." Cocteau, for example, has had a far more influential role in the practicing world theater than Gordon Craig, whose position through history books looms larger, year by year, more shadowy and out of scale than his own unrealized renderings. Cocteau's divinations through Diaghilev channels imposed much of the quality of ballet taste and style which has become our commonplace. He spelled out the policy simply and early: the rehabilitation of the everyday, the use of magic in the ordinary; circus, cinema, choreography, or wherever the usual could be tricked by retouching into the humanly touching. Cocteau substituted a lyric contemporaneity for historic revivalism, the actual for the decorative: *Parade* (Satie-Massine-Picasso, 1917) in place of, for example *Le Pavilion d'Armide* (Tcherepnin-Fokine-Benois, 1909). He took the ballet out of the realm of bureaucratic administration and gave it hectic life from the boulevards, that busy Bohemia of *la fourmillante cité* which has been Paris' gift to the rest of the world at all times, even today. When we watch our jazz ballets in dungerees it is only an extension of the deliberately 'poor' style which Cocteau first tapped forty years ago.

STYLE: The lively classic tradition in performance depends upon the style in the dancing which is, like stoicism or elegance, a moral virtue. Individuals as well as companies can be recognized by particular qualities which, when analyzed, define their particular manner. The style of companies reflect their sponsorship, social, economic, personal and political. The style of soloists is determined by private character and temperament. An artist tries to frame a performance as a self-portrait in action distilled from dross, cut and polished to flash from fiery footlights like fifty diamonds in the face of helpless adoration. The conquest of untidy egotism, the elimination of self-consciousness, the ragged preoccupation with personal inadequacy, the denial of unsureness which renders watchers doubly insecure, and a visible concern in his public self for others, audience as well as colleagues on stage, mark the start of style. Then, with all technical considerations conquered or presupposed, begins to appear that graciousness easing all risk, disability or ineptness which is the dancer's free-will offering of a simulacrum of perfection. Its height is the most simple pleasure in pleasing. Selflessly, the artist gives his all

22

and it's not too much. Here is the ultimate gauge of elegance. It becomes the face or mask of individual style.

There are stylistic ornaments, some borrowed from history, others acquired in the present, affected or inherited, but none useless or merely decorative when great persons absorb them into their own rhetoric. The grand manner is elaborately transparent; it displays the purged personality like the insides of a glass anatomical model. The whole complex apparatus functions, but with self-illuminating light rather than vital juices. Grace seems to wipe out every trace of vulgar toil. In the reflection of this fierce inner glow the gratitude of audiences for revelations of super-human capacity dissolves in tears and cheers. The bravos of balletomanes mean: thanks for your elegance. You do what we hardly believe can happen. You are what we never can be. You redeem our meanness and weakness by hints of strength purified. Pardon our mortality by stillness in sound and unarrested action. In your balance is our chance.

Style is braided with manners, morals and morality. Manners indicate mutual concern, embracing a conservative tone determining the presentation of Self, its harnessing, pruning and cultivation. Ego is at the heart of style; the somatic energy in self must be granted its immediate and concrete expression. I must be seen and brightly; but how? As a master, with the manners of mastery. I am so marvelous, so capable, so full of potential that, in my performance, in all the betrayals of personal behavior bridging my purely acrobatic skills to fuse them as art, I must seem really kind, genuinely gracious, truly pleasing, relaxed, generous in an acme of attention to my partners and my public.

Distinction between the performance-manners of a ballet dancer, a bull fighter and a circus acrobat are matters of scale since all make motions determined by the limits of necessity. A circus-arena is circular and enormous; so is a bull ring. All eyes are riveted on defiance of gravity and death. The bodies in play are as vulnerable as they are essentially nude, but they find an impersonality from being at so great a distance from the watchers. The scale of presentation must be broad to be legible. In bull fighting, where some creature's death is always desired, manipulators are clad gloriously in raiment of heavy light; the sequins at once dehumanize and glorify the player. Concentration in the passes is terrific, but movement must be comparatively compact. The risk is so appalling that, to survive,

23

fighters diminish the apparent weight of danger by neatness; this makes it tolerable. Diminishment or deprecation adds up to nobility, disdain of hazard.

Ballet has its risks, too. Snapped Achilles tendons are no jokes; sprains and strains are the gorings of the dance. There is exhaustion, too, but unlike in rings for lions, tigers or bulls, death is not a present partner. Hence the style of physical domination is lighter, more transparent, sweeter and less stern. But there is parallel striving to reach pinnacles of spectacular intensity. Discipline, hazard and display are always in triangular polarity as factors to be refined, combined, calibrated and kept wide open. Elegance is laconic; ostentation is channelled as modest championship. Skill keeps its own secrets. The peak of ballet style strives toward power in all star performances, but lacking the iron needs of the bull fighter, some ballet soloists, if they are not constrained, topple over into sweeping effects more appropriate to the circus. On tanbark, this broadness is a normal response to necessity; in the opera house it seems pure selfishness, a flaccid style, swollen scale, bad manners. The big-star style veers easily towards parody, self-impersonation, the negative sincerity of burlesque and party-camping.[7]

STARS: First dancers hold a peculiar place in ballet repertory. Their position is hard to equate with stars of stage, screen or opera. There are relatively few starring rôles for the male specialist; he must content himself with divertissement, support of just fine dancing. Lady stars have their *Giselle, Swan Lake, Sleeping Beauty, Coppelia* and the few others. There is a received idea that Giselle is the Hamlet rather than the Ophelia of ballet. It is a charming two act work with a delicious score and a strong libretto. Anyone familiar with

7. Jim Brent, a British acrobat, described a Soviet circus-school over the BBC (August 21, 1958):

"In Moscow the circus school had just started. To this center came young people with talent and the right physique to be taught in the basic skills of circus. Their teachers were veteran performers, people with a rich experience, eager to pass on their accumulated knowledge to those following them. A stipend was paid to each pupil and academic subjects were fitted into the course. Many people saw the graduates of this school when the Soviet State Circus visited this country [England] recently. Perhaps, like me, they were struck with the neatness and grace of these artists; there is a ballet *barre* and mirror in every circus building in the Soviet Union. The circuses there are all permanent buildings with programmes running all the year round. The Russians are great circus lovers."

the correspondence surrounding its original collaboration knows that the great poets responsible for its book had their tongues firmly in cheek while they worked it up. Notwithstanding their witty canonization of an epoch in European taste, the work has become, thanks to the keepers of the true flame of ballet tradition, sacrosanct. It is also commercially powerful as a star-vehicle. It is the hereditary property of whatever ballerina can claim legitimate descent from the first 'romantic' ballerinas. In our memory, the line is conceded to stem from Anna Pavlova, to have included Spessiva, whom few in the West saw but who seems to have been the best if poets and painters are to be believed. When you see *Giselle* today it is not easy to know whom you really see, since there is always a double or triple-exposure of shadowy precedents. It is the star rôle par excellence but it seldom glows with genuine individual incandescence. The currently starring star is fated to borrow an ancestral prestige from all those who have shone before her. As she adopts the romantic hair-do, she assumes the habit of an order. So it remains a real test for an intelligent dancer, because there is a lively tradition to buck, or accommodate. Of course it may be said that many in the audience know none of this; to them, Pavlova is as remote as Taglioni or Elssler, and Spessiva does not exist. This is true, but it is also true that the ikons of the great ones of the past are very much alive in the minds and imaginations of reigning stars, and in those of the critics who prepare their images; those images blackmail as much as they inspire. Often they even cloud individual identity and jealously prevent a good artist from knowing who she really is.

Sometimes audiences identify the special language of the classic dance in its many facets of formal, informal and deformed styles with the personal idiosyncrasies of individual performers. It is sometimes difficult not to confuse dances with dancers. Serge Lifar thought that he invented *Apollon Musagète*. Many among the public even have the notion that a strong solo performer designs his or her own variations. This is only true to the degree that a clever choreographer will try his best to show off certain qualities or specialities calculated to fit a given temperament and body, rather than to impose an arbitrary expression of his own which might be against the star dancer's idea of himself or herself. Balanchine invented *Apollon* on orders from Diaghilev to create a star out of a splendid body that had little training in the orthodox classic dance. That such a tour de force also embodied the greatest modern rôle for a male dancer indicates the capacity of this choreographer, then twenty-three years old.

The more overweening the personal stamp of a star, the less relation he or she has to the company in which he or she appears. All most stars want is a concentrated chance to display breath-taking excercises. Weak dance-designs are sometimes salvaged, if rarely distinguished, by personal insistence. Many ephemeral compositions are contrived not as patterns interesting or lasting in themselves, but as expedient space-suits for popular jumping-jacks. In most ballets, apart from frank divertissements, which content most stars, their very presence may flatten out other aspects of the choreography if it has much intrinsic interest. The ballerina exists, not to demonstrate ideas of art, but herself: instrument and personality. This is acknowledged in most ballet-programming at least once an evening. It is natural for stars to prefer flashy brief numbers, starting slow, building to fast, ending in a dazzle to reap their rousing reward. The chief use of a star in repertory is to set a standard of execution at which competitors and aspirants aim. A star-turn is important on the evening's bill of fare. It allows other members of the company to relax through one whole ballet. It sharpens the eyes of the audience in a heightened focus on a single body or pair of bodies. It instructs the eye of the public into a dissection of what actually goes on in the basic vocabulary of the classic academic dance. It presents in small units, those chords and clusters combined and employed through multiple moving bodies which is the stuff of dance design.

It is almost impossible, however, for stars once more or less securely set in ballet's firmament to accept repertory rôles. Somehow, no part of newness seems ever really to fit them. New rôles have no precedent and each one has its logistical presumption of failure. Stars are helped to think of themselves as souls apart, locked in their private specialties, only pleased to display those aspects of their personality which they have lazily selected. This does not make them easy or grateful in working for a choreographer, who may have different and even broader ideas of what they might well do. Since stars know in advance what they want to look like in addition to what they want to do, it doesn't leave much room for a dance-designer. The worst of it is that pretexts for dictated vehicles don't add up to much in repertory, except in those 'dramatic' or 'psychological' ballet-pantomimes where emoting replaces dancing. But it is too much to expect that stars should be modest or analytical; would we adore them as much if they were?

It would seem normal that dancers have realistic ideas about ballets in which they appear; this is often true if it refers to them, individually. Stars consider almost any choreography composed without them in mind, and indeed without them uniquely in mind, uninteresting. They cannot be bothered with standard repertory. When they can be persuaded to perform in it, which happens now and then mostly for emergency reasons, they are not very rewarding since they have performed the rôles too infrequently to realize the most that can be derived from them.

It has been said that stars are born, not made, and that audiences, not managements, make stars. Both are true. And stars are useful as long as they are good dancers. As one Broadway director replied when told to hire a Hollywood name: Look, I have nothing against stars, if they can act. Stars are splendid, particularly when they have pretty manners, do not give offensive personal interviews and make few demands which the management cannot fulfill. But, alas, there is a professional deformation or occupational hazard, not confined by any means to ballet alone, but present in baseball, bull fighting, opera and every performing art. A self-generating egotism based on the awareness of special skills mastered, often manifest in ballet by an excessive sweetness or 'modesty' which can be a heavier bludgeon than brass knuckles, takes over. The persona, the self-awarded mask becomes the real iron puss. Stars begin to believe their personal press-agents. The self is won away from the fragile concept of balance in perfection that keeps great artists both on their toes and on their track. The greatest talent of the Thirties, at an unpardonably early age, turned into an ex-dancer who impersonated herself; grotesque, wasteful and very sad.

INVENTION: A term often confused with Creation, Originality or Novelty. In the Age of Faith, the word Creation, and its parent Creator, was a theological appellation with strict limits. It referred to Lord God, Creator of Heaven and Earth, before Whom there was no thing; or else the range of great nature brought into being, balance and movement through His Will. Later, in the Renaissance, a new artistic device was *trovata*, a finding, not a creation. Vasari praised the gifts of eminent masters as *belli invenzioni*, fair findings or fresh handlings. Towards the end of the Age of Reason such terms as Creative, Creativeness and Creativity corrupted the idea of the irreversible fact of a Prime Mover, from which all other moving and ordering is organized. As creation was from God, to be creative was deemed god-like. Artists became god-like creators. Craftsmen disappeared into self-expressors who created their own autobiographical myths, although there is no evidence that many artists, and particularly young choreographers, are even masters of a craft let alone of an art. Artists are now expected to make newness by projecting their selves, instead of redistributing observable elements according to their gifts, their energy to develop these gifts, the taste of their time and the needs of the ballet-repertory at a given moment. Talent to whatever degree of ignorance or indiscipline, since it belonged to the same big family of energy shared by the god-like masters, has been assumed to possess some unique and absolutely qualifying authority.

Invention, meaning to come upon (among much phenomenon), or discover, or sometimes rediscover, not from nothing, but from what is given or available to find, has been confused as creation in our massive dragnet for novelty. In ballet-repertory, a new work is novel to the degree that its elements have not been seen before, or recently, by a given public, in this form. In ballet, in our time, novelty has been recognized as a healthy or tasty inversion, a systematic or even apparently haphazard reversal of the academic or expected: broken phrases, deliberate denial of suavity, silence for sound and rest where movement would ordinarily have been awaited. One of the advantages of the iron-maiden of classic academic instruction is the violent launching towards a new liberty impelled by breaking its rules. But too often, shock in surprise is an end. It's hard to be surprised twice running if the only virtue in astonishment is the unexpected. The hope of every novelty is to remain in repertory. When analyzing the creativeness of a contemporary creator, it is useful to tally up his total number of works currently in use and their respective longevity, rather than the whole roster of first performances for which he has been responsible.

It will astonish few familiar with the story of theatrical dancing to find that while originality is the sine qua non of a dancing-master, this newness consists finally of neither shock nor surprise. True originality is rarer than uranium, and like it generates enormous power for influence in both positive and negative directions. Invention, apart from its essential drive towards discovery, uncovering or recovering is also dependent on the gift for designing consistent and fluid movement in continuous sequence, equations of joined or disjunct physical phrasing. The true inventor has an over-all concept of an audio-visual totality in composition, based on his analysis of the governing music, and a power to move many bodies about a stage with as much ease and freshness as the separate parts of a single dancer's body move by themselves in balance with its whole. It is this wholeness of mortised parts inlaid in the stylistic cabinet, which by its transparent clarity of structure demands to be looked at with skinned eyes, that stamps the master craftsman long after its initial unfamiliarity has worn away.

An original work, as opposed to one in which there is a studding of novel morsels set in a commonplace bed, is a self-illuminated whole which maintains its equilibrium by a conviction or a revelation of a chosen palette or serial octave of human movement which is parallel (one of unnumbered parallels) to the basic musical impulse. True originality refocuses the attentive eye, not alone on a new ballet, but after this has become domesticated, extending the whole language of moving on stage. It subtly modifies the rest of the repertory as well which becomes lit with a new light, appears in a new perspective, and serves as a point of departure, as one of many origins for further useful and even original works.

THE DANCER: He or she is the unit of human capacity which makes ballet possible in performance. The dancer's professional training may be equated with that of the medical interne; army, navy or air-corps cadet; divinity or law-student, piano player or bronze founder. That is, dancers must submit their bodies (and minds) to a specialized, rigorous and competitive discipline for at least ten years. This discipline is partly acrobatic, musical (either conscious or instinctive) and to a degree greater than is commonly recognized by the great public, moral, since it involves hard choices about the usual pleasures of youth.

Young dancers have no time for anything much but dancing in order to emerge at an age very much earlier than most masters of a craft, capable of activity immeasurably beyond those not so trained, and of making their living by it. Apart from a dancer's innate gift of potential virtuosity, which he or she is granted at the outset and which alone justifies the servitude of preparation—aside from a fair appearance (straight legs, small head, small hips, facial features either interesting in themselves or capable of being made so), inborn musicality and some (not a lot) of analytical intelligence—there is that supreme extra, but indispensable gift of being able to know how to exploit the (ultimately) comparatively few talents that are ever grudgingly given to any one person. The tragedy in lack of fulfillment of many aspirants is their inability to push their few real assets into that unique extremity which tests their triumph. How few artists of any sort recognize their identity; how few can tell you when you ask them with final exasperation: who do you think you *are*? An artiste? A dancer? A worker in theater? A lover of the Dance? A plumber? Me: who, ME? Yes, you.

The failure to risk identity is finally the failure of energy, physical and moral. A girl of fourteen pleads with her parents to let her go to the big city for advanced training: Darling mummy, dearest daddy, all I want to be is a brainless ballerina. That she was far from brainless goes without saying, for early, but at an age crucial to the dancer, she had already made her well-informed, realistic choice.[8] No college-education to fit the home-maker; no proms; no dating (or not much); not much fun as ordinarily understood by teenagers; little togetherness. Virgil Thomson says dancers are autoerotic and have no conversation. That they possess a special temperament is true, and if they do not feel eminently suited to their life which is a secular retreat, they will be, however accidentally endowed, unhappy in it. Either they cannot stick out the training or they may take an easier route. With what they have managed to pick up in studios, combined with what ambition they have been able to husband, they can carry their little bundle of craft into the squalid routine of musical comedy, television or the deadly drudge of the Broadway hit-or-flop. In the one you die of boredom; in the other you don't eat. Dancers outside the classic, academic theatrical dance are in a separate category. Today you don't find many younger students de-

8. "Baseball is an endless chain of unconscious actions. A batter's swing is composed of reflexes. Once he started to think he'd be as lost as a ballet dancer starting to think. She'd wind up in the orchestra pit. Students of the sport claim that the only ballplayer who was master of his reflexes was Ty Cobb. He was thinking sixty seconds per minute." (Arthur Daley, The New York *Times,* September 23, 1958)

termined to make a career in the so-called 'modern' dance. Those who enter it take this vocation comparatively late. They are not un-like lay-analysts who for a variety of reasons, good and bad, cannot stand the long internship or long residency in institutions that tradi-tion determines. Some dancers stand on the periphery of theater just as some therapists on the brink of medicine.

A ballet-dancer's training includes the assimilation, indeed the mastery of boredom in repetitious practice, excercise, rehearsal; prac-tice, exercise, rehearsal; practice, exercise, rehearsal. They must ab-jure a 'fascinating' social and personal life or anything approaching that dissipation which would be useful education for poets, but which would prevent prompt attendance at early morning practice, exercise or rehearsal. In Colette's marvelous novel, Chéri taunts his icy wife, then busying herself as a volunteer hospital superintendant, when she won't cuddle snugly in bed. "It's as if I'd married a ballet-dancer. Nine o'clock sharp, the Class: it's sacrosanct. It has to come before everything else."

What keeps dancers going (and there is that point of no return when passed; like a ship launched, you can't stop it), is a one-tracked dedication to an increasingly less vague idea of perfection in performance. This standard must finally be set by the individual dancer alone; only he or she can know of what he or she is ultimately capable. Sometimes they will be surprised, not always agreeably. The higher the aim, the nearer approached (and every useful memoir of a famous dancer's career is filled with sincere and convincing admis-sions of various degrees of failure at each epoch of their careers), the more intense the self-competition. No records of speed, honors or dollars are inscribed on class-room or rehearsal-room walls to in-spire their surpassing. There is no four minute mile to smash. One does not go on practicing year after year because Mount Everest is *there*. The dancer's energy, like that of other artists when possessed by the muse rather than the self, is somewhat akin to the talent for indignation in saints and martyrs, a longing towards super-service or super-performance, approaching divinity in execution. Why are su-preme opera-singers hailed *diva*? Why is Maria Callas veritably *La Divina*? Why was Sarah Bernhardt recognized *divine*? And to make masochism more maddening, dancers must always be at the mercy of choreographers to whom they entrust themselves. They remain the creatures of the choreographer, but without them he is hamstrung.

31

The dancer's career is not viewed kindly by that American family who is depicted as the core of our country, backbone of TV, supermarkets, automobiles and eaters of mass-media, except those who have been sufficiently tenderized by television to bank on a chance for a quick Hollywood contract for home-grown starlets. Infants are mildly abused all over the nation by unscrupulous teachers who force toddlers up on toe-point about as fast as they can talk, and trick them out annually in pink and green recital tarletans (of nylon) for toe-tap or baton-twirling routines. Most of these kids, some of whom might have had promise, are wrecked for any practical purpose but cheer-leading by the time they are ten.

While professional dancers make a poor to fair living, they can teach long and quietly after they quit the stage, and their stage career is quite long. If you start from sixteen to eighteen, you can dance anyways for more than twenty years. It is a craft naturally determined by the physical ebullience of youth but the greatest performers are those well along in their thirties; ripeness is all. Very few dancers persist in their hard lives from any false hope of high pay. They dance because they are possessed by the gods or demons of dancing. They dance because they want to. Security is not a consideration. They throw their lives away and find them. Naturally, any cautious parent would worry, but dancers eat more regularly (and a great deal more) than other artists (painters, sculptors, poets, composers). They are healthier, support themselves sooner, are cleaner and live longer.

The problem of the young male dancer in the United States is awkward. In Soviet Russia today, as in other countries where the state assumes responsibility for the talents of those children who may be expected to bring them glory, irrespective of their parent's capacity to pay (artists, as well as scientists), boy dancers have long worn the same style of uniform as military or navel cadets. The only distinction is in the collar insignia; dancers wear lyres, sign of Great Apollo, Leader of the Muses, rather than crossed rifles or anchors, the badge of Mars or Neptune. In America, where skills at speculative ball-games are fixed at a premium past any other human capacity, dancing to good music on a stage has an effete smell. A talented youth, unless, he happens to come from a theatrical or musical family, or one so low in the social structure that even dancing is some sort of advancement, must kill his parents, symbolically at least, if

32

he is finally to achieve his heart's desire. It would be better for most artists, except novelists, to be orphans. For the Dance there is the crucial moment in the ritual encounter: "Son, if you persist in this folly you will Kill Your Mother." Mother rarely allows the same for Dad, but it would, be more honest if she did. The worst of it is that by the time Son has had the sense to blast this blackmail, the guts to leave home and get a job operating an elevator to pay for his lessons, he will be too old to profit by them. The very few brilliant (i.e. well-trained) male dancers bred in the West have all had, by some fluke or another, ten or more years of hard training before they were twenty. To make matters worse, the army demands its pound of flesh, and while some boys get themselves deferred, it is the rule that the best young dancers must waste two years at the very instant when they could be serving their country far more usefully, appearing in State Department tours to impress our hoped-for allies with our spiritual superiority.[9]

The prejudice against male dancing (which never extends to high-paid performers in variety, TV, films or Broadway, or to visiting British or Russians) has its roots in the position of the Ballerina in the last century. By 1850 male soloists were reduced to almost no activity but supporting ladies; they were called porteurs and transported girls about the stage. The men became so uninteresting that they were replaced by other girls who were dressed in men's uniforms. Opera ballet had whole categories of performers *en travestie*. Girls look good in tights. Ballets, such as those enlivening the first famous extravaganzas that were shown in this country (*The Black Crook*, 1866; *The White Faun*, 1868) gave our great-grandfathers and their young sons a serious trauma. The women were painted hussies to be sure, but those boy-things were straight from Sodom. Girls they

9. In a brilliant article analyzing the national interest in watching sports, Edward L. Rousseau wrote in "The Great American Ritual" (*The Nation*, October 4, 1958):

"Unlike basketball or football, the so-called national game (baseball) does not have the nostalgic association with high school or college days glanced at above. Like any ritual which has not degenerated into a relic, it is a unifying factor in society, imitating real life and yet different from it. The comparison sometimes made with ballet is false. The center of interest both in sports and in American life is a compulsive concern with what the score is. You don't keep score at the Ballet Russe—one reason why the American male is not at home there, in spite of the appetizing scenery. The world of professional athletics is as remote from the everyday round of American life as any art form, but sport—while sufficiently exotic to serve as an escape—appeals to a motive that is immediately intelligible. . . ."

might be, but they were called "ballet-boys." "I'd rather see my daughter (son) *dead* than on the stage." These atavistic, murderous, half-voiced and half-remembered sentiments still obtain among a majority of families who could easily provide as good boys as they have, grudgingly indeed, good girls. They deprive that department of the dance of what is perhaps its greatest glory since the man's body is capable of athletic extension denied the (mechanically) weaker sex.

Only with the emergence of the Russian Ballet in Western Europe before the 1914 war, did our time catch the first breathless astonishment of dancing men, perhaps unequalled at any epoch before or since. And ironically enough, the appearance of the boy dancers of the Moiseyev folk-ballet on American TV in the winter of 1958 may have accomplished more than anything else in showing the mass-public how good youths can look if given the full chance to be well schooled. Ted Shawn in our Twenties and Thirties did pioneer work on an evangelical rather than an aesthetic level. His men were strong and athletic. But flexed deltoids are only a superficial apology for male dancing; elegance is the real criterion. Americans now understand elegance in small foreign cars, cravats, sports-clothes, TV cabinets and the typography of luxury-advertising.

Contemporary male Soviet ballet-dancers (as distinct from their character-dancers) are strong as weight-lifters; indeed this is the way they are mostly used. The whole climate of native Russian ballet is retardative, even in its vast efficiency; men are generally considered as carriers or mimes, just as in the mid nineteenth century. Nijinsky was exiled from the Imperial Theaters. He made his great reputation not in Russia, but in the West.

In the best dance-theater, there is a polarity of male and female on an equal see-saw of elegance and muscularity. The power of the male for leaps in the lateral conquest of space sets off the softness, fragility, speed and multiplicity of the ballerina's action on pointe and in the sustainment of held, breathless equilibrium. Male dancers make girls more feminine and vice versa.

THE AUDIENCE: Lacking the patronage of princes, a privy purse or state subsidy, audiences in the United States (but not in Europe) are what finally pay for the ballet. Ballet is now far too expensive to support for single patrons even with means, as was the rule for three centuries. And Diaghilev had a devilish time finding enough

34

money even for his earliest seasons. Nor is this to say that a ballet-company costs more annually on the basis of its service than a symphony orchestra, opera company, library or museum. Actually, a first-class company playing forty weeks of work a year, maintaining a fairly progressive policy of commissioning new works, keeping the old ones spick and span (sweat rots clothes fast), paying the artists at least on the minimum union level, needs about $100,000.00 a year over and above an approximate $1,000,000.00 gross. In America, ballet is just on the brink of being institutionalized. Ballet, like Shakespeare, Verdi and Beethoven must be institutional, public-service theater. (The public in one way or another even has to pay for the housing of Raphael and Degas.) Ballet is not speculative theater, like Broadway, where people buy shares hoping for hits. Ballet can more than make its own way if it has a revolving fund for an intelligent management to play with. Ballet has partially supported itself, and also very handsomely those entrepreneurs who import foreign troupes. Native managers don't much like the native product. Native companies lack the selling prestige of the appellation Royal or even National. It's hard to sell the provinces without a massive commercial organization. The condition for the expansion of ballet into a future situation worthy of its great capacity, by the coherent and comprehensive training of a dancer-pool from all over our nation, like the training offered by the new Air Corps Academy, and a logical program for the commanding and production of new works, as well as the steady maintenance of a superior trained personnel, can never be assured. Most Americans don't care, and those who do can't pay. Yet there are signs that the fascinated audience (sometimes stated to be larger in number than the gross public for live ball-games) having at least tasted a promise of development, might mobilize itself into annual support for organizations with attractive programs and policies, who are capable of guaranteeing dancers a year-round job, and who know what history has taught them about repertory, its revival and renewal. There are at least three kinds of audiences: a general public, a special public and a critical one.

THE GENERAL PUBLIC includes those who like theatre in its multiformity, including music, drama, sport, films and Shakespeare. They are, by and large, unprejudiced, attentive, if not habitual customers, and promptly throb to broad or massive effects without demanding, or indeed noticing refinement in detail. Like those ignorant of chronology, to them the past is simultaneous. They neither know nor care which choreographer anticipated which, or if ballet is actually Russian, British, or American. They are satisfied with what appears to be technical prowess and they applaud obediently if a single movement, no matter how simple or tiresome, is repeated more than three times. To them, apparent physical fireworks are more satisfactory than energy robed in elegance. They like wide stages filled with scads of dancers moving more or less in unison to a strong beat and swinging tune, hoked up with costumes and scenery that cost money. Some of them develop into a more responsible

SPECIAL (or BALLETOMANE) PUBLIC which corresponds to opera lovers, boxing, baseball or bull fight enthusiasts. These have strong personal preference in dancers, companies and choreographers, and share a passion for the performance, if neither the art nor science of stage-dancing. They loyally attend first-nights of new seasons and new works, providing an electric social air of anticipation, although their initial reaction to a debut is frequently ambiguous and insecure. They have endless good-will and always expect a smash-hit which justifies or corroborates their interest in being in the theater just ahead of the great indiscriminate audience. They are by no means sure that they know what they like. If a season has been latterly distinguished by a 'new' score of Igor Stravinsky (his twenty-first in nineteen years) this serves as standard. Here is gilt-edged security. Correspondingly, they may be shocked (well, yes, *shocked*) by a new number to music by John Philip Sousa, previously tagged as a hack of military marches. This balletomane public is custodian of serious and significant ballet, conservative at core, constituting itself guardian of tradition, which means they identify excellence with past performances they may have seen or happen to remember. They have no knowledge of the idiom or vocabulary of the classic dance, even to the extent of some of them snapping photographs, painting abstracts or playing the piano. They should be made to pay, but it is too much to expect that they will pay well.

THE CRITICAL PUBLIC numbers among it poets, painters, musicians, journalists, diplomats, dentists and lovers of fine furniture, gardens, dogs, books and cooking, who bring to their observation of theatrical dancing some schooled sensual analysis from the parallel criteria of their own vocations or avocations. A working background in architectural logic and style, musical history and composition, poetic metric or landscape gardening enables a member of this specialist public to make responsible judgment past mere enthusiasm or accidental personal revelation, without in any way removing the 'pleasure' from a performance. There is a common American superstition that if you know too much about an art you will be deprived of that first fine rapture which absolves you from learning anything more about it. You cannot know too much. Few people who don't know anything about it *do* know what they like. They can't, because their eyes and ears are only open to a surface slice of spectacle. However, they need to be far less instructed in the particulars of the classic dance, the various names of steps or combinations, than about the existence of skill in other art or craft. If one has a qualitative opinion about a new office-building that pretends to be monument rather than shelter, if one recognizes the difference between two civic orchestras, and if one honestly cares about The Dance (many do not; why should they?), chances are that this unit of the critical public does actually know what he likes, that how he likes it is not small talk, and that if he likes a certain new work it will probably be continued in the repertory until it has a chance to be generally inspected. There are also

CRITICS, in the formal or professional sense, those who are paid for their opinions of performances; these also form a division of every audience—general and special. Critics are working journalists who earn their living by servicing each group, reporting for the daily, weekly and monthly press, and for less than half-a-dozen high-brow quarterlies, all of whom feel an urge to encourage dancing and dancers if they possibly can. Very often they are music critics on detached service. It would make more sense to let art-critics cover choreography, since in spite of a musical base it is essentially a visual matter; just as some painters are tone-deaf, so many musically trained writers are form and color blind. Professional critics are neither very discriminating nor very harmful; the weekly press takes its tone meekly or lazily from the daily press; the weekly recapitulations in the two most influential New York papers make the most sense and can be read as the record over the years, allowing for over-generosity in the encouragement of secondary activity, which is legitimate educationally and from charitable aspects. The audience—general, special and critical—over the last decade has come to by-pass the working critics who are read more for curiosity or corroboration than for advice. Individual poor notices of a new ballet cannot kill it to the same degree that a play is assassinated by the two major New York drama critics. Apathy in personal conviction is greater in the field of speculative theater. People don't want to be wrong about an investment, but they can exercise a modicum of personal preference when money is not involved; everyone knows new ballets are a dead financial loss, although some of them have their triumph through survival in repertory.

In our provinces, critics advise but are not able to fill a theater unless the program contains *Swan Lake*. Some provincial critics have a ferocious local reputation; this is a reflection of the area's vacuum: we love Teacher, she's so mean, particularly to all those phonies from foreign parts who are trying to put something over on us. The provinces do not suffer novelty with patience. Poets make the best critics and always have. Baudelaire, Gautier, Mallarmé, Claudel, Cocteau, Yeats, Marianne Moore, Carl Van Vechten, Edwin Denby have written words that transcend reportage and achieve a poetic permanence in fixing the ephemeral. It is the nature of poets to observe closely. Their pleasure in finding words which are equivalents of action, their precise sense of a verbal image related to visual pattern and musical form make their memoirs delightful, even illuminating. But poets do not often make very good journalists, and the more careful they are with their words and ideas, the less likely they are to fulfill the requirements of workaday journalism and the demands of the city-desk. Poets don't write about news in the dance, but the essential residue, if any, that stays in their minds, and in the echoing minds of parts of the public, after an event has ceased to be novelty and becomes history.

Historians of the dance are more archivists than critics; they record but rarely vitalize performance. Most of their researches are simple antiquarianism, useless to choreographers whose business is not archeological gossip but invention. A smug and obedient revivalism is no substitute for a search for new steps nor are documents proof of successful reinterpretation. Except for a few chronicles in the high-brow quarterlies, ballet has been spared that ratiocination which smothers famous literary figures, substituting free fantasy on themes from Kafka, Joyce, Proust, Melville, James, D. H. Lawrence, etc., for attention to the intention of the authors. Ballet won't stand still long enough to be mauled.

It is sometimes feared that the critical audience or its journalistic voice, issuing snap judgments from which there is no appeal, determines the span of a novelty at its debut. There is infrequent correspondence between what many journalists write at first and what the general public ends up by liking later, if the new work under observation has any genuine claims to invention, newness or originality, which few works ever have. The general amorphous and unconsidering audience ends up by liking, after a certain period of repeated exposure to the novel ballet, (it may take years; the dancers who first made it may have quit the scene), choreography of the greatest internal consistency, vitality and strength of structure. Durability does not depend upon a debut.

Time and *The New Yorker* are so committed to the wise-crack and their idiosyncratic rhetorical tone that their comment on dancing is only news-worthy. This is odd, since the reporting on horse-racing, popular music, architecture, science, even politics have high degrees of professional capacity. Both magazines are famous for the dim visibility of their art-coverage; *The New Yorker* is rather worse, since *Time* makes no bones about its mass-soothing Philistinism. Reports from great cities of the world in *The New Yorker* are written by observers of care and conscience; its critics of painting, sculpture, serious music and the dance are incompetent; that is, they are not equipped with the materials of the craft which they attempt to judge. Their air of smug domestication, the reduction of any unfamiliar sight or sound to patronizing intimacy, dismissal past damnation, is the exact reflection of the style of luxury-advertising copy for which the magazine now chiefly exists. A recent English critic called Stravinsky's last ballet, written at the age of seventy-five, 'experimental.' He was referring to the score; he had not then seen it performed. *Agon* is not an experiment; it is a masterpiece. But this is characteristic: Stravinsky innovated; he must have experimented. He still innovates, hence, he must still 'experiment.' How experimental can you get? Critics who serve the drain of audience apathy are recommended by their own looseness. If there was not this exact equation they would not hold their jobs, as the mass public can only swallow a drop at a time.[10]

For the last twenty-five years, from a variety of sources—musical comedy, films, television, ballet itself—the general public has been provided with a very eclectic repertory of permissive taste, all the way from revivals of nineteenth century full-evening, triple-length 'classic' monuments to free-form concert-recital 'modern' dances. The general public might not be able to answer a quiz-program based on ballet but one way or another they have seen a lot of it, and neither ice-skating nor modern-dance have won out as popular favorites. Theatrical dancing to most people means the academic classic dance. Ballet, beyond about five couples is quite lost on TV, but it must finally come to terms with popular theater or it can't afford to exist, as its apparatus is so costly to maintain. This was the prime fallacy of the Modern Dance. It thought it was too grand for the gross public. This public is blessed in its ignorance. It no longer expects any fulfillment of a preconceived formula. The special public can be more upset than any other since it feels it knows what is and what is not *the* ballet. The general audience just thinks good ballet is good dancing and is often right.

RUSSIAN BALLET: Formerly, dance-spectacle as organized at the Imperial Czarist courts in Petersburg and Moscow, ca. 1750-1910, founded on French, Italian, Scandinavian and Central European models, but with excellent native specialists starting from ca. 1865. Then, 1909-29, the dance and musical repertory called into being by Serge Diaghilev, the emigré aristocrat and ex-amateur bureaucrat of the Imperial Theater in Petersburg, with overwhelming influence on painting, music and theater in London, Paris and New York. Then, 1930-45, the exploitation in dilution of this repertory by his direct heirs in Europe and America, with notable additions invented

10. When *Agon* was presented by the Royal Ballet in London, compulsively but perfunctorily, with a cast augmented beyond the indications of its composer, *The Times* (August 28, 1958) continued the loyal service of the official press to this master, unaltered through fifty years: ". . . But there are limits to penury of invention if a choreographer is to make a satisfactory pattern of movement. *Agon* represents bankruptcy of melodic invention, which was anyhow never Stravinsky's strong point, disintegration of rhythm, which was once his forte, and collapse of texture, which is his principal interest in musical composition. Mr. MacMillan [the choreographer] has somehow made bricks without straw, a silk purse out of a sow's bristles. . . . It is true that it could have been better played . . . but it would need more rehearsal than the music is worth . . . for the ballet is a total loss."

by his final collaborators. Now, (1925 to the present), the establishment and repertory of the State Academies of the Classic Dance in Leningrad and Moscow, of massive splendor, prowess, efficiency and security but which bear absolutely no effect of the revolutions in music, painting and choreography exercised for our era by Stravinsky (left Russia, 1914); by Picasso (entered Russian collections, ca. 1909 but then unshown for forty years), or by Balanchine (left Russia, 1924). The institution of ballet in Russia presently enjoys the highest political and diplomatic prestige. Foreign statesmen make mandatory visits to the Bolshoi Theater to meet and greet the ballerinas and have their pictures taken, which does not happen at either the opera or drama. Contingents of dancers from the Bolshoi pool are sent east and west as prime examples of Soviet cultural achievement. But the Soviet ballet (and theater), after the fall of Lunacharsky, the first and only (from our standpoint) progressive minister of education, has been cut off from any international advance-guard movements since about 1930. Contemporary Russian taste in the plastic arts, music and architecture is a blank vulgarization of the retrograde official taste of 1890, which was then already provincial, except for small liberal circles in Petersburg, compared even to Rome or Berlin at the same period.

If unlimited government subsidy, social security, a great personnel pool to draw on, political necessity and selfless concentration in administration can accomplish high art, the Soviet ballet can be said to lead the world, nor need it heed the West's strictures that it is also the bald expression of gross style and brutal taste. For purposes of domestic policy, refinement has been of slight use. Character-dancing, as witness the Moiseyev company, is excellent. Long stretches of operatic pantomime are executed with a conviction and detail known nowhere else in the world, except Japan, where the tradition is older, more stylized and far more interesting. To Western eyes there is a heaviness in the women (except for those two stars Europe has been permitted to see) and a lack of imaginative approach which characterizes our own comparative material poverty with all its gentle elegance and intellectual piquancy. The Russians have the real sputnik-style; is it an index of our self-indulgent decadence and general decline?

However, there is evidence that the Russians themselves are not entirely happy with all they do. This has come to light as their companies make foreign tours and are forced to face up to international developments that have proliferated outside the Iron Curtain for the last quarter century, to say nothing of the still active effects of Diaghilev. Under Lunacharsky, who tried to persuade him to return and head the state theaters, the October Revolution stood for the international advance-guard in theater, dance and film. Meyerhold, Goleizovsky and Eisenstein had not yet been immolated. After all, it was not the United States that offered Isadora Duncan, the most famous dance-revolutionist of her era, a state-supported school; it was the Russia of Lenin, who had first hailed her in the days of the 1905 revolution.

We have seen in Russia, Czarist as well as Soviet, that intellectuals and artists were not only expendable but were a recognized danger to crown and state. Experiment was interpreted as obvious insecurity, and the novelty of choice as attack on the normal establishment. Russia had frozen, but long before the epoch of our own Big Freeze. Petrification set in as the taste of the Nineties, before Diaghilev launched his own reforms, when the Imperial theaters were ruled by ex-army officers and all the proprieties preserved for the sake of the puritanical governesses of a Germanophile court. Now, Russia feels the need of showing her dancers to the West, and we have been gladdened by their demonstrations of academic proficiency, political prestige and brio. We have been saddened by the sounds of their new music, and its consequent curse on choreography. However, Russian dancers have seen Western works. It is interesting to read the notices of Balanchine's *Symphony in C* (Bizet, 1947) recently performed in Moscow by the French Opera Ballet, in a version which did not benefit by the restorative powers of its inventor. M. Gabovitch, artistic director of the Bolshoi Theater, writing in *Sovietka Cultura* (June 6, 1958) said *"Le Palais de Cristal* of G. Balanchine had a very great success before the public. I think nevertheless that the development of such a genre is however limited, for finally this might lead to an end in itself, and there is the danger that the classic dance might transform itself purely as a demonstration of technique." This is the orthodox Marxist attack on 'formalism' (art for art's sake); any work must have elementary social-content (as if any work can avoid it, since before everything it must come from *some* society), every work must fulfill an ameliorative social function, like first-aid, or else it is useless or rather, dangerous. Oddly enough this attitude was attacked by an official Soviet voice. In an article dated July 10, 1958, only a month after the visit of the French company, B. J. Cutler of the New York *Herald Tribune* reported:

Russia came out today with a real man-bites-dog story: a ballet dancer criticized the state of modern Soviet ballet.

The surprise which this caused came from the position ballet holds in the Soviet Union. It is one artistic field in which Russia excels and its famed Bolshoi ballet has invariably been the Kremlin's most successful cultural ambassador abroad.

The courage to tell proud Russians that all was not well with their ballet was found in Viktorina Kriger, sixty-two, who joined the Bolshoi in 1910, won a Stalin Prize in 1946 and is not in awe of prima ballerinas or producers.

Her indictment was brief. In classic pre-revolutionary ballets such as *Giselle, Swan Lake* and *Don Quixote,* no one can touch the Russians, she said. But the bosses of new Soviet ballet have forgotten one ingredient: dancing.

The outspoken woman took dead aim at *Spartacus,* perhaps the most successful new Soviet ballet. It came well recommended, with music by Aram Khatchaturian and choreography by Igor Moiseyev, whose folk-dance troupe was a sensation in the United States.

Naturally, Mrs. Kriger found no fault in the ballet's ideological line. It tells of a slave uprising in ancient Rome. Spartacus, its gladiator hero was a favorite historical character of Karl Marx, and its theme is thoroughly approved by the Communist party.

But, Mrs. Kriger said, it is a spectacle and not a ballet at all. Its hero does not dance once, and the role could be performed by any dramatic actor with a stately figure and the ability to pantomime.

She said the country has many talented dancers, both male and female, whose active years are passing without the chance really to dance. She added that heavy acting, known here as 'suffering' has taken over ballet.

"When will the ballet dancer dance?" She asked.

FRENCH BALLET: Dance spectacle as performed by the state troupe of the National Academy of Music and Drama at the Grand Opera in Paris, for the last twenty-five years usually under the direction of Serge Lifar, the last premier danseur of Diaghilev, a choreographer of vast compulsion and few gifts.[11] Visually luxurious in dress-making and scenic decoration, it corresponds to the demands of the Parisian public. A typical manifestation (outside the Opera, but in no way alien to it) was reported by Laura Sheelen in the June-July, 1958 *Dance Observer*:

> In Paris, not all dance is doomed to failure. The French company of Janine Solane enjoyed undisputed success. The afore-mentioned Palais Chaillot [a theater about the size of the New York City Center] was swarming with people and the intended run was extended by popular demand. There was enthusiastic applause, with the adoring audience shouting "Bis, Bis" (Encore, Encore). One could only gasp in amazement as one sumptuous costume outdid another, in all about two hundred. The eyes were assaulted by the color and glitter, and the ears were ravished by some of the best Bach and Vivaldi. The heroine of the extravaganza fully justified the 'richesse' with which she had surrounded herself. Her ego quite eclipsed her company of forty and her passions were limitless. I am sure the more materialistic Americans in the audience were the only persons stunned into quick computations of the fortune invested; for it was impossible to believe the immorality of such an expenditure in the face of the present economic and political crisis which is crippling France. Perhaps only a few embitted foreign dancers, eating sour grapes, labeled this parading of flapping posteriors and amateurish skipping about with distended emotion an artistic treason. . . . . . .

Within the Grand Opera, the administration has suffered from the intrusion of a disorderly bureaucracy so that the normal scheduling of consecutive seasons is often rendered problematical by a series of crippling work-stoppages. This only reflects the lack of central authority endemic in France. It is not surprising that no new native ballet-masters have been developed for the Opera, no repertory has been invented which is representative to the degree that French letters, architecture or painting is exportable, while any dancers of promise always feel forced to leave the official house in an attempt to discover some open future. It might be demonstrated that the disorganization of French ballet and the petrifaction of Soviet is the result of state-sponsored bureaus which must always tend towards the

11. Mme. Misia Sert, who originally placed him in the Opera: "Serge, tu es le spectre d'un faune dans l'aprés-midi d'une rose."

44

mediocre, the weight of historic precedent, bureaucratic tenure and self-perpetuating incompetence. It is the echo of the political matrix rather than individual personnel that are finally to blame.

ENGLISH BALLET: Dance spectacle as performed by the Royal Ballet companies at Covent Garden, London, the leading administrators of which were developed under the Diaghilev aegis or immediate influence. British ballet reflects the present social climate of the Court of St. James; its Royal Patent is no token symbol. At our period in world history, there have been recent petulant attacks on the manipulation of the Crown Establishment, but there is no real general disloyalty to the idea of a need for the dynastic principle. The English predeliction for matriarchy is evident in its great queens from the first Elizabeth, Anne, Victoria, through the second Elizabeth, her able mother, grandmother and her beautiful great grandmother. This is reflected in the management of the Royal Ballet Company, with its Queen, Dame Margot Fonteyn, and its Winston Churchill, Dame Ninette de Valois. The male principle is recognized and admired when manifest, as everywhere else in the world, but is seldom encouraged into reckless independent thought or dashing action.

Correctness of execution, efficiency in administration, devotion to the tradition of the Diaghilev canon; a sweet, moderate graciousness and a heavy load of painted decoration have not encouraged much active competition towards choreographic exuberance or invention. Its most successful repertory has been revivals of the full-evening nineteenth century ballets, or imitations of them, with a strong interest in pantomime in which the English have shone for centuries. *The Sleeping Beauty* alone has had some three hundred performances at its lovely home theater. However, in contemporary British ballet there is slight trace of the fire or ferment present in today's English painting, sculpture, drama or fiction. Today, the richest vein of energy in Britain's plastic arts and literature is an activated protest of a still powerful people against blank political decline. The chief vein of British classic dancing is a discreet homage to feudal echoes clad in occasional borrowings from Parisian chic. Paris has always been a lovely place for a holiday. Good-taste is always a dire threat to progressive policy; this has been widely recognized ever since Diaghilev was enshrined in history, where it is shown how he was the enemy of accepted good-taste as soon as he had found Cocteau to

45

astonish him. The British firmly believe that the only legitimate bad-taste is Parisian; Italian and U. S. bad-taste are just Bad Taste. The British confuse the Paris of dress-makers with the France of poets and painters. But the London audience naturally gets what it likes. An editorial in *Dance and Dancers* (London, August, 1958) puts it neatly:

> . . . . .by ballet what you really mean are vast companies performing well-worn classics whose music you can hum in your baths and whose stories are so familiar that you don't have to think. . . . . .
>
> There should be a place in every country for small mainly experimental groups. . . .for they have a vital part to play—a part, moreover, which is quite outside the limited terms of reference possessed by the large or State-owned companies. Workshop performances are fine, but there is also a mezzanine between them and the major companies—on this half-landing appear the professional performances of more off-beat works by choreographers tried and trying. . . . . .
>
> London has already done pretty well in discouraging foreign dance visits, with the result that New York City Ballet avoids the place like the plague, American Ballet Theater by-passes us and goes to Ireland, Maurice Bejart's company only appears in Devon, Roland Petit wriggles out of a London engagement to appear in America, the Danes are reluctant to come, etc. etc. . . . . . .

Custodial discretion, reinforced by the stupendous financial success of many American tours has placed the Royal Ballet at the pinnacle of local and world prestige, yet at the very instant of its grant of a Royal Charter ensuring its descent as an independent organization, it must find itself at its most problematical period, regarding both repertory and personnel. The resuscitation of the distant past is no longer a working policy; the nineteenth century has been sacked of works to revive. The perpetuation of part of the repertory of the first half of the twentieth century has not resulted in a sequence of invention which has added many works to the international repertory. What British ballet could do with is some untidiness, intrusions from underprivileged taste, a sense of legitimate outrage and some red-brick energy. This is not easy to manage in a court-theater by means of a royal company. But maybe there is a public in Britain that might welcome an Angry Young Man on his way to rouse the Sleeping Princess right out of Windsor Forest.

AMERICAN BALLET: Dance spectacle as performed by native dancers in New York City, through our provinces and the world entire in an international (melting-pot) manner, combining elements of the more suave and acrobatic Russian Imperial and Soviet Academies (the best of our teachers still derive from the Petersburg-Leningrad tradition), with notable additions from jazz, free-form or individual lyric developments, pushed into a sharp, percussive, hard, clean accent, athletic and metrical which seems when exported to South America, Europe or the Orient, heartless, anti-theatrical (i.e. antipantomimic), under-clad, ill-decorated and relentlessly ingenious in its insistence on the academic classic dance as a propulsive or compulsive basis. In France it is greeted as *le style Frigidaire,* dismissed as mechanical and dowdy. The British hate it on principle since the dominant American repertory is both against Tradition (except in vocabulary), and has no Establishment. The Russians admit our jazz ballet is all right but think we should leave *Giselle* to them; we should, too. In Japan, critics expressed pity for poor dancers who were forced to fly about the stage with such soulless rapidity in Balanchine's merciless flagellation for every spirit of time-less grace. The sense of time is the heart of the matter, our American sense of time. Mr. Sumio Kam'bayashi, Press and Program Manager of the Tokyo American Cultural Center, distilled the essence of the Japanese ideological conflict with the New York City Ballet's repertory, (April, 1958):

> For the Japanese who are aesthetic (that is, sense-ly) rather than intellectual or volitional, who appreciate more leisurely tempo and less bustling activity, who prefer contemplation to action, etc. (Japanese may be in favor of the first part of the pair of dualisms that follows: introvert-extrovert, aggressive-fatalistic, adagio-allegro). Too much speediness is vulgar. That's why Kabuki (the Japanese traditional classic drama) and even Japanese film move on in a slow tempo. Pauses in which an actor strikes an effective pose are the order of day with our theater. Often you find the slow-speed film technique in Kabuki as pointed out by Eisenstein. This love of stillness, void or *nirvana* is typically Buddhistic Japanese. For such nations as we are, the ballet that moves with

presto tempo is almost unbearable if you want to watch it emotionally. Many dancers said they wanted the *Swan Lake* [Balanchine version] danced more slowly so that it gives time and room for them to identify themselves emotionally with the dance.

In his conversations with Robert Craft, Stravinsky said:

> I myself have no habit of anything oriental, and especially no measure of time in oriental music. In fact, my attitude resembles that of Henri Michaux: in the Orient I recognize myself as a Barbarian—that excellent word invented by Attic Greeks to designate a people who could not answer them in Attic Greek.

What most people complain of in the dominant American style of classic dancing is our sense of Time, which is often speedier than moderate. The best trained Americans move faster, fill in more steps in a minute to more elaborate and concentrated music than most other Western performers. Also, the dominant American repertory uses music impelling dancers to a density in sharp, silhouetted and plastic action demanding a more attentive eye and ear than previous gentler numbers. The American sense of Time is not static; time does not pass; we pass through it, but we impose on it an active analysis; we break it up for our fun and games, a sometimes insolent imposition on a fourth or fifth dimension. Stravinsky says that portions of *Agon* contain three times as much music for the same clock length as some of his earlier pieces. Hence Balanchine's choreography for it needed to contain an equivalent dosage of choreographic concentrate, requiring much more looking-at than less packed compositions. The sonorous analysis of time, due to possibilities not alone in electronic devices but in researches in serial forms from Schoenberg and Webern through the later Stravinsky, opens up a whole new world in the temporal structure of the classic dance. Balanchine's choreography to Hindemith, Charles Ives and Schoenberg, his interest in Varese and Webern indicates an extension of possibility never closed to the limitless perspectives in the academic dance. The reason that Balanchine has imposed his personal vision on the world of theatrical dancing in our time to the degree that he has stems from his technical interest in and technical mastery of musical form. An analytical study of a score at his piano, often culminating with a personal piano transcription for rehearsal purposes, starts his choreographic analysis; the oscillation of his interest in certain types of scores and certain clusters of composers tells us much about his method, for it is a logical procedure and corresponds to needs that he senses in the development of his company and his audience at a given period. In a recent season, anticipating export values necessary for an extensive Far Eastern tour, he composed four ballets for American dancers with scores by Vivaldi-Corelli, Gounod, Stravinsky (a commission) and Sousa (a discovery). The fast and sharp music gave the dancers no trouble, but the tender, transparent and gentle modulations of the Gounod symphony were not mastered by his own dancers whom he had over-instructed in a fast percussive beat. He did not have time enough to teach them to dance slowly. Balanchine handles time as some painters, color; for him, time is the plastic definition of movement in its sequence and separation; he requires unfamiliar music, music which has not been too much heard, music devoid of association, with a temporal urgency and strangeness, to be heard newly, at least in the season of its introduction.

The American response to new music is not a question of nationalism; *Billy the Kid* (Copland-Loring-French, 1938) had a charming score based on folk materials. The ballet had success since it was then a popular response to an historical need; but its choreographic value was slight, in few ways equal to Martha Graham's *American Document* from which its processional portions largely derived. It is not Americanism but the American dancer's capacity to utilize music which most nearly corresponds to his unprejudiced energy which makes American ballet as strong as it is, with the American ability to recognize changes in time, sensitive also to relentless mutations in history. Robert Craft writes of Pierre Boulez in the recent Columbia LP recording of *Le Marteau Sans Maître*:

> One of the most difficult items in *Le Marteau* is speed. Whether or not the world is moving more quickly than ever before, fast tempi today are faster than any past period. Boulez's characteristic fast tempo is 208 beats per minute whereas only a generation ago Webern's was 168. . . . . . . Beethoven begins the race by breaking through the conventional tempos designated by Italian words. He greatly extends the ranges and varies the kinds of tempos and, at the same time, adds new speed. But Beethoven's *allegro molto* is 144 (the "Eroica") and 144 is only *molto moderato* for Boulez.

In *Le Marteau* speed as a whole, not only the speed of fast movement, is much greater than in any music of any earlier period. . . . Perhaps if the tendency continues we will be able in the future to learn to hear the motor of the hummingbird.

Perhaps one day also we will be able to mark the discrete motion of the hummingbird's wings. Certainly there is no physiological barrier to what American dancers can, properly schooled, manage. The capacity of a good dancer in our corps de ballets today would have amounted to star (technical) capacity thirty years ago. The requirements of the post-Russian Stravinsky repertory have precipitated the increase of automotive efficiency; what could be, or can be, done if there were an all-out effort towards a real crash-program in ballet might be amazing. Most American dancers have some chance at adequate training, but let us assume for a moment that the academic dance was considered a legitimate exercise in the (cultural) defense of our nation by the Congress. Even in a dream, one could not ask for $133,000,000.00 which the newly opened Air Corps Academy in Colorado cost so far. There, some eleven hundred picked young men would be given training which no expense of mind or money could improve. Ballet is not a necessity. If it were, the efficiency in the instruction of dancers, the quality of human material, and the prestige involved, would be, to put it modestly, superior. So much for a social and economic absolute; as far as the physiological absolute, which depends practically on the first two, there seem to be fewer limits here, too, than one might think. Roger Bannister, the young Oxford physician who smashed the four minute mile, said in *Sports Illustrated* for August 18, 1958:

What is the ultimate in miling? Four minutes was only a milestone with the magical ring of round numbers on the path to a physiological absolute which axiomatically runners will never reach, though they will approach it more closely. Unless there is a process of eugenic selection of athletes—horrible thought—the limit depends on the athlete's ability to transport oxygen to his muscles. Over this distance without oxygen the muscles can no longer be driven by the mind. . . . . A mile in 3 minutes 30 seconds is impossible with the present human physique, but there remains a no man's land of 24.5 seconds. Gradual improvement is inexorable.

Even if it is not welcomed with open arms, even if our dancers on foreign tours do not always make the residual total impression so nervously hoped for by our State Department, there is no doubt but that from a progressive standpoint, American ballet, even lacking a state or national theater, dominates the epoch. Nor is envy entirely absent when foreign critics speak of the presence of Soul in the home team and its absence in honored guests. Since the dominant American repertory depends upon the most eclectic and advanced musical basis now available, since it has borrowed benefits from the researches and inventions of the greatest contemporary specialists in new rhythms, new harmonies, new balances of form in sound; and since we materially deprive ourselves in the departments of dress-making and decoration, our choreographers have had a wrenching of their imaginations to disassociate themselves from the expected, the easy or the merely decorative. We have a rich local vein of character-dancing in popular music and dance forms, which has contributed one master-mason in Jerome Robbins. The basic beat in jazz is perpetually liberating, not alone through syncopation, but from the ingenuity in the improvisational style of its reversible rhythm. Seemingly invented out of nothing, it embodies the exuberance of virtuoso playfullness. The style is hard to dry out because our popular music changes seasonally with a new hem-line or a waist-line. It keeps us, literally Up On Our Toes.

The American Style is disciplined but irreverent. Since we have no mythic national gallery to which we must always pay homage and no prototypes but the dubious heroes of Pioneer, Mechanic and Athlete, we are not bound by servitude to a sacred past, either personalities or sacred monstrous works. Everything we do is done to be done again and again, invented each time new, with new gags. This breeziness may seem brash to older communities, but mark how blue-jeans have conquered the world. What we dig is a new and fancy sharpness. We appear to the rest of the world exasperatingly capable of anything, good and bad. But there are not any paths of invention or range of performance that our home-grown dancers of energy and determination find shut to them. This now happens to be untrue anywhere else in the world.

ARGENTINE, AUSTRALIAN, DANISH, DUTCH, SWEDISH and SOUTH AFRICAN BALLET: The problem of the provinces is delicate. Possibly it should never be mentioned, but there is activity in the field in many remote parts of the world, each place bidding for its quota of prestige and getting it. The Danes have a moderately interesting history, but it is no absolute service to their modest excellences to over-exaggerate it. Dancing-masters in Scandinavia did influence the Imperial Russian schools in the last century, but Bournonville was no Petipa, no Ivanov. Canadian, South African and Australian dancers have become valuable members of the Royal Ballet and American companies, which proves the point: provinces are interesting for what they can contribute to capitals. Mr. Anatole Chujoy has written a valuable monograph on "Civic Ballet" which he has done much to foster:

> National Ballet Festivals were held in Canada every year for six years until 1955. They were discontinued for a very interesting reason: most of the talented dancers in the non-professional companies, which participated in the festivals were absorbed by the then newly established Canadian professional companies, the Royal Winnipeg Ballet and the National Ballet of Canada, and the television programs originating in Toronto and Montreal.

Provincial ballet-directors are always being betrayed in their selfless efforts to bring national or local companies into being, for their best dancers will always be picked off by bigger companies. The smaller troupe at its best, is usually in a state of hopeful evolution, interesting to those responsible, and to a very small, if passionate, portion of the local public, which is always dismayed that there is less energy for money in them than, for example, in the art-museum or symphony orchestra. The art-museum often has an endowment, and objects of known value; the orchestra plays a repertory of famous works; the ballet has neither. To persist, the managers of provincial companies must always ignore the true state of their place's history, geography and economy. When one is building a South African, a Canadian or an Atlanta, Georgia company, one can have no patience with the historian who tells you it can't be done, or that everything done here derives from centers far away, and everything good developed here will revert to those centers. It can, too, be done; we are doing it. More power to you. You are doing part of our work for the rest of us, and even if we are not very grateful you may find your names in the histories. But you are in the education business, not in the theater business, and if you doubt it, ask any of your dancers

52

where they would rather perform: Vancouver or Covent Garden? There are local excellences, local strengths, in some cases gifts and resources, even superior to those sometimes enjoyed in the big gardens of culture. We can admire the devotion, envy the fun, smile at the smugness and forgive the innocence, hope and heart break. But, except for practical training of dancers and choreographers who will do their best work in some larger town, the prognosis is limited. Auden wrote of the Portuguese colony of Macao:

> A weed from Catholic Europe, it took root
> Between the yellow mountains and the sea,
> And bore these gay stone houses like a fruit,
> And grew on China imperceptibly . . . . .
>
> Religious clocks will strike; the childish vices
> Will safeguard the low virtues of the child;
> And nothing serious can happen here.

MODERN DANCE: A loose idiom of idiosyncratic, free-form movement, identified with careers and contributions of half a dozen individuals, all in their prime by 1935, when their loose connection (there was no formal association) represented an unorthodox attack on the academic classic ballet as it was then known (or unknown) in the United States and Central Europe. Its chief inspirer was the Californian, Isadora Duncan at the turn of the century and the following decade; while Jaques Dalcroze, a Swiss musical theorist, seemed to provide an anti-academic, as well as anti-theatrical body of instruction in measure and rhythm. His big point was that the Russian dancers of the Diaghilev company could not 'keep time' to their music. He was interested in theater if it was in the open air. Rudolf Laban, a Hungarian theorist, was even more puritanically anti-theatrical. Most modern dancers had strong ethical objections to the over-decoration of stage dancing, some of which was salutory, but much of which was a rationalization since they developed outside official theatrical institutions and had neither home base nor localized public.

Martha Graham, like her historic ancestors Loie Fuller, Isadora and Ruth St. Denis, is in a different category. Acclaimed over the world as America's leading 'modern' dancer, her method is hailed both as justification and salvation for the Modern Dance as a legitimate, legible and transmittable vocabulary. This is neither fair to a remarkable personality nor accurate as apologia for a movement. Graham is an exceptional artist, not comparable to Isadora, because Isadora had only the rudiments of training. She didn't need any for what she actually danced. She was an improviser of great personal magnetism who arrived at that moment in history when there was a corset around every woman in the West, aching to be thrown off. Isadora robed herself in the three-century old prestige of Hellenistic sculpture and the century old repertory of German symphonic band music. Swept in on a healthy breath of California poppies, her performance was a danced sermon with Whitman as gospel. Her influence was ethical and social rather than theatrical.

Graham is an accomplished and meticulous artist who served a long and arduous apprenticeship in eclectic presentations of the dances of Spain and the Orient, including enough classic ballet to have respect for it as a training aid. Graham's mistress was Ruth St. Denis, who as anybody who has read her fascinating autobiography knows, is a creature of enormous appetite and intelligence, an impressive historic figure. With nothing at hand to borrow from, she filled an epoch in the American theatre, bringing the idea of Dance, as well as American Dance, to more lands than Duncan ever knew. Her instinctive passion for the East, her later knowledge of it from first hand, made her evocations and her evocativeness in the minds of the young dancers like Graham, an experience far livelier for them than the Diaghilev Ballet. Ruth St. Denis knew theatre from vaudeville, variety and from what Ted Shawn called "A Thousand and One Night Stands."

Graham is also the professional, outside the descent of the academic tradition, but she has contributed to it in a variety of openings-up, even as Isadora did more ambiguously. What is more important, she has been exactly right for herself, possibly for herself alone. She has a consummate analytical gift for expressing her particular intensity. Her face and form are not what they are by any chance. She worked for them, and they show it. But just as there was little in precedent to promise her, there is not much that directly descends from her. One has only to see her own well trained young dancers in those rôles she first created for herself. Not that she lacks choreographic talent for pattern, gesture or oddity. Simply, she has

analyzed her own assets and their place in our present; what she decided to do corresponded with what she felt she could do plus what
needed to be done; her repertory was both self-assertion and oblique
critique. There was only herself to do it; this was what she was born
for, just as Isadora and St. Denis had their call and saw their light.
You never had to ask Martha Graham who she thought *she* was. She
was Martha, and she did dances for and around Martha, and they
have been of lasting interest around the world.[12]

As an original, one of the rare ones, what is evident as her personal tone refers only to herself and its theatrical framing; this limi-
tation she has embraced and used as strength. That she is the only
contemporary figure outside the academic dance to be able to do this
demonstrates her intensity as well as the wide uses of the academic
traditions, beyond which she alone found a unique path. *Herodiade*
is the name of one of her famous dances, based on Mallarmé's poem.
Years before Graham, Yeats had written words which also apply to
her:

> Yet I am certain that there was something in myself com-
> pelling me to attempt creation of an art as separate from every-
> thing heterogenous and casual, from all character and circum-
> stance, as some Herodiade of our theatre, dancing seemingly
> alone in her narrow moving luminous circle.

But lacking other equally powerful personalities, the Modern
Dance *soi-disant* produced no second generation of performers of intensity, little repertory disassociated from first-performances and no
extensible code of movement. While there were flashes, or fragments
of spiritual grandeur of some depth if extreme narrowness, the future
of Modern Dance either as program or philosophy is obscure. What

12. Stark Young, perhaps the most sensitive and exact critic of theater-as-a
whole who has ever written in America, said of Graham:
"There are times when the Graham programme or some number in it seems
too long. If you have full faith in the dancer you get an unpleasant sense that,
with so much given to it, more must be being said than you are taking in; a
sense of inadequacy of perception is laid on you as it were. There are times, too,
when the motif and the effect seems overpresented, and you are reminded of
Talleyrand's remark that whatever is exaggerated is insignificant. And we may
have found not too infrequently an evasion of the dramatic, a concentration on
the stark pattern for the design-idea of the composition. The benefits of this—
for a period of time, that is—are manifest in the fine cleanness and purity of
her dancing. We have the sense that, no matter what has been left out, nothing
has entered a composition that has not grown into it organically. . . ." (*Immortal
Shadows: A Book of Dramatic Criticism*)

was most legible or negotiable of its thesis moved into the field of physical education in state-colleges, replacing gymnastics, or into musical-comedy dance-numbers where it instilled a little life of no greater importance than the vehicles it adorned. On Broadway it is dilute and serves as a base for an embroidery of jazz-character steps.

BALLET MUSIC: Skipping the long history of what past music has accompanied what lost dances, it is important to analyze what present music may serve us. Not everything available is suitable. Even the convinced preference of a certain choreographer for a chosen composer is no guarantee of sensibility. The most important thing to consider, if one works for a company with a musical conscience, is the size and quality of the available orchestra. How many men can you afford to pay to play those pieces you have chosen to use as your dancing-floor?

In the 1930s there was a vulgar tendency to seize large scores, the symphonies of Beethoven, Berlioz, Brahms, Tschaikovsky and Shostakovitch. The strength of the orchestras playing these pieces often bore little resemblance to the indications on the partition. The public, then a rather rudimentary audience without benefit of high fidelity radio stations or the LP record, was sufficiently familiar with the Pastoral, the Pathetic and the Fantastic, to bring them along half-memorized, to the theater. The attending choreography was naive, too. A first statement was proposed by a solo dancer; the corps chimed in at the tutti and pre-tenderized ears guided innocent eyes to fill up all the blank bars with partial correspondences in a musical visualization. It is not by accident that none of these works are any longer in repertory. Their interest was exhausted due to the over-familiarity of their music. And it is now far too expensive to employ on casual circuits the apparatus of the German state theaters where one hundred and ten men were the normal post-Wagnerian requirement. Approximation of Richard Strauss, and of Wagner himself, on a reduced scale, particularly if the pieces have acquired fame in the absolute symphonic repertory, were for a while acceptable; but today, in large part due to the greatly expanded service of the recording industry, the audience is better educated in their realistic demands for a scale of sonority fulfilling the original intentions of composers. A state-supported opera house is needed to maintain a great orchestra, which even reduced to fifty plus men, on the union scale must always cost more weekly than the total group of dancers.

Increasingly for us, the modesty of the orchestra's size determines a selection of music, but here economic necessity is not censorship. On the simplest restriction, there is a large catalogue of string-music, and in a variety of other combinations whose balance, scale and scope is suitable for dance. A clever choreographer gains piquancy by uncovering scores with unexpected provenance in divisions which can be incorporated within the body of an orchestra at his disposal. A ballet is launched by the choice of its music far more than any pretext of plot, libretto or literary idea. Music determines dances more than any single element. Naturally the choreographer must do things with it or to it. His analysis, his measurings, not in formal structure alone, but on the floor of its atmosphere, its charm or lack of charm, determines his range of gesture or motion and tells the most, at the same time about the nature of his own gifts.

The most able ballet masters are not those necessarily who are most prodigal of invention, or those who are compelled to attempt an approximate dancer's equivalent for every musical concept. Sometimes, even in the most propelling or suggestive music, too much goes on for its own accommodation. If some absolute consistency was forced equating entries and reëntries, restatements, variations and reversals, the visual part might collapse from the pressure of the aural. Synthesis of music and movement is what commands taste and ingenuity. When Balanchine was making *Jeux de Cartes* (1937), he found an ingenious device in which the pack unfolded itself in fan-like conformations, from the suite King, Queen, Jack, etc., held in a poker hand. He made the dancers vary the sequence three times, each totally different. Stravinsky, with the parsimony of experience, told him simply to repeat the first one unchanged three times: "They won't see it the first, nor applaud till the third."

Concepts of time in rhythmic divisions are the base of any truly contemporary dance-style. Pastiche is unsatisfactory, however nostalgic, because it only recalls and is neither superior to nor the equal of an original model. Stravinsky's method of revival is resuscitation through metamorphic transformation. It was the score of *Apollon Musagète* (1928) which made us listen anew to Delibes as a serious composer of dance-music. A general acceleration of incident and accident all over the world in the last sixty years has generally found its prophecy in Western music. Stravinsky marks the beginning of musical thinking which determined a new idea of dancing based neither on poetry nor painting but on analytical sonority and rhythmic play. He has led dancers since 1909; only those who follow him closely have been able to extend the repertory by amplifying the academic classic vocabulary. This is not to say that he has written the only dance scores of use or interest, but it is to insist that his initial contributions to the twenty Diaghilev seasons, and his masterpieces over the most recent thirty have affected every aspect of theatrical music as the seminal influence. What is remarkable still is that he can even presently, after half a century's history arouse consistently strong differences of opinion. His gifts are medicinal; his invention has the pungency of fresh iodine and the impersonal freshness of clean linen sheets. His atmosphere has the astringency and dis-comfort of certain therapies. His music has massaged the body of the dance; he offers super-sonic devices against arthritic choreographers, and an accumulation of calcium on passive hearing or snobbish seeing. On November 9, 1913, Claude Debussy wrote to Stravinsky to thank him for the score of *Le Sacre du Printemps*:

> For me, who descends the other slope of the hill but keep, however, an intense passion for music, for me it is a special satisfaction to tell you how much you have enlarged the boundaries of the permissable in the empire of sound.

The problem of musical taste, the choice of one piece of music rather than another upon which it is prudent to risk dancing forms the principal policy-decision of ballet management. Often accident seems the best policy. A choreographer, seldom a trained musician, is permitted to choose something he happens to have heard and liked and blandly proceeds. Or there are instances when vague outside pressures, overheard in conversations of critics and connoisseurs insist that some contemporary composer demands to be commissioned. When this happens on the basis of prestige rather than preference, the result has its compulsive nervousness in composition. Fulfillment is achieved only by conviction and collaboration. The streets of choreography's hell are paved with paid-for scores which though produced were unproducible.

People refused to take Balanchine seriously when he said of the music of John Philip Sousa: "I like to listen to it." Stravinsky makes a distinction between hearers of and listeners to music. Similarly, in the dance, a difference may be drawn between those who watch it and those who see it. Some choreographers have an instinctive awareness of sights and sounds, but their gifts, unclarified by analytical intelligence, are not sufficiently powerful to precipitate vague feeling into formal passion. This betrays basic lack of energy, for the schooling necessary is available if a mind is willing to be as rigorously exercised as a body. Listening to music systematically is in itself training; not just attending haphazard concerts, but the subjection of the ear to considerable sequences of many composers' products. In our times we have seen poets and musicians of the advance-guard swarm back to scores by Tschaikowsky and Puccini, two names proscribed in Paris at one time (although never by Diaghilev, who died singing *Butterfly*). Catholic taste and an eclectic policy are matters of discrimination rather than promiscuity. It is not by accident that Balanchine has done three works by Georges Bizet and two by Emmanuel Chabrier, although their music had not been previously considered promising for ballet.

It is not alone the choice of a score for its own unique quality that should be wholly determining, but also the choice of a piece in relation to all others against which it will be shown in combination in a given repertory. Choice is, or at least should be in order to serve and survive, something governed by necessity. We have the pieces we need to open an evening, and while it stretches analogy to think of every program as a menu, there are certainly soup as well as salad ballets. There are hors d'oeuvres, second courses and deserts. Some, like melon, can serve as a first-course, too, but at banquets we won't start with the beef. Surprise, re-freshness, re-creation are prime ingredients. It is not that our palate is jaded; it is seldom very profoundly stimulated. Our ears have heard some sounds so often that they are no more alive to them than our bodies to the chairs we sit in. An energetic choreographer must uncover new noises by old composers and even commission new noises by new composers. This last is tricky, expensive and comes off about one time in ten, but the attempt must never be abandoned, even though chances of even a semipermanent success are slim.

Part of the trouble lies with the commissioning choreographer. He chooses a composer, not for what this craftsman can finally make but for the purpose of getting a new piece formularized as much as possible like scores which have already been proven. New noises, new rhythms, new suggestions do not in themselves attract him. The choreographer naturally wants a hit; a hit is a ballet by Tschaikowsky. The trouble with Stravinsky's masterful suite of ballets is that they are all by him, including the one dedicated to Tschaikowsky. By trouble one means the trouble that must be taken by a ballet-master to find choreographic treatment worthy of scores of such savor, expertness and so much mystery. Cocteau, in the finale of his letter to Jacques Maritain, speaks of it best:

> In 1916, Satie was our schoolmaster. From the year 1923 we heard Stravinsky speaking our language better than we. The lack of appreciation he enjoyed in this new period proves to what point our language is disdained.
> *The Critics*: "Mr. Stravinsky discovers the classics."
> *Stravinsky*: "Exactly. I knew them; I knew them as you did; I had not discovered them."

Of course Cocteau meant discovered, uncovered from long neglect and recovered, through his own gifts of devination and composition.

It is difficult for musicians to know what is grateful for dancers to do. Few are interested in theater; their business is the orchestra. Whatever a choreographer does it can never be the complete answer to a musician's notion, since, even though he may be vague about movement, he knows what he would wish by way of dynamics and emphasis, while the choreographer, quite possibly will have wholly other feelings. It can't hurt a composer to know something about dancing, any more than it hurts a dancer to read music, and to know not alone counts, beat and tune, but what is actually being played in all its wholeness. It is more important that the choreographer know what he really wants in relation to what he can reasonably expect to get from a given talent. It is not always the composer's fault if the delivered score is useless. Maybe he did to the best of his ability what he thought he had been asked to do. When done, it did not correspond to what the choreographer had loosely imagined he had wanted. Neither Tschaikowsky nor Stravinsky had any failures in the great music they have showered on us, although their thoughtless choreographers have had many. To be sure, at the outset, *Swan Lake* was considered a Wagnerian disaster, *Nutcracker* a hodge-podge of opera-dances and *Le Sacre du Printemps* a madman's joke. You-can't-do-this-to-us is the accolade with which most great and many good new works are kissed, but debuts don't count. Scores survive, and if not for the stage, for which they may be too interesting, then like *Le Sacre,* for the concert-hall.

One way to have a final failure, although sometimes a quick hit, is to make parody music in which the composer conspires with the choreographer to flatter the public by making noises they already know, at the same time poking sly fun both at audience and at the original source of the material. The parody score, derived from the French *musiquette* of the 1920s has all the predigested sophistication of a book-club or record-library choice. You have seen or heard it all before.

BALLET SCENERY: The suggestion and adornment of space and atmosphere in which dancing happens. Ballet is a repertory operation; few theaters in the United States, even opera-houses, have much storage space. Most ballet scenery is soft, painted on large cloths, to be rolled and folded. Heavily built, solid practicable pieces are hard to move and stack. We dislike intermissions over fifteen minutes, for they break the flow of an evening. While the nineteenth century theater of illusion contained platforms, traps, aerial ballets on wire, simulations of fountains, oceans, fireworks, volcanic eruptions, forest fires and earthquakes, our minimal dance spectacle in the mid twentieth century is, comparatively, a tame affair, depending mainly on dancing, except in Russia. The Bolshoi still enjoys a maximum theatrical apparatus but their aesthetic is still that of a century ago. As possibilities for stage scenery in the West have shrunk due to the cost of union labor, real-estate, shifting taste and an accelerated sense of time altered by the scope of spectacle in wide-screen films, a consequent spareness has favored dancers. Our audience would rather watch dancers move than wait while scenery is shifted. Hence, ballet scenery has become the most naive mechanism for big scale spectacle, usually consisting of a back-drop with side wings.

In the seventeenth century when painted moveable scenery started to be hung in designed theaters rather than transformed ball-rooms, the aim was, by simulation of grand architectural or natural elements, to imitate an enclosed heroic space, gigantic, symmetrical and metamorphic. An enchantress's palace transformed itself before your eyes by having hauled up stretched, painted and cut canvas, into a subterranean dungeon which burned away into the splendor of glorious sunbursts. The dancing itself must have been far less amusing than the parade of such tableaux. The language of the dance was then comparatively undeveloped, but perspective illusionism was extremely sophisticated.

In the eighteenth century, frontal symmetry having been somewhat exhausted, there entered freer devices of forced and steeply precipitated vanishing points. Asymmetrical collonades replaced blocked twin corridors, and were pushed off-center to a deep apex. Columns were bent, enfiladed pillars warped and divided into a visual syncopation of modules, suggesting an increase of movement even in static paint. Vaguer spaces were suggested, triangular rather than cubed, and the stage-floor triangle, since it corresponded to the actual working area dancers used had more possibility for legibility and packed movement. Exotic archeology, Babylon and Peru, Ceylon and Muscovy, Martinique and Morocco, every sort of fantastic geography offered stupendous backgrounds against which regiments of dancers and figurants defiled.

Stage illumination was rudimentary. Oil lamps with reflectors gave way to gaslight. At the turn of the last century electricity began to be controlled. Paint was primarily illusionistic, like an architect's dead rendering. It strained to re-present literal imitations on plane canvas surfaces of the look of woodgrain, marble, tapestry, water, sky, with unchanging shadows from a single source of light, creating a papery plasticity, put in with a straight-edge, always illogical in some detail and under most light.

When Diaghilev became attached to the Imperial Theater, the tradition of scene-painting (designers not infrequently were the painters themselves) was inherited from the Franco-Italian opera houses. Foliage, cut leaf-borders on netted drops were broad in yardage but small in scale and photographic in detail. A painstaking literalistic naturalism was the rule. He brought with him to Paris two gifted designers, Bakst and Benois, and these took advantage of a revolution in rendering that had already been accomplished by the Post-Impressionist easel-painters. Broken color of Seurat and Signac, the daring chromatic contrasts and broad generalized vibrating areas of Bonnard and Vuillard and the forced night-illumination of Lautrec and Degas, who had instructed themselves in theaters and circuses, made the great cloths of the first seasons of the Ballets Russes an important revolution in visual taste.

The bravura brushwork in Delacroix, Courbet and Manet had not touched the stage-decoration of their epoch, but by 1905, later researches in palette intensity, poster-display and electricity had already triumphed. Essentially, Bakst and Benois were pasticheurs of taste, in love with an historic past, period by period, which they reconstructed on documents from the archeologists of their time with the broad effects of contemporary paint-handling. When Diaghilev became finally acclimatized to international Paris, which took him some five years, he was able to proclaim far more daring steps in the aims of stage-decoration for the non-realistic or lyric theater. At the start he was satisfied to use his professional theater designers, who had hoped to be, but who were certainly not, primarily easel-painters. While the early Cubists, Picasso, Matisse, Gleizes, the Post-Impressionists and Fauves were available to him by 1909, as well as independent lyricists like Modigliani, Dufy, and Pascin, he was then not thinking in these terms. It was still the epoch of exportable Russian nationalism: Golovin, Korovin and Roerich. It remained for Jean Cocteau to carry the painters of the School of Paris to the theater in the collaboration of *Parade* (Satie-Picasso-Cocteau, 1917). This was, so far, the single most influential manifestation of modernity in the century. It proposed, through splintered facets of Cubism, American rag-time and the journalism of megalopolis, aspects of that permanent 'modern life' of great cities which Baudelaire first found in Constantin Guys, but which the lyric theater had rarely ever employed with so frank and full an apparatus of painter's eyes and poet's vision.

In many cases, Diaghilev's late decor was accidental, insistent and had little to do with dancing. Scenery was often more striking than choreography and it needed have only the slightest relation to music. Stravinsky complains of Matisse's decor for *Le Rossignol* (Balanchine, 1926). "Diaghilev hoped Matisse would do something very Chinese and charming. All he did, however, was to copy the China of the shops in the Rue de la Boetie." Braque and Juan Gris were easel-painters too preoccupied with their personal plastic studies to take stage-decoration seriously, and Diaghilev himself leaned to a slapdash execution as a violent shift from the early over-meticulous detail and pinched scale of the official styles. Some of the painters used their stage-space as a kind of laboratory, but these were rarely decorators. At its period of greatest importance to him, Diaghilev thought of scenery as enormously enlarged sketches, never carried too far, more often than not seeming to be slight and unstudied but actually executed with fantastic virtuosity by Prince Schervachidze. Part of their piquancy came from the huge area of their playfullness, their apparent lack of serious intent. Picasso threw ingenious devices into the arena and his caprice was always the most monumental. These were tremendous one-man shows, or rather one-tableau (or two, or three) poster-like demonstrations which announced the next big exposition of a new period of the easel-pictures. André Derain, a painter of less depth than some of his colleagues, was, nevertheless, perhaps the most brilliant of the decorators, for he filled his space with a consistent painterly richness, the paint itself appetizing and luxurious, a glow of vast visual luxury on a human scale.

The Diaghilev repertory which enjoyed the most brilliant painting was not the strongest in terms of the dance. As an example, *Le Tricorne* (Falla-Massine-Picasso, 1919) has had numerous revivals due perhaps more to musician and decorator than choreography. Picasso and Matisse pinch hit for a large corps de ballet; the Diaghilev seasons launched the international success of many of the most expensive artists of our time.

Today, except in those companies which are still under the shade of Diaghilev's formula without enjoying the distinction of his collaborations, painted cloths are recognized to have many disadvantages. Contemporary conceptions of space are not entirely satisfied by boxing in a stage floor with static paint, however atmospheric, dashing or suggestive. The broadness of an easel-painter's sketch blown up to the scale of a proscenium opening must be coarse to be legible. Huge sketches were astonishing when they took the place of naturalistic drops, but the scale of the dancers was dwarfed by the very imitation of broad brush strokes. Today we desire, with our most progressive choreography, the form and light which enhance the three-dimensional plasticity of bodies in motion. To serve as foils to dancers we sometimes need objects as real as they are, unveiled in their own air, lit in their own light, not a simulated one. The decor that Gabo and Pevsner constructed in oilcloth and mica for *La Chatte* (Sauget-Balanchine, 1927) and the objects sculptured by Joan Miro for *Jeux d'Enfants* (Bizet-Massine, 1932) were among the first statements of detached forms which framed dancers by their architectural shape. The big shift in the scenery of our day has been the change of emphasis from paint and color to form and light.

Instead of providing a flat surface with indications upon it which could be read as three-dimensional, veritable three-dimensional objects were presented as light-traps, as facetted or curved surfaces upon which light was bounced or absorbed. Great changes came with the possibilities of the incandescent bulb, and our engineers have by no means finished with the enormous facilities offered by new kinds of light, its pre-setting, monitoring and the subtlety of an organ-like play in delicate balance of circuits in series. The American dancer, Loie Fuller had her own small experimental theater in the Paris Exposition of 1900 (which she shared with the first Japanese classical dancer to appear in the West). She took full advantage of the most recent inventions of Thomas A. Edison by strapping poles to her forearms upon which were hung huge wings of china-silk. These she waved and turned, and the light hitting them seemed like fire, water, petals or clouds under the shifting lamps. The movement of her veils in air, under light made more of a dance than her feet, but something of the Tiffany Glass incandescence of her act has been caught in Toulouse-Lautrec's lithograph.[13]

The painter Pavel Tchelitchev, in the ballet *Ode* (Nabokov-Massine, 1928) used a great range of visual devices for creating spacious air on stage with no pigment, only forms in light. He forced perspective by hanging rows of puppets, diminishing in size which merged with real dancers identically dressed; there was back-projection of cinema film, and a cat's cradle of ropes which made a variety of metamorphic vanishing points. Dancers became self-lit sculptural units; sometimes immobile when confused with the inanimate dolls, at others active, with their mobility enhanced by the mysterious opposition of live and dead; the principle unifying element was light. Later, Tchelitchev proposed a further step in increased plasticity: scenery was not to be any longer a lit surface but rather, in itself, the source of its own illumination. With the development of plastics

13. "A large American woman, rather ugly and bespectacled, standing on a transparent trap-door, uses rods to manoeuvre oceans of light veiling, and sober, active and invisible like a hornet in a flower, she stirs up the orchid of light and fabric which billows out, flares up, opens, roars, turns and floats, changing shape like clay in a potter's hands, twisted in the air under the sign of the torch and the hair. . . ." (Cocteau: *Paris Album: Portraits Souvenirs*)

which were weightless or nearly so and could be moulded into any shape, lamps could be placed on dimmers inside sculptured forms. The dancer's energy, action and dynamics illuminated his or her body; Tchelitchev wished his forms that framed them to be in a parallel self-illumination. Paint laid on, no matter how close the brush-strokes imitated the sketches of a painter, or however well lit the canvas might be, was finally static and hence dead. Light itself, vibrating in and on changing forms, had the fluency of motion. In subsequent productions, notably *Errante* (Schubert-Balanchine, 1933) and *Ondine* (Giraudoux-Jouvet, 1937) he pushed the principle of self-illumination further than it has ever been seen before or since. He made that influential part of the public which first recognizes innovation and remembers it longest impatient with the passivity of painted drops. The beautiful flow of the silk act-curtain for Noguchi's *Orpheus* (Stravinsky-Balanchine, 1947) was first seen in the finale of *Errante*.

Today, wherever the prime interest in ballet is dancing, choreography, its investment by performers, and neither pantomime, interior-decoration nor dress-making; the desideratum in decor is absolute plasticity. Bodies are robed in light to proclaim their three-dimensional properties. Paint on cloth can be lit and back-lit in a great range of color and atmosphere, but the plane basis is fixed. Luminescence, however, faced on an impalpable cyclorama plays back and around moving dancers and gilds their shifting silhouettes with the most legible accents and highlights.

Among the important inventions of Martha Graham are her stage-settings, which in spirit recall the mastery of scale, substance and plastic pruning of Japanese gardens, where shrubs, stones, moss and gravel make a mosaic of real objects, sometimes delimiting a landscape and at once enlarging it infinitely by the most subtle alterations of exact placement and diminutive scale. Her most notable designer has been Isamu Noguchi, a distinguished sculptor of Japanese tradition who has moulded and constructed separate objects of considerable size and complexity helping to order her space-forming doors, beds, frames, grills, trees, through and in which she weaves her movement and fixes her important gesture. The objects themselves are keys to her mysteries, opening up action. Painting, unless it is tapestry, has to be translated into other terms of form; sculpture is form itself.

Ballet is about dancing and scenery can help when it does not smother. There are not, however, many ballets of primary choreographic interest which could not get along quite well without much more decoration than is seen at a circus, where the great width of space is contained by tied lines, wires and nets of the trapeze, bars of the cages, the platforms and pedestals for man and beast. These linear divisions are real lines in continuous space. Everything is subordinate to the action of acrobats and animals, and dancers in their genre, have the same athletic physicality; they are the greatest race of big cats and are best viewed when naked.

Ballet-scenery requires far greater tact in design and discipline in the designer than opera or dramatic decoration. Songs are to be sung with a necessarily static delivery and can be launched before splendid surfaces. The movement in the control and release of breath and voice can be made the more thrilling from the depth and richness of the launching-site. Plays happen in a certain space and special time; period and locality must be proposed or suggested. Dancing happens in general space, in its own intense time, whatever the pretext of incident that can be imposed on movement. Space is passive, ready to be stamped and filled with the impress of bodies. A perfume of light and, even sometimes painting, is an aid but the best space is that in which the dancers move freest without being pinned on a grid of dead outlines, obtrusive shapes or insistent masses of unchanging color.

WHAT IS BALLET ABOUT: How does the audience feel about it? Is ballet about music? Must the steps danced be a literal transcription of music played? Is it indeed possible, even if it were desirable, to equate the filling of ears with sights or eyes with sounds?

Is ballet about scenery and costumes? When a performance is all but forgotten from its first impact, is it the scenic investiture that salvages the most vivid memory?

Is ballet about star-performance? When we recall a single dancer, fixed in light, approaching the super-normal through personal domination, grace or physical capacity, is this disassociated from every other theatrical element? If so, how often can we count on it to happen? How much has it to do with the temperament or soul of an artist, or with what the performer has been given by way of tradition, training or design?

67

Is ballet about choreography? Is the chief interest a maze of ordered movement which is woven for and by the dancers?

Ballet is, of course, about all these in varying degrees of importance at different periods of history, or at different moments in the same evening, but it is about one thing constantly, supremely to the despair of every scene-painter who attempted to compete with a choreographer, despite the music which is the base of the business, and at the expense of the choreography which is exhaustable after two seasons or five or twenty-five; for just as opera depends on song alone and its singing by a singer, as the spoken drama upon words embodied by players, so does ballet depend upon dance, the dancer, dancing whatever is calculated to raise public and performer to some transitory terrestrial paradise. Ballet is about dancing in time.